# Waiting for Pegasus

A vignette by Julio Ruelas, dated 1901. Reproduced from *Revista Moderna de México*, 6, No. 8 (Oct. 1904), 73.

# Waiting for Pegasus

*Studies of the Presence of Symbolism and Decadence
in Hispanic Letters*

EDITED BY
ROLAND GRASS AND WILLIAM R. RISLEY

An Essays in Literature Book

Western Illinois University
Macomb, Illinois 1979

The drawing by Julio Ruelas on the cover is reproduced from *Revista Moderna,* 3, No. 17 (Sept. 1900), 269.

The epigraph on page 6 is the last stanza of Rubén Darío's "Sonatina," from *Prosas profanas,* 1896.

Copyright © 1979 by Western Illinois University
Manufactured in the United States of America
Printed by Yeast Printing, Inc., Macomb, Illinois
Library of Congress Catalog Card Number 79-64810
ISBN 0-934312-02-8

To Anna Balakian, who has done so much, in her writing and in her teaching, to make the scholarly world aware of the international aspects of the symbolist movement.

*¡Calla, calla, princesa—dice el hada madrina—*
*en caballo con alas hacia acá se encamina,*
*en el cinto la espada y en la mano el azor,*
*el feliz caballero que te adora sin verte,*
*y que llega de lejos, vencedor de la Muerte,*
*a encenderte los labios con su beso de amor!*
—Rubén Darío

[*"Hush, hush, little princess," says the fairy godmother,*
*"on a wingèd horse headed here has set out,*
*with a sword on his belt and a hawk on his hand,*
*the happy young knight who adores ere he sees thee,*
*and who comes from afar, defeater of Death,*
*to warm thy lips with his kiss of love!"*]

# Contents

A vignette by Julio Ruelas, dated 1901. Reproduced from *Revista Moderna de México*, 12, No. 2 (Oct. 1907), 78.

# Introduction

*. . . simbolismo, alma de la mayor
parte de las escuelas modernas.
—Amado Nervo, 1897[1]
[. . . symbolism, the soul of most
of the modern schools.]*

Symbolism and decadence are so inseparably intertwined that the subtitle of this book could simply be "Symbolism-Decadence in Hispanic Letters." They are the two major terms—both of which have been used to refer to artistic technique or style and to a basic world view—that are most frequently applied to the literature of the extraordinarily rich and complex *fin de siècle* period, whose nucleus is approximately three decades, 1885-1914. Out of dissatisfaction with the materialism, mass-ism and impersonality of industrial-bourgeois civilization, with the rationalism, objectivity and analytical spirit of positivistic science, and with the reflection of all these in the literature of realism and naturalism; and perhaps more directly in response to a loss of faith in God, man and traditional values, a new artistic sensibility was born which required new forms of expression. Arthur Symons, a sympathizer with this alienated, refined, egocentric and hypersensitive spirit, wrote in 1893 that "After a fashion it is no doubt a decadence: it has all the qualities that mark the end of great periods, the qualities that we find in the Greek, the Latin decadence: an intense self-consciousness, a restless curiosity in research, an oversubtilizing refinement upon refinement, a spiritual and moral perversity." If the classical (perfect simplicity, sanity and proportion) is the supreme art, said Symons, "then this representative literature of to-day, interesting, beautiful and novel as it is, is really a new and beautiful and interesting disease."[2] In fact, one year earlier, Max Nordau had declared this life- and art-style to be clear evidence of physical and spiritual degeneration, a personality disorder: the French symbolists "had in common all the signs of degeneracy and imbecility." He had characterized the literary atmosphere as one in which obscurity, ghost stories, puppet shows and occultist writings were fashionable and in which "Mere sensuality passes as commonplace; elegant titillation begins where normal sexual relations end. Vice looks to Sodom and Lesbos, to Bluebeard's castle and the servants' hall of the 'divine' Marquis de Sade's *Justine* for its embodiments. Readers intoxicate themselves in the hazy word-sequences of symbolic poetry. Ibsen dethrones Goethe; Maeterlinck ranks with Shakespeare; Nietzsche is pronounced by German and even French critics to be the leading German writer of the day; society persons wipe away a tear over Paul Verlaine's invocations to the Virgin."[3]

Like the cosmopolitan Paris from which it radiated, and like the entire nineteenth-century European intellectual and literary world, this new spirit, *decadence,* and the literature it created, *symbolism,* were thoroughly international, pervading Western civilization. The symbolist movement deeply enriched and was enriched by the Hispanic literatures, by which we mean those of Spain and Portugal, Spanish America and Brazil. Nevertheless, a full awareness of the rich Hispanic symbolist harvest has been delayed by an interesting combination of myopia, moral outrage, national pride and a good deal of honest confusion on the part of literary critics and historians and even the writers themselves who belonged to the movement. In spite of the immense bibliography dedicated to the *fin de siècle* period and to the fruits it bore long after the advent of World War I, Hispanic criticism still suffers from an incomplete appreciation of symbolism-decadence and thus has a need for even such a modest book as our own.

There is still no uniform terminology for dealing with the symbolist period. An entire book could be written solely to gather and sift through the varied, conflicting or overlapping meanings attached to such major labels as "naturalist," "impressionist," "pre-Raphaelite," "Parnassian," "symbolist," "decadent," *"modernista,"* "Generation of 1898" and "expressionist," as well as to many less precise or minor ones: "mystic," "aesthete" or "aestheticist," "idealist," "hermeticist," *"saudosista,"* *"romaniste,"* *"instrumentiste,"* "Byzantine." Such terms are often hyphenated to argue for their inseparability ("symbolist-decadent") or set in impossible oppositions (*modernismo* vs. Generation of 1898). Their usage is equally unstandardized. Sometimes they are capitalized and other times, lower-case—or both: the Portuguese language has *Simbolismo,* noun, but *simbolista,* adjective, standard in Brazil but not in Portugal, where both words may be written without a capital letter. The terms may designate one literary school or an entire movement or epoch. Their meaning is often restricted to a style or technique, or to an ideology or world view, as if stylistic norms somehow were unrelated to deep convictions about the nature of reality and man's relationship to it. In the case of *symbolism* and *decadence* some writers distinguish between them, others use them interchangeably, and still others give them very personal connotations. Furthermore, the evolution of our two key terms over nearly a century has not always been taken into account. All of this has led to confusion. A major culprit has been the classificatory mania, with its need for sharply drawn boundaries even where there are only hazy ones or none at all. Each school and each revolutionary movement in the arts opposes and rejects a preceding one (e.g., symbolism reacting against Parnassianism) without a realization that, deep down, one is really assimilating the other and continuing it in many ways. Hence, criticism may fail to recognize the proximity and interrelatedness of currents it conveniently supposes to be antithetical. Partly because the symbolists believed they were reacting against naturalism, naturalism and symbolism-decadence may appear to be polar opposites: the one stresses objectivity and exteriority, systematization-mechanization, description or direct presentation of visible things of a given society here and now; while the other values subjectivity and individualism, idealism and spiritualism, the intimation and suggestion of things invisible and transcendent. Yet in their marked preference for the abnormal and the "ugly" in subject matter; in their detailed attention to disease and decomposition, especially neurasthenia; in their desire to capture and reproduce sensations and to seek out nuances; in their deep interest in the workings of the inner self; and in their manner of visually fixing an object and then rendering it symbolic through careful elaboration, naturalism and symbolism have significant points of convergence not only with each other but also with realism, impressionism, Parnassianism and later movements. In a sense, the terms by which we distinguish literary currents are a matter of emphasis. To recognize this is especially important for understanding the vast fabric of the symbolist movement, whose thirst for complete freedom in artistic expression led it to harmonize opposites, to fuse together the literary genres and even the various arts themselves, and thus to embody many apparent contradictions.

Hispanic literary history and criticism have some special circumstances with respect to symbolism-decadence. The first, a strong moral reaction on the part of literary critics contemporary with its development (not to mention the general reading public) which distorts aesthetic judgments, is reflected in the essays by John Kronik, Geoffrey Ribbans, Lily Litvak, Raymond S. Sayers and Catherine Vera in this volume. Second, because of the internationalism of the intellectual and artistic climate of the late nineteenth century and the cosmopolitan literary climate of the great cities of Spanish America and Brazil, symbolism could radiate directly from Paris to the American "offspring" without passing first through the mother countries, Spain and Portugal; thus it could develop in America at the same time as or even before it influenced aesthetic evolution on the Iberian Peninsula. This fomented Latin America's literary "independence" from Peninsular literature and allowed America to influence developments in the lands of the mother tongue at the same time that it was influenced by them in a rich cross-fertilization. Third, Spain and Spanish America have a long tradition of using the syncretic term *modernismo* rather than *simbolismo* to refer to the period. This term will require some discussion in its own right and does not coincide with usage in Portugal and Brazil. Symbolism is a regular category in Luso-Brazilian criticism, but the Portuguese word *modernismo* refers to two different movements which occurred after symbolism and which coincide in nature and time with vanguardism. In view of these special circumstances, we must explain our terms and explore their background briefly.

"Symbolism" has designated a literary school, a French and then an international movement, and now it is proposed for an entire literary period. Max Nordau reported that in Paris in 1884 a group of young poets who followed Stéphane Mallarmé and called themselves the "Hydropaths" changed their name to the "Decadents," wearing defiantly an epithet applied to them in derision by a critic.[4] Thereupon, Jean Moréas, the French poet of Greek extraction, protested that "Les prétendus décadents cherchent avant tout dans leur art ... le pur Concept et l'éternel Symbole"[5] [the so-called decadents seek before all else in their art ... the pure Concept and the eternal Symbol] and proposed the name *Symbolistes* to replace "Décadents." A smaller group which retained the insulting label broke away and was officially inaugurated in April 1886 by Anatole Baju's periodical *Le Décadent.* The break was meaningless: "Both groups hated each other, yet no distinction is possible between them, and Symbolism was always equated with Decadence by contemporaries."[6] Around the same time, Moréas founded the review *Le Symboliste* and published his manifesto, "Le Symbolisme," in *Le Figaro* of September 18, 1886, soon followed by René Ghil's *Traité du Verbe* (1887) on the meaning of Symbolism. Although the major contemporary poets disavowed the term and Moréas himself proclaimed *Symbolisme* dead in September 1891, "Symbolism" endured as the term denoting the Parisian poetic *cénacle* of the decade 1885-1895. Eventually, it broadened to encompass French poetry from Nerval to Valéry, centered in Baudelaire, Verlaine, Mallarmé, and Rimbaud. Finally, thanks to key works such as Arthur Symons' *The Symbolist Movement in Literature* (1899), Edmund Wilson's *Axel's Castle* (1931), Maurice Bowra's *The Heritage of Symbolism* (1943) and Anna Balakian's *The Symbolist Movement: A Critical Appraisal* (1967), the international aspect of symbolism has been recognized. "Symbolism" has been formally proposed by René Wellek as the "general term for the literature in all Western countries following the decline of nineteenth-century realism and naturalism and preceding the rise of the new avant-garde movements: futurism, expressionism, surrealism, existentialism or whatever else."[7]

Although the broadest meaning of the word applies to expression via the use of symbols, a central process of art in general, we use *symbolism* in the present volume in the international sense, accepting Wellek's recommendation "to call the period of European literature roughly between 1885 and 1914 'symbolism,' to see it as an international movement which radiated from France but produced great writers and great poetry" in many other countries as well, and to extend the meaning of symbolism to prose, drama, and literary theory and criticism.[8] Our own preference is to write symbolism without a capital letter except when referring to the Parisian *cénacle;* but some variations will be seen in the essays of this volume, notably in the essay by Geoffrey Ribbans, which takes up the terminology problem.

But what is symbolism? The word as we use it here shall include "decadence," for the terms are inseparable. Our governing concept is the careful synthetic overview provided by Anna Balakian, which finds the essence of symbolism in "three prevailing constants: ambiguity of indirect communication; affiliation with music; and the 'decadent' spirit."[9] The first two constants could be viewed as one, for music—fluid, abstract and ineffable, supremely evocative—is the means of indirect communication *par excellence.* These constants underscore the suggestive nature of symbolist expression as against direct statement or allegory. Partly in reaction against Parnassian objectivity, the subject matter of poetry becomes the intimate emotional and aesthetic experience of the individual; poetry arises out of the mediation or interpenetration of self with the exterior object, which creates the symbol. Here the vagueness of romanticism is wed to the precision of realism and the impressionistic techniques of naturalism. "Pour être symboliste," says the Larousse encyclopedia, "il suffit d'exprimer les secrètes affinités des choses avec notre âme"[10] [to be a symbolist it is enough to express the secret affinities of things with our soul]. This nebulous phrase does not reflect how symbolism sought to give the *effect* of indefiniteness through the imprecise precisely expressed; yet the statement is in keeping with the fact that the symbolist movement reached no agreement on what a symbol actually was, nor did it have a unified aesthetics. A. G. Lehmann's indispensable study describes eight different notions of symbol held by prominent symbolists.[11] Symbolism had a basic *harmony* rather than a unity of thought. Vagueness, mystery, enigma, dreamlike suggestion, hermetic or purified language, synesthesia, analogues to musical composition, nuance and exquisite construction are essential elements of this delicate process, for the poet seeks not to describe but to evoke through the magical powers of words and their arrangement an emotion or mood (*état d'âme*, state of soul), so as to make the reader actually *experience* that emotion or complex of emotions. Because it contains and conveys "the ambiguous relation between the inner consciousness of man, the poet, and the physical world outside him,"[12] the well-wrought symbol often "lifts the veil" from normal quotidian reality, embodying and evoking a higher, transcendent reality and giving a sense of the underlying unity of all things. Ricardo Gullón's essay in this volume, on techniques of poetic condensation in Antonio Machado, is a lucid and compact introduction to "the fascinating abbreviation" that is the symbol, i.e., the symbol as it was conceived by the majority of the symbolists. Distinguishing between image and symbol, and metonymical and metaphorical symbols, Gullón stresses the symbol's ability to function in different ways in different contexts. Studying Machado's skill at subtly expanding a natural image into a complex and deeply suggestive symbol, he demonstrates how personally and how powerfully Machado synthesized the symbols his epoch offered him.

Wallace Fowlie has remarked that "each [symbolist] poet developed and represented a single aspect of an aesthetic doctrine that was perhaps too vast for one historical group to incorporate."[13] Nevertheless, nearly a century after their heyday, we can discern that three figures are largely responsible for the initial and fundamental symbolist notions regarding music and of "the ambiguity of indirect communication," the true core of symbolist technique and its most enduring contribution to modern literature. They are Baudelaire, Verlaine and Mallarmé. Baudelaire, either the extraordinary precursor or the first great figure of symbolism, influenced by Richard Wagner, found that words, like musical notes, could suggest and evoke mood without conveying specific meaning. Above all, he formulated admirably the age-old notion of "correspondences" between matter and spirit, between the visible and the invisible, which led to the great importance of synesthesia; and he underscored the multiplicity of meanings contained in words, objects and images, i.e., the essential ambiguity and mystery of poetry. Verlaine's famous "music before all else" statement was uncomplicated, meaning "pleasing sounds above all else," verse as nearly pure music. He created a simple, melodious but subtle lyricism in a minor key, conveying intimacy and mystery and achieving both the "precise nuance" and a delicate ambiguity. His poetry truly seemed to embody the aesthetic goals of symbolism: "he found words for the sensations of the soul, for the fine shades of feeling," said Arthur Symons.[14] This expressive genius and accessibility made him the most influential French symbolist in the Hispanic literary world; "Padre y maestro mágico" [Father and magical master] Rubén Darío called him.[15] Mallarmé, the high priest of the movement, went furthest in adapting to poetry the *form* of music, the structure and techniques of musical composition. He was also the great theorist and codifier of symbolist allusion and ambiguity as well as a maximum example of the obscure, hermetic poet and of that striving for absolute perfection and rarified expression that seeks the very essence of poetry.

The symbolist notions concerning music and indirect communication are not accidental characteristics to be listed in literary manuals. As Guy Michaud has shown in *La doctrine symboliste,* they reflect a vast idealism-spiritualism based in mysticism and transcendental philosophy.[16] Synesthesia, for example, is far more than a dazzling stylistic device in some of *modernismo*'s more "decorative" works, or the virtual essence of the modern spirit in literature, as Ramón del Valle-Inclán thought in 1902.[17] As Theodore W. Jensen's essay in this volume demonstrates, it is a natural manifestation of an important idea which can be traced back to Greece and even to Egypt. Swedenborgism is only its modern avatar that centered upon language and spawned Baudelaire's "universal analogy" or "correspondences." The interest in synesthesia derives ultimately from Pythagoras' "Kosmos" or harmonious universe populated by organisms (microcosms) which contain within themselves the structural principles of the Kosmos (macrocosm). Because this concept became the basis for most theories of the occult, Jensen's study reinforces John Senior's view that occultism is the metaphysical foundation of the symbolist movement.[18] Unanism or the world soul (Rubén Darío spoke of "el alma de las cosas" [the soul of things] ), the interrelatedness of all objects and beings in the cosmos, the essential harmony of the universe: all are notions derived from Pythagorean metaphysics and Platonic thought. They underlie symbolism's synesthesia and also its desire to harmonize opposites (e.g., Valle-Inclán's "armonía de contrarios") and to resolve the self-world conflict through a synthesizing vision. Thus they reflect the aspiration to harmony which lies at the very core of symbolism.[19]

The third constant of symbolism in Anna Balakian's definition, the "decadent" spirit, is the nearest this intuitive and suggestive form of expression comes to ideology or to having a consistent world view. Now the immediate connotations of "decadent," especially in Hispanic cultures, are moral and negative because they cluster around the figure of the egocentric and ultrarefined dilettante, the seeker of rare and exquisite sensations: narcissism, aestheticism, artificiality; hypersensitivity, neurosis, feverish hedonism, exaggerated and aberrant eroticism, perversity; cruelty, sadism, morbidity, necrophilia, and so forth. Yet these characteristics are "natural" manifestations of a deeply serious attitude toward reality, the *maladie fin de siècle.* As we noted earlier, decadence was no mere rebellion against what privileged cerebra viewed as bourgeois mediocrity, stultifying daily routine, conventional morality, philistinism, dehumanizing industrial civilization, and modern corruption in general. Nor was it born out of a world-rejecting apathy. True, it did view the end of the century as a waning, a passing, a decay or "falling away" in the etymological sense of the word *decadence.* Fundamentally, though, decadence is the battle against the Void—the brevity of life, impermanence, the nothingness beyond death, the unknown, the impossibility of complete fulfillment, the futility of human accomplishment, the realization that human putrefaction cannot be purified or transcended. And it is an exercising of mankind's supreme right to thirst forever after the infinite and the new. In the words of Holbrook Jackson, it is "a demand for that uniting ecstasy which is the essence of human and every other phase of life" and an effort "towards the rehabilitation of spiritual power."[20]

*Where* the ecstasy is sought, however, marks a major difference between the introspection and subjectivity of romanticism and that of the symbolist movement:

> The symbolists who had come into a waning and disillusioned century no longer aspired toward the beyond dreamed of by the romanticists, but thought of simulating it here and now in the mystery of mute things, in invisible phenomena which were conveyed by the ambiguities of communication. Theirs was an intimate dialogue between man and his shadow, not an ascent toward higher spheres as in the case of the romanticists, nor a transformation of reality into surreality, but a descent into the abyss; the dream for them was not an indication of a superior reality or a replenisher of ordinary reality, but an emblem of the unreal, of the ideal that can exist only if art gives it dimensions.[21]

Some found in decadence's restless curiosity a cause for optimism and spiritual regeneration. W. B. Yeats celebrated the growing interest in occultism and the supernatural, dreams and visions, mental telepathy and other paranormal phenomena denied by "positive science" and said, "We are, it may be, at a crowning crisis of the world, at the moment when man is about to ascend, with the wealth he has been so long gathering upon his shoulders, the stairway he has been descending from the first days."[22] For many, though, the "intimate dialogue between man and his shadow" could only be a "descent into the abyss," a fall into deep pessimism and dejection—in John Senior's phrase, "the way down and out." The self and art were the *only* domains; for Nature, worshipped by the romantics, had had its day. Art and artifice were vastly superior.

The cult of artificiality has been called by A. E. Carter "the key to the idea of decadence as the nineteenth century understood the term."[23] Oscar Wilde summed up a prevalent attitude by saying: "The first duty of life is to be as artificial as possible. What the second is no one has yet discovered."[24] Such flippancy veils the dark side of the symbolist psyche. Decadence reacted not only against the long-standing myths of Arcadia and the Noble Savage, but against things natural in general. Nature is seen as monotonous and boring in its eternal sameness, even as cruel and destructive; on all counts it deserves to be violated, altered, improved upon and replaced by artificiality. "The abnormal becomes a proof of man's superiority to natural law, a demonstration of free will. . . ."[25] Here is a dimension of the decadent's seemingly schizoid personality (e.g., the beauty of the horrid, pleasure in suffering, etc.): "a hatred of modern civilization and a love of the refinements modern civilization made possible."[26]

While there is little need to survey the development of *fin de siècle* decadence (A. E. Carter and others have done an exemplary job), some high points deserve mention because "from about 1880 till the beginning of the present century the idea of Decadence was the turning-point around which the literary world revolved."[27] Its origins are in waning romanticism (for

Mario Praz, "Decadence" is *equivalent* to "Later Romanticism"),[28] in the notorious Marquis de Sade. Théophile Gautier's writings celebrate artificiality as early as the 1830s, but not until the towering figure of Baudelaire do we have the real creation of the cult of artificiality and of the decadent as a type (dandyism, make-up, joy in depravity, sexual promiscuity and perversions, drugs, sadism, Satanism) as well as the full identification of the *modern* (civilization and technology) with the *artificial* and with *decadence:* Baudelaire used the three terms synonymously. Key "documents" are his treatises on drugs (1851, 1860), his revolutionary *Les Fleurs du Mal* and *Notes nouvelles sur Edgar Poe* (1857), and his essay on the painter Constantin Guys, with its "Eulogy of Make-up" (1860). Perhaps the finest piece ever written on decadence is Gautier's *Notice* to the 1868 edition of *Les Fleurs du Mal,* which states that the literary style required to express the neurotic sensibility of decadence was "le dernier mot du Verbe sommé de tout exprimer et poussé à l'extrême outrance"[29] [the last word of the Word called forth to express everything and thrust to the furthest extreme]. Zola's naturalism touches heavily upon decadence (which to a great extent Zola equated with the Second Empire his novels were ostensibly a history of) since "he had set out to write a study of manners, and he ended with a description of moral and aesthetic degeneracy."[30] In the 1870s and 1880s the very personification of decadence in daily life and in art was the melancholy Verlaine, at once feverishly sensual and feverishly devout, of whom Arthur Symons later said: "To fix the last fine shade, the quintessence of things; to fix it fleetingly; to be a disembodied voice, and yet the voice of a human soul: that is the ideal of Decadence, and it is what Paul Verlaine has achieved."[31] Verlaine's 1883 sonnet "Langueur" ("Je suis l'Empire à la fin de la décadence" [I am the Empire at the end of the decadence]) is often cited as a summation of the entire concept of decadence. It was Mallarmé, however, whose life and work most truly delineated the real decadent spirit of symbolism, the battle against the Void which can be waged meaningfully only through art. A profile of this spirit emerges especially from the ennui and desire for the "voyage" expressed in "Brise marine" (1865) and the escape into voluptuous sensuality in "L'Après-midi d'un faune" (1876); the obsessive narcissism of its companion piece "Hérodiade" (composed 1864-67) which discovers emptiness and sterility and suggests self-destruction; the prose poem "Igitur" (1867-70), portraying the poet's descent into self to battle the demon of impotency; the quest after poetic immortality and an "Orphic explanation of the earth" in the strange anti-poem "Un Coup de Dés" (1897), which attempts a "mirroring of infinity."[32] Jules Laforgue, too, epitomized the decadent spirit in his *Moralités Légendaires* (1887), parodying some of the greatest myths (Hamlet-Ophelia, Lohengrin, Pan, Salomé, Diana). So did Axël, the hero of Villiers de l'Isle Adam's play of the same name (staged in 1894 in Paris), who takes the "sacred leap," committing suicide with his Sara so as not to stain the moment of true spiritual beauty they have found in love. Unmatched, however, as an example of the cult of artificiality, and universally characterized as the breviary or catalogue of decadence, "the pivot upon which the whole psychology of the Decadent Movement turns,"[33] is the extraordinary novel *A Rebours* (1884) by Joris-Karl Huysmans. Its hero, the Duke Jean Floressas des Esseintes, is considered the prototype of decadence and certainly represents the quintessence of artificiality, living his life, as the title has it, "against the grain," in violation of nature. Des Esseintes finds railroad locomotives more beautiful than even the most painted mistress. Tired of depraved sexual excesses and disdainful of humankind, he cloisters himself away in the refined solitude of his villa on the outskirts of Paris, to live in the aestheticism of his imagination and sensations. Ultimately, suffering nervous attacks and unable to digest food normally, he ends up nourishing his body through enemas—and enjoying it as a victory over nature! Hereditary neurosis is the axis not only of Des Esseintes' sensibility but of his entire personality as well; in that his decadence is both pathological and aesthetic, Des Esseintes—whose creator was a disciple of Zola and a member of Zola's *cénacle*— represents the transition between naturalism and symbolism. *À Rebours* set the pattern for Oscar Wilde's *The Picture of Dorian Gray* (1891) and Gabriele D'Annunzio's *Trionfo della morte* (1894) and *Il fuoco* (1900). Des Esseintes was imitated in many later novels and carried to the extreme, most notably in Octave Mirbeau's *Jardin des supplices* (1899) and Jean Lorrain's *Le Vice errant* (1899, pub. 1902) and *Monsieur de Phocas* (1901). After the latter's protagonist, commented Enrique Gómez Carrillo, "no se distingue, a lo lejos, sino los muros blancos del manicomio"[34] [nothing is visible in the distance except the white walls of the insane asylum]. The decadent novel could now lead only to parody, as in the *Sonatas* of Valle-Inclán.

Hispanic literature is hardly without its decadents, for the *maladie fin de siècle* was thoroughly international. The Guatemalan-born Parisian, Enrique Gómez Carrillo, exceptionally well-informed about the European intellectual world and adept at transmitting his knowledge to Spain and Spanish America, represents the enthusiastic, energetic and optimistic variety of decadent, brimming with intellectual curiosity, wanting to "verlo todo, probarlo todo, amarlo todo, lo bueno y lo malo, lo amargo con lo dulce, lo tranquilo como lo peligroso"[35] [see everything, try everything, love everything, the good and the bad, the bitter with the sweet, the tranquil just as the dangerous]. In the other vein, contrasting with Gómez Carrillo's apparent ebullience and enjoyment of the artistic climate of Paris, is the unhappy decadent poet, Julián del Casal, unfit for life in colonial Cuba and obsessed with death. The hypersensitive soul is often the greatest dreamer as well as the one who finds everything in life imperfect, unsatisfactory, less than ideal. But Casal's melancholy, disenchantment and alienation were indeed exceptional: in his own words, he suffered from "ese hastío prematuro, ese profundo descorazonamiento, ese escepticismo glacial, ese adormecimiento de los sentidos, ese apetito desenfrenado de lo raro y ese estado de catalepsia en que se encuentran a los veinte años"[36] [that premature disgust, that profound dejection, that glacial skepticism, that numbness of the senses, that wanton appetite for things strange and that cataleptic state in which [artists] find themselves submerged at age twenty]. Luis Felipe Clay Méndez' essay in this volume shows how Casal, heavily influenced by French symbolism, sought an escape in self and art and developed a full aesthetic of artificiality, becoming—out of spiritual kinship rather than voluntary imitation, and with the expected moral reservations of his culture—a sort of Hispanic Des Esseintes.

If Huysmans' name keeps appearing in our discussion, it is because his importance can hardly be stressed enough; truly it was enormous among his contemporaries, in America as well as in Europe. Casal, in one of the last letters he wrote to Gómez Carrillo, confessed that only two desires made him wish to stay alive a bit longer, "dos cosas que ... son sagradas para mí: abrazar a Verlaine y darle la mano a Huysmans"[37] [two things that ... are sacred to me: to embrace Verlaine and to shake hands with Huysmans]. Strangely, though, one of the least studied aspects of the symbolist movement is the prose it produced, in spite of the fact that nineteenth-century writers were fully aware of the novel of symbolism as well as of its poetry and drama. The symbolist novel was a major vogue within Spanish American *modernismo,* as we shall soon see below. The symbolist narrative of Brazil and especially of Portugal is considerable, as Raymond Sayers' essay in this volume points out. In Spain the prose of Valle-Inclán, Azorín, Unamuno, and Gabriel Miró (as well as of minor figures such as Antonio de Hoyos) is profoundly influenced by the symbolist movement. Why, then, this lacuna in the important area of symbolist prose?

The problem can be traced back to French Symbolism and especially to the prestige of its maximum theorist, Mallarmé. Just as Edmund Wilson found within a symbolism a "serious-aesthetic" tradition (Mallarmé, Yeats, Valéry) and a "conversational-ironic" one (Corbière, Laforgue, T. S. Eliot),[38] it is fair to distinguish at least two separate theoretical-critical traditions with respect to the matter of symbolist prose-narrative-novel. The first apparently stems from Mallarmé and conceives of symbolism almost wholly in terms of poetry. Believing that a serious tone and the expressive and suggestive intensity common to poetry are indispensable to authentic literature, this tradition rejects narrative prose—especially the novel—as a genre alien to symbolist expression, accepting as artistic only the prose poem, "prose d'écrivain fastueux, ... ornementale"[39] [the prose of a sumptuous writer, decorative prose], as Mallarmé called it. He disdained narration and description as mere journalism (*reportage*). The second tradition begins with the textual evidence of the 1870s and 1880s but is based also on the *evolution* of symbolism; so it is broader and more flexible than the first: it believes in the existence of symbolist prose narrative and novel and does not exclude irony from its concept of symbolism. If the essence of the poetry tradition could be summed up in several key passages from Mallarmé about suggestion, the prose tradition owes a good deal to the important concept T. S. Eliot called the "objective correlative": "The only way of expressing emotion in the form of art is by finding an 'objective correlative'; in other words, a set of objects, a situation, a chain of events which shall be the formula of that *particular* emotion; such that when the external facts, which must terminate in sensory experience, are given, the emotion is immediately evoked."[40] Anna Balakian considers this part of the dilution of the symbol's ambiguity and expressive intensity which occurred during symbolism's "afterglow" in European literature and as a bridge which extended symbolism to narrative prose.[41] Eliot's "objective correlative" surely has influenced the broad definition of William York Tindall, labeled "hopelessly general" by Tindall himself but very applicable to narrative fiction: "The literary symbol, an analogy for something unstated, consists of an articulation of verbal elements that, going beyond reference and the limits of discourse, embodies and offers a complex of feeling and thought. Not necessarily an image, this analogical embodyment may also be a rhythm, a juxtaposition, an action, a proposition, a structure, or a poem."[42]

Unquestionably, symbolist narrative and novel existed both in practice and in theory. *A Rebours,* widely considered the prototype of the genre, inspired the "symbolic conception" of the novel described by Jean Moréas in his 1886 manifesto, profiling the passive hero or "unique personage" who uses the world as a pretext for his own sensations, transforming it through his temperament and hallucinations into a mere extension of his psyche, and its empirical objects into symbols, a "unique reality"; in doing so he transforms himself into "a clown whose mask mirrors a deformed world as artifice."[43] Although this narcissistic form has been the dominant concept of the symbolist novel, we believe that Ralph Freedman's statement about the flexibility of lyrical novels is valid for symbolist fiction as well: "Their repertoire of possible techniques includes many variations of narrative form which they use in the manner of lyrical poetry, extending from a pure stream of consciousness to a controlled pattern of figures and scenes manipulated by an omniscient author."[44] The symbolists adapted the methods of poetry to prose narrative and portrayed inner consciousness. The three main constants of symbolist poetry—ambiguity of indirect communication, affiliation with music, and the decadent spirit—were constants of many novels as well. Techniques of suggestion and musical composition were placed at the service of a carefully elaborated poetic prose which rendered the "world" through the perspective, moods and sensations of (usually) a passive, contemplative and often aestheticist protagonist and thus transformed it into a network of images and symbols, many times an analogue of the protagonist's (and the author's) psyche. As the "drama" was one of the flow of perceptions and feelings, of inner consciousness, external action was minimal and atmosphere all-important; the extreme inward turn of narrative devalued traditional factors such as chronological time, cause-effect, historical environment, character development. Reflecting the ideal of a poetic, intensely expressive and suggestive prose (as in the prose poem, adored by the Symbolist coterie), narratives were far briefer than the voluminous novels of realism and naturalism; the short story, the novella, the novelette and the short novel were the preferred forms. Irony and satire (present in the fundamentally serious *A Rebours*), even parody, formed an important dimension of symbolist narrative, even in its origins, since decadence incorporated in its mystical idealism both libertinism and the critical-analytic spirit of positivism and naturalism. Major contributors to the symbolist novel were Villiers de l'Isle Adam, Remy de Gourmont, Edouard Dujardin, Huysmans, Maeterlinck, Paul Adam, Teodor de Wyzewa, Jean Lorrain, André Gide, D'Annunzio, and others. René Wellek finds symbolist prose in "the late Henry James, in Joyce, in the later Thomas Mann, in Proust, in the early Gide and Faulkner, in D. H. Lawrence"[45]—figures mentioned or studied, along with Hermann Hesse, Virginia Woolf and others, by Freedman, and by Tindall, who had added E. M. Forster and Joseph Conrad to the list.[46]

These names, however, do not allude to the deep influence and presence of symbolist fiction in the Hispanic world. If the symbolist novel was only a "tenuous" genre for France,[47] it was vigorous and very much in vogue in Spanish America, within *modernismo*. Its orbit includes—to name only a few of the possible titles—the following representative works: *Amistad funesta* (1885) by the Cuban José Martí; *El donador de almas* (1899) by the Mexican Amado Nervo; *El extraño* (1897) and *La raza de Caín* (1900) by Carlos Reyles of Uruguay; *Idolos rotos* (1901) and *Sangre patricia* (1902) by the Venezuelan Manuel Díaz Rodríguez; *Claudio Oronoz* (1906) by Rubén M. Campos of Mexico; *La gloria de don Ramiro* (1908) by Enrique Larreta of Argentina; *La lámpara en el molino* (written 1906) by the Chilean Augusto D'Halmar; and, later, *La reina de Rapa Nui* (1914) and *Alsino* (1920) by Pedro Prado of Chile.[48] As Raymond Sayers' essay in this volume studies in detail, Portugal had the novels of Raul Brandão (*História de um Palhaço*, 1896; *A Farsa*, 1903; *Os Pobres*, 1906), Mário de Sá-Carneiro's novel *A Confissão de Lúcio* (1914) and his short story collections *Princípio* (1912) and *Céu em Fogo* (1915), the Visconde de Vila-Moura's novel *Nova Safo* (1912), and António Patrício's story *Serão Inquieto*. In Brazil the prose tales of Henrique Coelho Neto's *Rapsódias* (1891) and Rocha Pombo's novel *No Hospício* (1905) are symbolist, and Lima Barreto's novel *Vida e Morte de M. J. Gonzaga de Sá* (1919) uses symbolist techniques.

As for Spain, the "Generation of 1898" and later authors were deeply influenced by the symbolist movement. It left its mark on narrative, especially in the unclassifiable Valle-Inclán, who learned much from Maeterlinck and D'Annunzio; in the deeply subjective and introspective works of Azorín (who translated Maeterlinck's play *L'Intruse* into Spanish in 1896) and of Unamuno; and—although his contentment and joy of living free him from the decadent spirit—in Gabriel Miró. Miro's belief in the word (". . . quizá por la palabra se me diese la plenitud de la contemplación" ["perhaps through the word I may be granted fullness of contemplation"]), akin to Mallarmé's theories of poetic language or to Valle-Inclán's in *La lámpara maravillosa*, reveals the aesthetic philosophy underlying his sensual prose: "Es que la palabra, . . . como la música, resucita las realidades, las valora, exalta y acendra, subiendo a una pureza precisamente inefable, lo que por no sentirse ni decirse en su matiz, en su exactitud, dormía dentro de las exactitudes polvorientas de las mismas miradas y del mismo vocablo y concepto de todos" ["For the word, . . . like music, brings realities to life, gives them value, exalts and refines them, raising to a 'precisely ineffable' purity what, when it was neither felt nor said in its nuances, in its exactness, was lying dormant within the dusty exactness of the same gaze, the same speech and concept that are possessed by everyone"].[49] Unamuno's "tragic sense of life" makes him "a Spanish participant in the symbolist experience,"[50] but he belongs to symbolism also in the techniques by which he dramatizes the probing of his soul. Both *Niebla* (1914) and *San Manuel Bueno, mártir* (1933) are, in different ways, deeply suggestive "objective correlatives" of his complex mood inspired by his overriding concern with the problem of human impermanence. *San Manuel*'s complexity and ambiguity, well studied by Carlos Blanco Aguinaga,[51] are due not only to the novelette's multiple perspectivism but also to the skillful symbolic elaboration of the lake and mountain of Valverde de Lucerna. These are two of the finest interdependent and composite symbols in all of modern Spanish literature—and symbols only possible thanks to techniques developed by the symbolist movement. The syncretic Valle-Inclán is a far more obvious case of how symbolism enriches a profoundly original artistic temperament. His early or *modernista* prose of the decade 1895-1905—especially the definitive edition of *Jardín umbrío* (including the two novellas "Rosarito" and "Mi hermana Antonia"), the *Sonatas* and *Flor de santidad,* each very different in tone from the others—is so thoroughly imbued with symbolism that he is probably Spain's major symbolist prose writer.[52] These works have a great deal in common with the flexible profile of the symbolist novel we have sketched out above. So, too, does Valle's unique and misunderstood *La lámpara maravillosa* (1916), which shows how deeply symbolist aesthetics were ingrained in his artistic consciousness. Guillermo Díaz Plaja claims that in the entire history of Hispanic aesthetics, including Rubén Darío, there is no book which even comes close to it, in doctrine and in density, for explaining the aesthetic foundations of *modernismo,*[53] and Emilio González López calls it the "manifiesto magno del simbolismo expañol"[54] [ great manifesto of Spanish symbolism]. Carol S. Maier's essay in the present volume goes to the very heart of Valle-Inclán's symbolist affiliation, and to the heart of Spanish symbolist prose in general, by studying Valle's concept of poetic language as it is presented, embodied and dramatized in *La lámpara maravillosa.*

In view of the importance of symbolist prose in the Hispanic literatures, our overview of "symbolism and decadence" requires that we touch upon the relationship of symbolism to Spanish and Spanish American *modernismo.* The term *modernismo,* not synonymous with "modernism," is not the Hispanic equivalent of "symbolism" (though it has been used nearly as such, for example by as perceptive a writer as Manuel Díaz Rodríguez);[55] but it is indeed the reason why *simbolismo* is not a broad category or period-encompassing term in the Spanish-speaking countries today. *Modernismo* has been used to designate the following: a literary school, a particular affected manner (the French-inspired *preciosité* of the early Rubén Darío, roughly during the decade 1888-98, later called *rubendarismo*), a new poetic language or a technique ("modernismo es, ante todo, una técnica," says Dámaso Alonso[56] [*modernismo* is, above all, a technique]), a formal revolution, a revolution in both form and spirit, a new sensibility, and so forth. More broadly, it has signified a movement, an epoch, and, of course, in Federico de Onís' now-classic study (1934): "El modernismo es la forma hispánica de la crisis universal de las letras y del espíritu que inicia hacia 1885 la disolución del siglo XIX y que se había de manifestar en el arte, la ciencia, la religión, la política y gradualmente en los demás aspectos de la vida entera, con todos los caracteres, por lo tanto, de un hondo cambio histórico cuyo proceso continúa hoy"[57] [*Modernismo* is the Hispanic form of the universal literary and spiritual crisis which initiates around 1885 the dissolution of the nineteenth century and which was to manifest itself in art, science, religion, politics, and gradually in all the other aspects of life, with all the marks, therefore, of a deep historical change whose process continues today].

For our purposes, it is important to observe that *modernismo* was an eclectic and syncretic movement which incorporated a wide variety of elements from (essentially) neoromanticism, impressionism, Parnassianism, symbolism and, *avant la lettre,* expressionism—but particulary Parnassianism, which dominated during the period from roughly 1875 to 1892 (although symbolist tendencies may be detected early on), and symbolism, the impact of which was stronger after 1892. *Modernismo* brought together disparate and even seemingly incompatible elements, attitudes, techniques, and tendencies, blending them in what Pedro Salinas called "el acomodaticio crisol del modernismo" [*modernismo*'s accommodating crucible].[58] It could do this, as Onís explains, because of the Spanish American's ability to assimilate and view as his own all forms of foreign culture. Literary tendencies which in Europe developed in successive phases coexist in Spanish America, often in a single author. And so it happens that the Spanish American *modernistas* are at the same time classical, romantic, Parnassian, symbolist, realist and naturalist.[59] At the same time, the *modernista* writers could be—indeed, these may be regarded as three constants of *modernismo*—cosmopolitan, innovative, and extremely individualistic. Just as *modernismo* represents Spanish American literature's full entrance into world literature, ultimately the *modernista* writer seeks out and affirms his individuality and uniqueness through the universal. As Martí said, "Conocer diversas literaturas es el medio mejor de libertarnos de la tiranía de algunas de ellas"[60] [to know many different literatures is the best way to free ourselves from the tyranny of any of them].

*Modernismo,* then, is more comprehensive than symbolism, which it subsumes. Nevertheless, there is a growing awareness in Spanish-language criticism of symbolism in its own right, apart from or within *modernismo,* and the present volume is a response (and, we hope, a contribution) to that awareness. As Parnassianism is seen to have produced the more decorative, precious vein, symbolism emerges both as the source of a more "essential" *modernismo*—of ambiguity, suggestion and musicality as well as of the underlying mysticism and idealism that seeks essences—and as the major element of *modernismo,* the current of most lasting influence. Just as Juan Ramón Jiménez declared long ago that *modernismo* was composed of two basic currents but "Lo que entra en España no es el parnasianismo sino el simbolismo"[61] [What enters Spain is not Parnassianism but symbolism], Ricardo Gullón declares that the most vigorous of the tendencies that join in *modernismo* is the symbolist one.[62] Similarly, looking back at symbolism from the standpoint of European vanguardism, Renato Poggioli finds that symbolism was indeed "the principal poetic movement, the richest source of modernism [not to be confused with *modernismo*] in the field of literature."[63] This thinking has entered Spanish criticism as well. In his recent book which seeks to prove that Antonio Machado is above all else a symbolist poet, J. M. Aguirre reduces the importance of Parnassianism, affirming that the symbolist movement is the origin of modern poetry in the Western world and that symbolism is the fundamental reality not only of Spanish *modernismo* but of European letters from the beginning of the twentieth century until the 1930s.[64]

The new emphasis on symbolism in Peninsular Spanish criticism may be especially helpful for Spain, whose earlier lack of awareness of symbolism is not typical of all Hispanic culture. If Portugal and Brazil seem to be missing from our brief profile of the present concept of symbolism in Hispanic literatures, it is because *simbolismo* has long been a standard category in Luso-Brazilian criticism, as noted earlier, and because Raymond S. Sayers has covered the matter in the review of symbolism in Portugal and Brazil he has written for this volume. Spanish American literature, with its eyes wide open and its gaze unrestricted in space and time, has not suffered as Spain has from her long-standing cult of Iberian individuality and uniqueness and from the canonization of the "Generation of 1898" concept, a corollary of which was that *modernismo* was a superficial stylistic spark-shower incompatible with the serious metaphysical broodings and existential agony of an Unamuno or an Antonio Machado. It hardly needs to be said that to have been influenced by the international symbolist movement in no way signifies a lack of originality. On the contrary, it is normal and inevitable that a writer be part of the literary spirit of his age. True literary comparatism would want to understand the evolution of symbolism as it became international, and to study its varying adaptations to new cultural environments and to each new writer it touches. Above all, we should want to know not *whether* an author is a symbolist but rather how his particular temperament rejects, assimilates or transforms the essentials of the movement.

Spanish America seems to have accepted symbolism somewhat more easily than Spain, in spite of the fact that their common tongue allowed them to share the same sources of the diffusion of symbolism. Spanish and Spanish American writers alike flocked to Paris, the Mecca of the art and literary world in the 1890s. Books and articles studying the leading writers of France and Europe appeared in Spain and Spanish America throughout the decade and later. Among the most important sources were Darío's *Los raros* (1896) and Enrique Gómez Carrillo's series of articles and books—*Esquisses* (written in Spanish, Madrid, 1892), *Sensaciones de arte* (Paris, 1893), *Literatura extranjera* (Paris, 1895), *Almas y cerebros* (Paris, ca. 1898), *Sensaciones de París y de Madrid* (Paris, 1900), *El alma encantadora de París* (Barcelona, 1902), *El modernismo* (Madrid, ca. 1905) and many others. Among the authors treated in his studies and personal interviews are Verlaine, Charles Morice, Anatole France, Huysmans, Paul Bourget, Moréas, Catulle Mendès, Maurice Barrès, Jean Lorrain, Henri de Régnier, Georges Rodenbach, Villiers de l'Isle Adam, Maeterlinck and Verhaeren. John Kronik's overview of Gómez Carrillo's role as a "Francophile propagandist" points out that "of the numerous French authors Gómez Carrillo propagandized, many had never been mentioned before by a Spanish-language writer" and that his role in spreading Verlaine's name in Spain "was greater than that of anyone before Darío and more sustained thereafter," so that all in all, "he made Spanish writers aware of a modern sensitivity in art."[65]

The importance of reviews and journals was great, especially as a unifier of Spanish American *modernismo*. Alongside *La Nación* and *La Razón* of Buenos Aires, many new ones came into existence: in Argentina, the *Revista de América* (1894), founded by Darío and Ricardo Jaimes Freyre and succeeded by *La Biblioteca* (1896-1898) and *El Mercurio de América* (1898-1900); in Mexico, *Revista Azul* (1894-1896), founded by Manuel Gutiérrez Nájera, and *Revista Moderna* (1898-1911), founded by Jesús E. Valenzuela; in Venezuela, *Cosmópolis* (1894-1895), founded by Pedro César Domínici; to mention but a few. In Spain, the dailies *El Liberal, El Imparcial, Blanco y Negro* and *ABC* carried articles on contemporary European literature. Gómez Carrillo's three articles on "Los poetas jóvenes de Francia," published in the *Revista de América* in 1894, explained with precision what Symbolism of the Paris *cénacle* was and who its major figures were, apparently so well that after the *Revista de América*, Parnassianism was no longer confused with symbolism in the Río de la Plata region.[66] These same articles, with important additions, were published the following year in Gómez Carrillo's book, *Literatura extranjera*. In keeping with the all-important role literary journals played in the literary life of the period, Catherine Vera's essay in this volume documents conclusively Spanish America's awareness of symbolism in major periodicals of 1896-1910, key years in the evolution of *modernismo,* between the publication of Darío's *Prosas profanas* and *Los raros* and the beginning of the Mexican Revolution.

In spite of the enthusiastic reception of symbolism by leading Hispanic writers, its acceptance was hardly unanimous. Within the general ethical norms of Spanish culture, *modernismo* and symbolism, with their mixture of mysticism and sensuality, posed a conflict (insoluble for many) between aesthetics and morality. The decadent life-style, narcissism, and aestheticism in general were viewed as immoral. The reaction of superficial temperaments is predictable and often amusing. In his essay for this volume, John Kronik uncovers the interesting case of the Spanish expatriate Leopoldo García Ramón, a Paris-based contributor to major Spanish periodicals during the 1880s, the key decade in the development of French Symbolism. Ironically, García Ramón's impassioned negative reaction to Jean Moréas' *Manifeste* and to "deplorable" Symbolism in general, helped make him—albeit unintentionally—one of the first publicizers of French Symbolism in Spain. Lily Litvak has shown that this sort of moral outrage and confusion over the new literary currents, which we laugh at today, were typical of the years 1888-1910,[67] and Catherine Vera's piece herein shows that the same reaction was common in Spanish America. Yet this moral conflict occurs in Spain's most sensitive temperaments as well. In this respect the Machado brothers offer a contrast. Allen W. Phillips' essay in our volume points out decadent elements in Manuel Machado's life-style and in his poetry prior to 1910, in *Alma* (1899-1900) and especially in *El mal poema* (1909)—the sad, monotonous, nuanced poetry of refined baseness in the manner of Verlaine, fusing mysticism and sensuality. If Manuel Machado embraced decadence and Verlaine, Geoffrey Ribbans' essay herein delineates Antonio Machado's more complex and ambivalent attitude toward French symbolism: how as a practicing poet fascinated by the new mode he achieved the *galerías* (of *Soledades, Galerías y otros poemas,* 1907), a peak of European symbolism, while also revealing dissatisfaction with major features of French symbolism's life-style and with some concepts of its poetry—narcissism and artificiality, fleeting and etherial Verlainian poetry, and the cult of mystery and imprecision. Ribbans also shows how, looking back from his maturity, virtually as a literary historian, Machado was able to view symbolism within its nineteenth-century context and make a keen appraisal of its strengths and weaknesses.

What, then, is the present status of symbolism in the Hispanic literatures that do not have it as an established literary category? Happily, both Spanish and Spanish American criticism are moving toward a clear concept of symbolism and its influence. In recent publications, Emilio González López has urged critics to recognize symbolism, long hidden beneath *modernismo,* especially with respect to Valle-Inclán.[68] Nevertheless, González López' article dealing with the major critical terms presents too limited a view of symbolism (equating it with a search for eternal essences) and makes Parnassianism and decadence secondary and "wholly accessory," which certainly they were not. His two books on Valle's poetry and theater furnish neither a working definition nor a consistent concept of symbolism. A broad, somewhat chaotic, but still helpful definition of symbolism emerges from Luis Antonio de Villena's recent article "Simbolismo y decadentismo en *Alma,* de Manuel Machado" (*Insula,* No. 377 [April 1978], pp. 1, 12), which considers symbolism a technique and decadence an attitude within the large cultural orb of symbolism, the dominant one in Europe from 1871 to 1914. Perhaps the clearest view of the relationship of Parnassianism, symbolism and decadence emerges from many articles by Allen W. Phillips on *modernismo* and decadence, covering both Spanish and Spanish American authors.[69] There is no need to abandon the term *modernismo* in order to appreciate symbolism within it, as proven by the work of Phillips and Ricardo Gullón (especially his *Direcciones del modernismo*) and by the recent volume *Estudios críticos sobre la prosa modernista hispanoamericana,* edited by José Olivio Jiménez, cited earlier. The latter reveals a sound appreciation of symbolism's relationship to *modernismo* and contains helpful studies on decadence. Jiménez' forthcoming Taurus volume of critical studies, entitled *El simbolismo* and scheduled for publication this year, will focus on symbolism in its own right and will be a most welcome contribution. David L. Anderson's *Symbolism: A Bibliography of Symbolism as an International and Multi-Disciplinary Movement* (New York: New York University Press, 1975), supervised by Anna Balakian, contains more than two hundred fifty items pertaining to literature written in Spanish and Portuguese including such authors as: Unamuno, Antonio and Manuel Machado, Valle-Inclán, Azorín, Juan Ramón Jiménez, Federico García Lorca, Jorge Guillén; José Martí, Manuel Gutiérrez Nájera, José Asunción Silva, Rubén Darío, José Enrique Rodó, Enrique Gómez Carrillo, Julio Herrera y Reissig, Richard Güiraldes, Ramón López Velarde; Eugénio de Castro, Raul Brandão, Camilo Pessanha, Fernando Pessoa, Cruz e Sousa, and Alphonsus Guimaraens. This bibliography complements a forthcoming critical history of symbolism, a huge collaborative effort by a team of some seventy-five internationally known scholars, organized by Anna Balakian for the International Comparative Literature Association, as a part of their continuing project on the comparative history of literature in European languages. This collection will contain several extensive and important articles by Hispanists. At present the best single Spanish-lanaguage introduction to symbolism (especially to its French roots) is found in J. M. Aguirre's *Antonio Machado, poeta simbolista* (1973). As if to remedy Spain's and Spanish America's incomplete awareness of the symbolist movement, Aguirre devotes the first 214 of the 380 pages of his text to a description and history of symbolism.

Obviously, much remains to be done. Efforts to discern symbolism within *modernismo* must move forward with greater precision. As for Spain, the "Generation of 1898" concept cannot continue to place metaphysical and ideological concerns in opposition to the period's major aesthetic currents. Above all, more studies of specific works by writers who have an unmistakable relationship to symbolism are needed: not just the Machados, Valle-Inclán and Juan Ramón Jiménez, whose symbolism has begun to be studied, but also Unamuno, Benavente, Azorín, Miró. Comparative studies which analyze rather than mention the influence of such key figures as Maeterlinck and D'Annunzio—like that of Susan Kirkpatrick[70]—would be most helpful. Because we are only at the beginning of the burgeoning interest in Hispanic symbolism, the present volume includes essays studying areas of the impact of symbolism that are fundamental. All the essays were prepared specifically for this volume. The piece by Ricardo Gullón is based on the conclusion of his book *Una poética para Antonio Machado* (Madrid: Gredos, 1970) but is presented here for the first time in essay form because we wanted to make it available in English to literary comparatists.

Foremost among the fundamental areas examined in this book are the introduction and diffusion of symbolism within Spain, Portugal, Brazil, and Spanish America, and the reluctance of Spain and Spanish America to accept the symbolist aesthetic and the decadent way of life so clearly present in the works of some of their most distinguished writers (in the essays by Kronik, Ribbans, Sayers, Vera, Phillips, and Clay Méndez). We have also been concerned with the underlying metaphysical and aesthetic roots of symbolism, specifically in occultism and Pythagoreanism (in the essay by Jensen), as with the theory and practice of symbolist aesthetics (in essays by Ribbans, Gullón, and Maier). That the Hispanic literatures were part of a thoroughly international movement is clear from two essays in our volume that are firmly in the vein of literary comparatism, those by Lily Litvak and J. M. Aguirre. Both reflect the European symbolist tradition in attitude and technique and touch upon the fundamental schism that lies at the heart of the symbolist personality. Lily Litvak shows Juan Ramón Jiménez wrestling with a problem closely related to the Hispanic aesthetic-moral conflict but which fits into the essential dualism of the symbolist personality, caught between sensualism and spirituality. J. M. Aguirre pursues a line of thinking which coincides broadly with Gaston Bachelard's and specifically with Edward Engelberg's in his anthology *The Symbolist Poem*: the window pane as the symbolist poet's "great divide" between many inner and outer worlds—man and object, beautiful illusion and sordid reality, subjective and objective, self and "other," perhaps even between meaning and nothingness. In that "the poet is trapped between his impulse to recover the transcendent world and his awareness of the utter impossibility of ever doing so, except by resorting to the illusion of the windowpane," the window is the constant reminder of the poet's separation and alienation from an ideal world and thus embodies and reveals the tension underlying all symbolist poetry.[71] Aguirre explores the self and the "other" in the suggestive context (or emotional construct) of window-mirror-room-street, tracing the values given to the window symbol by many poets and prose writers of the *fin de siècle* period and after. No essay could underscore more than his how clearly the Hispanic literatures belong to the international literary movement that was symbolism.

\* \* \*

We wish to thank the Editorial Board of *Essays in Literature* for the opportunity to produce this book. Special thanks are due to Rulon Smithson, the editor for foreign literatures of our sponsoring journal, who was available on several occasions for consultation on the fine points of French language and literature. Having said this, however, we should add that he is not responsible for any errors that we may have made when we were not wise enough to seek his advice. We are also thankful that we could call on David Wise at Washington University at a time when we were literally snowed in and could not get to a major research library to check some details. Finally, we are grateful to those who inspire us day after day and without whose affection and good humor projects like this would be difficult to complete—Rhoda Grass and Diane, Kristin, and Amy Risley.

R. G. and W. R. R.

## NOTES

[1] *Obras completas: Tomo II, prosas-poesías,* ed. Francisco González Guerrero and Alfonso Méndez Plancarte, 4th ed. (Madrid: Aguilar, 1967), p. 342.

[2] "The Decadent Movement in Literature," *Harper's New Monthly Magazine,* 87 (1893), 858-59.

[3] *Degeneration* (1895; rpt. New York: Howard Fertig, 1968), pp. 101 and 13, resp.

[4] Ibid., p. 101.

[5] Guy Michaud, *Message poétique du symbolisme* (Paris: Nizet, 1947), II, 331.

[6] A. E. Carter, *The Idea of Decadence in French Literature, 1830-1900* (Toronto: Univ. of Toronto Press, 1958), p. 138. This equation was true for much of Europe and America during the following decade. At a celebration in honor of Rubén Darío in Córdoba, Argentina, in 1896, a young man named Carlos Romagosa read an address on "la última evolución literaria llamada por sus adversarios *decadente* y llamada por sus iniciadores *simbolista*" [the latest literary evolution, called by its adversaries *decadent* and by its initiators *symbolist*] (Rafael Alberto Arrieta, *Introducción al modernismo literario,* 2nd ed. [Buenos Aires: Columba, 1961], p. 46).

[7] "The Term and Concept of Symbolism in Literary History," in *Discriminations: Further Concepts of Criticism* (New Haven: Yale Univ. Press, 1970), p. 90.

[8] Ibid., p. 120.

[9] *The Symbolist Movement: A Critical Appraisal,* 2nd ed. (New York: New York Univ. Press, 1977), p. 101.

[10] Quoted in C. F. MacIntyre, *French Symbolist Poetry* (Berkeley: Univ. of California Press, 1971), p. vi.

[11] *The Symbolist Aesthetic in France, 1885-1895* (Oxford: Basil Blackwell, 1950), pp. 306-07. William York Tindall has observed that "Neither Baudelaire nor his *semblables* drew fine distinctions between symbol, emblem, allegory, sign, and image, all of which meant symbol" (*The Literary Symbol* [1955; rpt. Bloomington: Indiana Univ. Press, 1971], p. 47); nor was the important distinction between symbol and allegory made by creators of the symbolist novel such as Huysmans and D'Annunzio.

[12] Balakian, p. 163.

[13] *Mallarmé* (Chicago: Univ. of Chicago Press, 1955), p. 264.

[14] *The Symbolist Movement in Literature* (1899; rpt. New York: Dutton, 1958), p. 49.

15 In the poem "Verlaine (Responso)," 1896. Typical is the reaction of the Guatemalan, Enrique Gómez Carrillo: "Verlaine es, para mí, el poeta más penetrante, más delicado y más sutil de nuestro siglo" [Verlaine is, in my opinion, the most penetrating, most delicate and most subtle poet of our century] (*Literatura extranjera: estudios cosmopolitas* [Paris: Garnier, 1895], p. 319).

16 *La doctrine symboliste (Documents)* (Paris: Nizet, 1947).

17 "Modernismo," in *La ilustración española y americana*, 22 Feb. 1902; rpt. in Eliane Lavaud, "Un prologue et un article oubliés: Valle-Inclán, théoricien du modernisme," *Bulletin Hispanique*, 76, Nos. 3-4 (July-Dec. 1974), 370-75.

18 John Senior, *The Way Down and Out: The Occult in Symbolist Literature* (1959; rpt. New York: Greenwood Press, 1968), p. xxiii.

19 A helpful synthesis of major sources of the symbolist aesthetic is given in Verity Smith, *Ramón del Valle-Inclán* (New York: Twayne, 1973), pp. 31-41.

20 *The Eighteen Nineties* (1913; rpt. New York: Capricorn Books, 1966), pp. 70-71.

21 Anna Balakian, "The International Character of Symbolism," *Mosaic*, 2, No. 4 (1968), 3.

22 Quoted in Jackson, p. 71.

23 "The Cult of Artificiality," *University of Toronto Quarterly*, 25 (1956), 464.

24 Quoted in *Realism, Naturalism, and Symbolism: Modes of Thought and Expression in Europe, 1848-1914*, ed. Roland N. Stromberg (New York: Harper, 1968), p. 243.

25 Carter, *The Idea of Decadence . . .*, p. 5.

26 Ibid., p. 6.

27 Mario Praz, *The Romantic Agony*, trans. Angus Davidson, 2nd ed. (New York: Oxford Univ. Press, 1970), p. 396. Much of the following summary is taken from Carter's *The Idea of Decadence. . . .*

28 *The Romantic Agony*, p. xxi.

29 "Notice" to Charles Baudelaire, *Les Fleurs du Mal*, 2nd ed. (Paris: Lévy, 1868), p. xvi.

30 Carter, "The Cult of Artificiality," p. 460.

31 "The Decadent Movement in Literature," p. 862.

32 Fowlie, p. 226.

33 Praz, p. 322.

34 *Primeros estudios cosmopolitas* (Madrid: Mundo Latino, 1920), p. 270.

35 Quoted in Juan Mendoza, *Enrique Gómez Carrillo: Estudio crítico-biográfico* (Guatemala City: Muñoz Plaza. 1940), p. 48. On Gómez Carrillo, see the recent study by Sophia Demetriou, "La decadencia y el escritor modernista: Enrique Gómez Carrillo," in *Estudios críticos sobre la prosa modernista hispanoamericana*, ed José Olivio Jiménez (New York: Eliseo Torres, 1975), pp. 223-36. Henceforth, this collection will be cited as Jiménez.

36 *Prosas* (Havana: Consejo Nacional de Cultura, 1963), I, 267; quoted by Joan Federman, "La visión decadente del mundo en los cuentos y crónicas de Julián del Casal," in Jiménez, pp. 124-25.

37 Enrique Gómez Carrillo, *Almas y cerebros* (Paris: Garnier, n.d. [1898?]), p. 137.

38 *Axel's Castle: A Study in the Imaginative Literature of 1870-1930* (New York: Charles Scribner's Sons, 1931), p. 96.

39 Stéphane Mallarmé, "La Musique et les lettres," in *Oeuvres complètes,* ed. Henri Mondor and G. Jean-Aubry (Paris: Gallimard, Bibliothèque de la Pléiade, 1960), p. 644.

40 T. S. Eliot, "Hamlet and His Problems," in *The Sacred Wood* (London: Methuen, 1950), p. 100.

41 *The Symbolist Movement,* p. 163.

42 *The Literary Symbol,* pp. 12-13.

[43] Ralph Freedman, *The Lyrical Novel: Studies in Hermann Hesse, André Gide and Virginia Woolf* (Princeton: Princeton Univ. Press, 1963), p. 35.

[44] Ibid., p. 30.

[45] "The Term and Concept of Symbolism in Literary History," p. 120.

[46] In *The Lyrical Novel* and *The Literary Symbol,* resp.

[47] Bernard C. Swift, "The Hypothesis of the French Symbolist Novel," *Modern Language Review,* 68 (1973), 784.

[48] See Hernán Vidal, "*Sangre patricia* y la conjunción naturalista-simbolista: La bancarrota social positivista en la novela hispanoamericana," *Hispania,* 52 (1960), 183-92, and the following by Roland Grass: "El *Claudio Oronoz* de Rubén M. Campos y el valor social del modernismo," in *Homenaje a Sherman H. Eoff,* ed. José Schraibman (Madrid: Castalia, 1970), pp. 117-36; "Amado Nervo y los comienzos de la novela modernista," in *Homenaje a Andrés Iduarte,* ed. J. Alazraki, R. Grass, R. O. Salmon (Clear Creek, IN: The American Hispanist, Inc., 1976), pp. 165-77; "Carlos Reyles and the Impact of the Symbolist-Decadent Novel in Spanish America," *The American Hispanist,* 2, No. 15 (Feb. 1977), 11-13; "The Symbolist Mode in the Spanish American Modernista Novel, 1885-1924," in *Symbolism* (prob. title), ed. Anna Balakian (Budapest: International Comparative Literature Association), in press.

[49] Quoted in Jorge Guillén, *Language and Poetry* (Cambridge: Harvard Univ. Press, 1961), pp. 159 and 161-62. Spanish texts are given by Guillén on p. 256; English translations are those supplied by Guillén.

[50] Balakian, *The Symbolist Movement,* pp. 116 and 141.

[51] "Sobre la complejidad de *San Manuel Bueno, mártir,* novela," *Nueva Revista de Filología Hispánica,* 15 (1961), 569-88.

[52] See William R. Risley, "Hacia el simbolismo en la prosa de Valle-Inclán," *Anales de la Narrativa Española Contemporánea,* 4 (1979), forthcoming.

[53] *Las estéticas de Valle-Inclán* (Madrid: Gredos, 1965), p. 262.

[54] "Bajo la sombra del modernismo y el impresionismo: la generación del 98 y el simbolismo," *Insula,* No. 350 (Jan. 1976), p. 11.

[55] See Diane Cornwell, "El modernismo hispanoamericano visto por los modernistas," in Jiménez, pp. 311-12. Still other definitions of *modernismo* fit closely the concept of decadence as we have outlined it above.

[56] *Poetas españoles contemporáneos,* 3rd ed. (Madrid: Gredos, 1965), p. 85.

[57] *Antología de la poesía española e hispanoamericana (1882-1932)* (1934; rpt. New York: Las Américas, 1961), p. xv; see also his "Sobre el concepto del modernismo," in *Estudios críticos sobre el modernismo,* ed. Homero Castillo (Madrid: Gredos, 1968), p. 37. The latter vol. will be cited hereafter as Castillo.

[58] "El problema del modernismo en España, o un conflicto entre dos espíritus," in Castillo, p. 25.

[59] "Sobre el concepto del modernismo," pp. 39-40.

[60] *Obras completas, XV* (Havana: Editorial Nacional de Cuba, 1964), 361.

[61] Juan Ramón Jiménez, *El modernismo: Notas de un curso (1953),* ed. Ricardo Gullón and E. Fernández Méndez (Mexico City: Aguilar, 1962), p. 227.

[62] *Direcciones del modernismo,* 2nd ed. (Madrid: Gredos, 1971), p. 167. A more extreme form of the idea is Emilio González López' statement that Hispanic literary criticism, "Ofuscada por la pérdida de la silueta del simbolismo en la niebla del modernismo" [obfuscated by the loss of symbolism's silhouette in the fog of *modernismo*], considered Valle-Inclán's pre-1914 writings sometimes as decadent art and at other times as Parnassian, when these two aesthetics were really nothing more than "simples adornos que no afectaban la esencia simbolista de la obra" [mere adornments that did not affect the symbolist essence of his work] ("Bajo la sombra del modernismo . . .," p. 11).

[63] *The Theory of the Avant-Garde,* trans. Gerald Fitzgerald (Cambridge: Harvard Univ. Press, 1968), p. 198.

[64] *Antonio Machado, poeta simbolista* (Madrid: Taurus, 1973), pp. 34 and 184, resp.

65 "Enrique Gómez Carrillo, Francophile Propagandist," *Symposium,* 21 (1967), 52, 54.

66 Boyd G. Carter, *Historia de la literatura hispanoamericana a través de sus revistas* (Mexico City: Andrea, 1968), p. 46.

67 "La idea de la decadencia en la crítica antimodernista en España," *Hispanic Review,* 45 (1977), 397-412.

68 In art. cit. and *El arte dramático de Valle-Inclán (del decadentismo al expresionismo)* (New York: Las Américas, 1967) and *La poesía de Valle-Inclán: Del simbolismo al expresionismo* (Río Piedras: Editorial Universitaria, Universidad de Puerto Rico, 1973).

69 Two recent arts. are "El primer José Juan Tablada: Modernismo y decadentismo," in *Homage to Irving A. Leonard* (East Lansing: Michigan State University, 1977), pp. 181-96, and "A propósito del decadentismo en América: Rubén Darío," *Revista Canadiense de Estudios Hispánicos,* 1 (1977), 229-54.

70 "From 'Octavia Santino' to *El yermo de las almas*: Three Phases of Valle-Inclán," *Revista Hispánica Moderna,* 37 (1972-73), 56-72. See also the very helpful articles by Graciela Palau de Nemes, "La importancia de Maeterlinck en un momento crítico de las letras hispanas," *Revue Belge de Philologie et d'Histoire,* 40 (1962), 714-28, and Lily Litvak, "Maeterlinck en Cataluña," *Revue des Langues Vivantes,* 34 (1968), 184-98.

71 Edward Engelberg, *The Symbolist Poem: The Development of the English Tradition* (New York: Dutton, 1967), pp. 31-32.

A vignette by Julio Ruelas, dated 1901. Reproduced from *Revista Moderna de México.* 6, No. 7 (Sept. 1904), 23.

# The Introduction of Symbolism into Spain: A Call to Arms

## John W. Kronik

The symbolist doctrine spawned controversies in Spain that raged on well past the turn of the century. Its partisans and dectractors south of the Pyrenees were still arguing their cases at a time when the movement had already made inroads serious enough to shape the style of some of Spain's most significant poets and to merit the attention of the important critics on the literary scene in Madrid and Barcelona. Symbolism's trials and conquests on the Peninsula have been amply documented in studies of Rubén Darío, of critics like Clarín and Emilia Pardo Bazán, of francophile expatriates like Alejandro Sawa, and of poets from the Machado brothers and Juan Ramón Jiménez to Jorge Guillén. The cries of shock and suspicion naturally rang loudest at the onset of the incursion when those reacting in hostility did so under the burden of an abbreviated historical perspective. Later generations, including ours, who have watched symbolism's purported linguistic absurdities and moral threats wreak esthetic miracles, tend to divide the opposing camps into the misguided and the enlightened. That symbolism has become a fact in the life of modern literature, even in Spain, understandably obscures the battle that its introduction triggered, especially in Spain. A glance at one who might rank among the misguided souls offers us a curious but telling footnote to the history of symbolism in Spain.

Leopoldo García-Ramón was a literary figure who today survives only among the marginalia to be plucked from a dusty shelf.[1] Born in Seville in 1849, he spent most of his life in Paris, where he mixed with French literati and Hispanic expatriates and visitors. Most of his books bore the imprint of the Parisian publishing house of Garnier and were directed back at his fellow Spaniards. The author of some fiction and of an occasional literary curiosity like *El arte de fumar. Tabacología universal,* he also prepared editions of Calderón, Alarcón, and Quintana and translations into Spanish of Boccaccio, Hans Christian Andersen, Maupassant, and others. The French translation of Pardo Bazán's *Bucólica* came from his hand, and she, in turn, wrote a prologue for his *Seres humanos (Estudios de mujer)* (Paris: Garnier, 1884). As a journalist he wrote for some of the more significant Spanish publications of his day, among them the *Revista Contemporánea, La España Moderna, La Revista de España,* and *El Correo de Ultramar.* Though not nearly so significant or open-minded as Pardo Bazán or Enrique Gómez Carrillo, García-Ramón was one link in the cultural lifeline between Paris and Madrid.

For a period of time García-Ramón contributed a series entitled "Cartas de París" to the *Revista Contemporánea,* a semimonthly magazine of wide-ranging contents published in Madrid. The first of these "Letters from Paris" appeared in the issue of August 30, 1886 (Vol. LXIII), the second a month later on September 30, 1886. Beginning with October 30, 1886, every number of the *Revista Contemporánea* carried one of García-Ramón's reports from the French capital until January 15, 1887, after which date they became quite irregular. The last of the "Cartas de París" was published in the issue of April 30, 1888. The third in this series of chronicles was an extended account of and reaction to Jean Moréas' "Manifeste littéraire de l'École Symboliste" [Literary Manifesto of the Symbolist School], which the French poet launched in the literary supplement of *Le Figaro* on September 18, 1886. Dated "París, 20 de Octubre de 1886," García-Ramón's "Carta" was printed ten days later in the *Revista Contemporánea* (Año XII, tomo LXIV [(Oct. 30,) 1886], 155-67). News of the Moréas manifesto thus reached the Spanish reading public barely more than a month after its proclamation.

But the news did not arrive uncolored. Hostility and derision mark the tone of this expansive essay from its opening salvo, which is a clarion call to Spaniards to be on guard against the "gravísimo peligro que les amenaza" (p. 155) [very grave danger that threatens them] from the shores of the Seine. Since he finds indifference and Olympic serenity in the Spanish press, the Academy, and the literary circles, his design is to be the first to sound the alarm, which he hopes will be heeded. And why such distress? Because in Paris a revolution has just occurred, a peaceful revolution in which only ink has been shed, but which is of transcendental proportions nonetheless.

La secta de los poetas *decadentes* o *deliquescentes* que ambicionaba la supremacía literaria desde el 1866 que se formó en las alturas de Montmartre, ha trabajado con tal ahinco, conspirado con tal ardor que, a fuerza de agitarse y dar saltitos, . . . ha acabado por topar con su Napoleón . . . Y este genio, que se llama Juan Moreás [sic], no ha hecho más que llegar, ver y vencer; suyo es el cetro de la poesía lírica . . . en un brillante manifiesto, ha reunido todas las aspiraciones y aberraciones, grandezas y ridiculeces, *decadencias* y *deliquescencias* de sus vocablos, bajo el nombre redundante y feo de SIMBOLISMO.[2] (p. 156)[3]

[The sect of *decadent* or *deliquescent* poets who from the heights of Montmartre aspired to literary supremacy since 1886 has labored with such zeal, conspired with such fervor that, by getting excited and hopping about, . . . it has finally hit on its Napoleon . . . And this genius, whose name is Jean Moréas, has simply come, seen, and conquered; the scepter of lyric poetry is his . . . [I]n a brilliant manifesto, he has gathered all the aspirations and aberrations, the grandeur and the ridiculousness, the *decadence* and *deliquescence* of their vocabulary under the redundant and ugly name of SYMBOLISM.]

Unsympathetic as he is to the symbolist cause, García-Ramón does not perceive it as a sham performance. On the contrary, he believes the danger is all the more acute because these are poets who write in good faith and must therefore be taken seriously. The problem is twofold. On the one hand, Spaniards are susceptible to anything French. As proof García-Ramón adduces the French pulp novels that are serialized in Spanish newspapers, French books that are sold in Madrid shops, French plays that are produced on the Spanish stage. By that token, "si Dios no lo remedia, pasará lo mismo con esta lamentable *decadencia* o *simbolismo,* sobre todo porque posee los tres requisitos: es malo, es feo y es francés" [if God doesn't prevent it, the same thing will happen with this deplorable *decadence* or *symbolism,* especially since it has the three prerequisites: it is bad, it is ugly, and it is French]. On the other hand, the symbolists are victims of neuroses, irremediably mad, given to morbid hallucinations, and deserving of study as pathological cases. "El pueblo que fingiese comprender semejante poesía—pues en realidad no la comprende nadie,—que la leyese y aplaudiese, sería en breve un pueblo de dementes, un Leganés monstruoso" (pp. 156-57) [A country that pretends to understand such poetry—because in reality nobody understands it—that reads and applauds it, would in short order become a country of madmen, a monstrous insane asylum].

Aberrant poets, eccentric poetry, and an impressionable public: ample cause for worry about the latest Parisian peril, according to García-Ramón. With his campaign thus launched, he sets out to seal his case and to forestall accusations of exaggeration by becoming more concrete. He has had to garner all his God-given patience, he says, and ingest a surfeit of decadentism so as to be able to explain to his readers what symbolism is. "El cual tiene por abuelos a Mallarmé y [V]erlaine y por dictador a Juan Moreás, y consiste en reemplazar las ideas con palabras, en producir en el ánimo la más supina intensidad de impresión con la sonoridad y el color de los vocablos" (p. 157) [In Mallarmé and Verlaine it has its grandparents and in Jean Moréas its dictator, and its aim is to replace ideas with words and to produce with the sound and color of words a most supinely intense impression on the spirit]. Divested of its suspicious overtones and taken as a straight and succinct description of the symbolist esthetic, this statement could have served the readers of the *Revista Contemporánea* as an informative encapsulation of symbolism and introduction to the names of its two major poets.

García-Ramón's task, however, is to take issue with this new art, so he turns to quote directly from the Moréas manifesto (in Spanish). He labels as a "tontería" [nonsense] and as an impossibility Moréas' wish to restore the simple, clear, and divine language of Rabelais and Villon and to bring their expressive perfection into a modern context. You do not recapture Villon, protests García-Ramón, by using archaic turns of phrase, by amassing metaphors, and by deriving pleasure from obfuscation to such an extent that it is quicker to decipher a hieroglyphic or a page of Sanskrit than it is to unravel a symbolist sentence that in Villon's style was crystal clear. García-Ramón objects to the symbolists' abuse of poetic license, to their inversions, to the liberties they take with the French language. Apparently affected by the threat of this engulfing wave, García-Ramón is guilty of some distortions. For example, Moréas does not propose the suppression of the idea, but rather its expression through an artistic form that takes on prominence in its own right. He defends the esthetic value not of obscurity but of ambiguity. But these are distinctions that García-Ramón is not prepared to make.

As proof of his observation that for the symbolist poet "el vocablo" reigns supreme, García-Ramón cites a lengthy paragraph from René Ghil's *Traité du verbe.*[4] Reference is to a passage where Ghil discusses Rimbaud's sonnet "Voyelles" and its attribution of chromatic values to vowel sounds as a transcendence of the more limited vision of the master, Verlaine, who merely had a vague sense of such possibilities. The quotation goes on to record Ghil's disagreement with Rimbaud's specific color equivalences, taken as Ghil was with the theory as such, and reproduces his own, beginning with an all-absorbing black A, the desert. García-Ramón prefaces Ghil's words with the assurance that commentators of the twenty-fifth century will find the challenge to analyze and explain them quite harrowing, and after the quotation he makes sport of the entire matter of colors and vowels, calling it "una deliciosa *chifladura*" (p. 159) [a delightful *whim*]. In the final analysis he is not amused and regards this vowel fixation as a confirmation of the symbolists' morbid tendencies. These dreamers, he writes, are possessed by "la monomanía del vocablo en sí mismo" (p. 159) [the monomania of the word for its own sake], and he accuses them of hunting in dictionaries because he cannot believe that they retain in their heads the abundance of words that they hurl at their readers. The pursuit of the recondite expression results in failure, according to García-Ramón, because the words that the symbolists conjure are not only strange and freakish but also anti-musical. Moreover, no matter how intense the effort to paint only with words, the idea, ever too powerful, comes to the surface.

His intentions notwithstanding, García-Ramón's negative posture in this section of his article does not prevent him from performing for his Spanish contemporaries a service that reaches beyond his stated aim. He draws their attention to Arthur Rimbaud, an important poet who was not to achieve in Hispanic circles the resonance that Verlaine did. He also introduces them to one of symbolism's most celebrated poems and to a theory and practice—synesthesia—fundamental to the understanding of symbolist art. More directly, García-Ramón admits to the possibility of value in an occasional symbolist composition, though he laces his confession with a redoubled warning:

> Tampoco debe V. suponer que no dicen más que absurdos o simplezas, pues no hay loco que no tenga su cuarto de hora de lucidez; y como quiera que las incoherencias son las verdaderas manchas negras, que no la vocal *A*, y las hay a centenares, cuando descubrimos una perla por estas lobregueces, nos parece la más hermosa y mejor orientada de cuantas en la vida admiramos. Y esto es un mal; pues los tontos que se deleiten con las poesías que entienden, podrán pensar que las incomprensibles son más bellas aún, sólo que su inteligencia no alcanza a tanto, y este galimatías será lo que más aplaudan y adulen, por lo mismo que se quedan en ayunas. (p. 160)

> [Neither should you assume that they say only absurd or stupid things, for there is no madman who does not have his moment of lucidity; and since the real black stains are not the vowel *A*, but incoherent statements, which we find by the hundreds, when we discover a pearl under all the obscurity, it strikes us as the most beautiful and best hewn of any we have admired. And that is bad, for the fools who delight in the poetry they understand might be led to believe that incomprehensible verses are more beautiful yet, but that their intelligence is not up to the task, and precisely because they remain in the dark, this gibberish will be what they applaud and adore most.]

In the final pages of his article, García-Ramón examines in some detail three brief, recently published volumes of symbolist poetry, thereby aiming to provide his readers with the opportunity to formulate their own judgment of symbolism. Significantly, García-Ramón here stresses that the symbolist theories as such have their virtues; but he evidently decries them when they are put into practice. Laying claims to objectivity, he announces his resolve to praise what is laudable but also to bring forward even the slightest defects. Forthwith he plunges into a mocking, destructive, and superficial analysis of the three books, *Les Syrtes* and *Les Cantilènes* by Moréas and Noël Loumo's *Vers de couleurs.*[5]

His method consists largely of quoting snippets of verses, some in the original French, some in his own Spanish translations, and subjecting them to ridicule. Here and there he indicates the moments of lucidity, to which he had referred before, with their elegance, clarity of expression, and good French syntax. García-Ramón is seemingly unprepared for a syntactic or linguistic revolution and rejects the symbolists' most daring and subtle innovations, labeling them as signs of madness. Baring his private tastes, he provides what can be taken as an explanation for this exercise in subversive criticism: he likes poetry that is healthy, energetic, and powerful. Moréas' poetry strikes him as desperate, whining, bland, sickly: the poetry of a eunuch. He quotes a full stanza from *Les Syrtes* in French, followed by his Spanish translation, as an example of verses that he cannot understand and which therefore prevent him from sharing the poet's feelings. For García-Ramón the poetry of Moréas—that "diablo de hombre" (p. 162) [devil of a man]—is hermetic and projects too singular a psyche. Looking for a human content of a certain order that he is unable to find in this poetry, he generally fails to consider it *as poetry.* At those moments when he does, he isolates as "curiosities" those of the poetic metaphors and images that are most audacious in their associations and sensory evocations. He cannot or refuses to embrace a union that seems bizarre, and he compels his rational processes to keep his senses separate and in restraint. Blue silences, for example, simply do not fall within his range of perceptions, and so we find him in battle against synesthesia.[6] He closes his survey of *Les Syrtes* in the following manner with a reference to its final six lines: "En fin, las *Sirtes* terminan reclamando un nuevo Mesías que *destruya la obra de la Mujer* y *siegue el deseo infame en las nuevas generaciones.* En lo cual estoy conforme, si la obra de la Mujer estriba en parir *decadentes,* y el deseo infame es el de escribir versos simbolísticos" (p. 163) [The *Sirtes* ends with a call for a new Messiah who *will destroy what Woman has wrought* and *mow down the new generations' infamous desires.* With which I find myself in accord if the work of Womankind means giving birth to *decadents* and the infamous desire refers to writing symbolist verses].

Passing on to Moréas' *Les Cantilènes,* García-Ramón deems it worse than *Les Syrtes* insofar as it is more "deliquescent," but on the other hand he regards it as better in proportion as its moments of intelligibility are more frequent. In fact, if some of its pages were deleted, the result would be quite worthy of esteem. In this volume of ballads and other poems, García-Ramón discovers common sense and good taste, even beauty, and he only laments that Moréas does not always write with such grace. He judges "Agha Veli" to be the best poem in the collection (pp. 89-94 of the 1886 edition) but says it is too long to translate. Instead, he makes the curious choice of presenting to his readers an example of what he finds murky and deficient, a sonnet that he reproduces in full ("Sous la rouille des temps je suis un vieux blason," pp.

106-07). Readers given the opportunity to study the two poems concurrently would have been—and still are—likely to agree with García-Ramón's preference, but both the comparison and the presentation seem promoted less by critical fairness then by the desire to justify and share an antagonistic appraisal.

García-Ramón identifies Noël Loumo, seven years Moréas' junior, as the youngest of the master's disciples. Loumo's poetry, too, ostensibly devoid of redeeming qualities, is the butt of García-Ramón's condemnation. He criticizes it for being improverished in ideas and thoroughly "disparatado" [absurd] from start to finish. He registers shock, dismay, and impatience and predicts that Loumo will end his days in a madhouse. As it turned out, the Count succumbed to old age in his ninety-third year, but it is a fact that he is better remembered for other endeavors than for his poetry.

By way of summary García-Ramón returns to the symbolists' impenetrability, their habit of clouding substance with linguistic pyrotechnics. He is convinced that they thumb the dictionary for the most singular words they can find, commit them to memory, and then dot their language with these discoveries.[7] As a conservative Spaniard transplanted to a land where clarity of expression had been a hallowed tradition, he considers this latter-day Gongorism a sure sign of neurosis. He ends his essay with these two paragraphs:

> Naturalmente, los decadentes no vivirán, pues no pueden vivir, pero durarán; y créame V., no les quiten ojo de encima; la locura es contagiosa, y estos poetas son muy capaces de pasar los Pirineos, si aquí los mandan con sus cantinelas a otra parte.
> ¡Líbrenos Dios del cólera, de los terremotos y del simbolismo, amén! (p 167)

> [Naturally, the decadents will not live, because they cannot live, but they will last; and mind you, don't take your eyes off them; madness is contagious, and these poets are quite capable of crossing the Pyrenees if here they send them and their ballads off packing to another region.
> May God deliver us from cholera, from earthquakes, and from symbolism, amen!]

History, of course, was to decree otherwise, and mad or not, the symbolists did cross the Pyrenees, both directly and by way of a transatlantic journey that Darío and others helped to pilot. Given that turn of events, the modern reader might well question García-Ramón's sincerity or his judgment. The jocular tenor of certain passages in this Letter from Paris can readily fan doubts about its critical authority. There is no way of gauging the extent to which García-Ramón is expressing his personal reactions to a newsworthy literary event and to what degree he is merely trying to be clever, to entertain and shock, to write a journalistic chronicle that would find readers and keep them reading. In his defense one can say that he engages here in a type of destructive criticism that was common practice in his time. The revered Clarín himself wrote such negative pieces in which the attack on the word quoted out of context was fundamental procedure. The tone of his contribution to the *Revista Contemporánea* is not in itself sufficient justification for doubting that García-Ramón was truly aghast at the examples of symbolist poetry that had come to his attention in the mid-1880's and that he considered it both defective and evil.

In that case this early commentary on the symbolist mode would seem to issue from an onlooker guilty of the severest parochialism. Faced with the examples that he cites, today's observer is likely to have the opposite reaction from the one that García-Ramón is trying to elicit. Testimony to his misguided impressions is that symbolism in its conquests proved no more injurious than any number of other artistic subversions. However, the temptation to condemn García-Ramón needs to be checked by several mitigating factors. One must point out that if García-Ramón cannot be counted among the more receptive critics, he was certainly not alone in his suspicions of symbolism. It is a matter of record that even in France there was no immediate and open embrace of this new doctrine (not to speak of the confusion surrounding its tenets and its denomination); and in Spain the detractors of the symbolist creed and practice were many in number, included some of the most conspicuous literary figures, and remained recalcitrant for a long time. It is doubtful that García-Ramón dealt a delaying blow to symbolism's entry into Spain; he was simply an early voice in a chorus that was to strike the same note. Even his association of decadence and madness was no private whim of his. An idea that was already in circulation at this time, it was to receive intensive discussion in the following decade as Cesare Lombroso's theories spread and as Max Nordau's *Degeneration* reached France and then Spain. In Spain the enemies of symbolism were soon to be joined by an even more vociferous bevy of *antimodernistas* who shared their concerns and dislikes.[8] If on the one hand García-Ramón was not an isolated and therefore errant specimen of an anti-symbolist stand, on the other he was witness to the birth of the movement, and that circumstance, too, merits consideration. He is not the first educated, literate, and well-informed writer to suffer the tricks of history. Literary criticism is an ephemeral venture under the best of conditions. If yesterday's critic is so often—and rightfully—forgotten, it is because today's historical reality speaks louder than his words. García-Ramón experienced and reported on symbolism's intial stages, from the perspective of private sensitivities formed by other esthetic and moral patterns and by different national circumstances. He could not view it at a historical distance. We who enjoy that privilege might well examine our first reaction, say, to Andy Warhol's notorious painting of a can of tomato soup.

The disparity between a Spanish expatriate's early reaction to French symbolism and today's assessment of that movement explains why García-Ramón's article in the *Revista Contemporánea* is a relic of the past. Its historical interest actually rests with the lack of clairvoyance that it displays, and, judging by later reactions, one can presume that its message descended on a public that, if not shocked into taking protective measures, was at least amused. Yet if García-Ramón's report caused his readers to laugh at symbolism, the last laugh is on García-Ramón, not because he miscalculated its significance, but because, as we can see from our perspective, he unwittingly became an agent of its spread into Spain. The primary contribution of the piece is the announcement of the event that impelled its composition: almost simultaneously with its publication in France, García-Ramón brought to his countrymen news of Moréas' symbolist manifesto. Concomitantly he supplied them with a rudimentary but serviceable explanation of the nature of this new movement. He ranks among the first to have publicized the names of Moréas, Ghil, Mallarmé, Rimbaud, and Verlaine in Spain. He brought to the pages of the *Revista Contemporánea* selections of poetry and excerpts from the theoretical pronouncements of this group. Whether in the original French or in García-Ramón's seasoned translations, these snatches were among the earliest examples of French symbolist writings to reach a Spanish reading public. The especially sensitive and critical spectator perhaps pierced García-Ramón's harsh editorializing to arrive at an appreciation of his own. Working closely with the texts himself, García-Ramón was acute enough to recognize that the symbolist esthetic as a whole was not without its significant aspects and that certain of its poetic texts exhibited positive features. The symbolist proposals and turns of phrase surely struck many of García-Ramón's contemporaries as crass instances of artistic *lèse-majesté,* yet they could not have shared his outrage had his contribution to the *Revista Contemporánea* not invited them to do so. Though his anti-symbolist stance was to be typical of many of his fellow Spaniards, García-Ramón shared with them the information that he garnered at the scene. His article is an introduction—perhaps a stimulus—to debates of the future and an unintended announcement of the winds of change.

*Cornell University*

## NOTES

[1] I have made passing reference to him in "Rubén Darío y la entrada del simbolismo en España," in *Poemas y ensayos para un homenaje,* ed. Eleanor K. Paucker (Madrid: Taurus, 1976), pp. 97-98.

[2] García-Ramón uses the terms "symbolist" and "decadent" indiscriminately, a common practice at the time that endured for many years in Spain.

[3] The emphasis in this and subsequent quotations is García-Ramón's.

[4] He has at hand the first edition, with a preface by Mallarmé (Paris: Giraud, 1886). A changed version published two years later (Brussels: Edmond Deman, 1888), which superseded both the 1886 edition and an intervening one (Paris: A. Lévy, 1887), does not contain this section.

[5] The first editions are: Jean Moréas, *Les Syrtes* (Paris: Presses de Lutèce, 1884); *Les Cantilènes* (Paris: Léon Vanier, 1886); Noël Loumo (with Louis de Germon), *Vers de couleurs* (Paris: Léon Vanier, 1886). Noël Loumo is the pseudonym of Henri Begouën.

[6] Lily Litvak has documented the special horror of synesthesia that the opponents of *modernismo* exhibited: "La idea de la decandencia en la crítica antimodernista en España (1888-1910)," *Hispanic Review,* 45 (1977), 402-03.

[7] It is interesting to note that this search for the odd word which García-Ramón rules so objectionable finds a direct echo in Antonio Machado, a poet not known for his flight from ideas. Compare the following example from Moréas' *Les Syrtes* ("Homo fuge," stanza III): "Et les Tentations pullulent,/ Et les Tentations ululent/ Dans l'ombre du Ravin fatal" ["And temptations pullulate,/ And temptations ululate/ In the shadows of the fatal ravine"], with Machado's well-known lines from *Campos de Castilla* ("Campos de Soria," stanza VI): "de galgos flacos y agudos/ que pululan/ por las sórdidas callejas,/ y a la medianoche ululan,/ cuando graznan las cornejas!" [With thin and pointed greyhounds/ Who pullulate/ Through the sordid alleys,/ And at midnight ululate/ When the crows caw].

[8] See Litvak, pp. 397-412.

# Antonio Machado's Attitude to Symbolism

## Geoffrey Ribbans

It is an unfortunate fact that the term Symbolism still has a somewhat uncertain connotation. We need not accept Paul Verlaine's cheerfully negative and unacademic approach ("Le Symbolisme? Comprends pas. Ce doit être un mot allemand, hein? Qu'est-ce que ça peut bien vouloir dire? Moi, d'ailleurs, je m'en fiche. Quand je souffre, quand je jouis ou quand je pleure, je sais bien que ce n'est pas de symbole"[1] [Symbolism? Don't understand. Must be a German word, isn't it? What can it really mean? In any case, I couldn't care less. When I suffer, enjoy myself or weep, I know very well it's no symbol] to find some difficulty in arriving at a definition. As so often happens with literary terminology, symbolism may be defined in several distinct ways: in a broad, all-embracing sense as a universal phenomenon, ever present in a latent form in poetry and remotely related to Plato;[2] or else as the culmination of a process which has by the early twentieth century finally distilled "poetry" from its "impurities";[3] or, alternatively, Symbolism, now duly accredited with a capital letter, may be conceived of as a specific technical term for a circumscribed poetic movement at a given place and time, namely France in the late nineteenth century.[4] Even here there is scope for differences of opinion: is Symbolism to be thought of as an exclusively French movement (encompassing, it is true, a few Americans, the odd Greek and lots of Belgians within its coterie) or as a wider Western phenomenon? And, within France, Symbolism can be narrowed down still further to the so-called "Symbolist school" or Generation of 1885: that is to say, the wave of poets who flourished about the time the term "Symbolist" was first brought into general currency by Jean Moréas.

Let me attempt, for the purposes of this study, to introduce some clarity into these conflicting concepts. On the universal quality of Symbolism, the distinction drawn by Wellek and Warren between "the 'private symbolism' of the modern poet and the widely intelligible symbolism of past poets" seems valid. Symbolism as it concerns us here is "private symbolism," which "implies a system and a careful student can construe a 'private symbolism' as a cryptographer can decode an alien message."[5] Regarding geographical extension, while my concern is basically with France and Machado's relationship with French Symbolists, I would stress the general scope of the movement. As Edmund Wilson declared long ago in *Axel's Castle*: "The Symbolist Movement proper was first largely confined to France and principally limited to poetry of rather an esoteric kind; but it was destined, as time went on, to spread to the whole western world and its principles to be applied on a scale which the most enthusiastic of its founders could scarcely have foreseen."[6] As for the narrow identification of Symbolism with the *cénacle* of 1885, this seems to me an over-subtle refinement which excludes the really great French poets of international standing from being considered within the ambit of a now established and recognized term, however arbitrary its adoption was and however inadequate one may feel it is in itself. Such a contemporary critic as Anna Balakian is at pains to emphasize the enduring quality of the movement, observing its "avatars" far into the twentieth century.[7]

The working definition I shall adopt for the purposes of this essay is taken from an unpretentious recent study of Symbolism by Charles Chadwick: "the art of expressing ideas and emotions not by describing them directly, nor by defining them through overt comparisons with concrete images, but by suggesting what these ideas and emotions are by recreating them in the mind of the reader through the use of unexplained symbols." This is Symbolism on a human plane; there is also a transcendental aspect present or implied in most of its poets, in which "concrete images are used as symbols, not of particular thoughts and feelings within the poet, but of a vast and general ideal world of which the real world is merely an imperfect representation"[8] (the Platonic ressonances of this definition are evident). To this we may add that since their aim is to capture the essence of Beauty, Symbolist poets employ a variety of cross-references—what Baudelaire called "correspondences" and critics call synaesthesia—between the various senses; since they seek to suggest, not depict, the analogous art is music, not sculpture or painting as for the Parnassians; because of its elusiveness, in which one of the terms of the comparison remains unelucidated, Symbolism tends inevitably towards obscurity; and finally, in its quintessential aims, it seeks to limit its scope to the poetic core—in Henri de Régnier's words "on veut en bannir délibérément, en toute conscience, ce qu'on appelle . . . les contingences, c'est-à-dire les accidents de milieu, les faits particuliers"[9] [one seeks deliberately, with full awareness, to eliminate what are called . . . contingencies, that is to say the accidents of environment, particular events].

Machado certainly thinks of Symbolism as the movement which owed its initial impulse to Baudelaire and had as its principal figures Mallarmé, Verlaine and Rimbaud; he also paid particular attention to Edgar Allen Poe and saw the novels of Proust and Joyce as the final results of Symbolist aesthetics. In a certain degree, too, he associates the philosophy of Bergson with one derivation of Symbolism and the poetry of Paul Valéry and the Spanish poets of the twenties with another. To examine his attitude to Symbolism, then, is to study a central issue in his poetry and his poetic theories. My purpose, therefore, is rather different from Dr. J. M. Aguirre's in his detailed study of Machado as a symbolist poet. Aguirre accepts the limited definition of Symbolism as referring to the Generation of 1885[10] and is therefore concerned to a great extent with poets like Régnier, Rodenbach and Vielé-Griffin, with whom he establishes some interesting points of contact. The book consequently overlaps less than one might expect with my subject, for I seek rather to trace the broad issues Symbolism raised for Machado than to catalogue specific cases of influence.

All his life Machado attached great importance to his two early stays in Paris and tended to exaggerate their duration: they lasted only three or four months each, in contrast with Manuel's total residence of over two years in the French capital. Although Alejandro Sawa[11] and others may have given them a foretaste, the brothers' real familiarity with Symbolism undoubtedly dates from these visits.[12] Of his first stay in 1899, Antonio said many years later: "París era todavía la ciudad del *affaire Dreyfus* en política, del simbolismo en poesía, del impresionismo en pintura, del escepticismo elegante en crítica. Conocí personalmente a Oscar Wilde y a Jean Moréas. La gran figura literaria, el gran consagrado, era Anatole France"[13] [Paris was still the city of the "Dreyfus affair" in politics, of symbolism in poetry, of impressionism in painting, of elegant scepticism in criticism. I met personally Oscar Wilde and Jean Moréas. The great literary figure, the hallowed writer, was Anatole France]. It was only on his second trip of 1902 that he met Rubén Darío.

The most important contacts the Machado brothers had in Paris were Jean Moréas, mentioned above, who was Greek by origin, and the Guatemalan *modernista* Enrique Gómez Carrillo. Moréas' exaggerated pretensions to literary leadership made him the center of a circle of younger writers, many of them foreigners, for his eccentric pronunciation of French made him appear ridiculous to most Frenchmen.[14] Antonio's reference to him leads me to believe that he knew Moréas' collection of essays entitled *Les premières armes du Symbolisme*[15] [Symbolism's first campaign] published in 1889. In this collection Moréas' influential and opportunistic *Manifeste du Symbolisme* [Manifesto of Symbolism] is reprinted, together with a rebuttal—elegant and ironic—by Anatole France, as well as a comment on impressionism. The fact that these subjects all converge in Machado's biographical note points to a close acquaintanceship with Moréas' book.

Gómez Carrillo took upon himself the self-appointed role of acting as guide and philosopher of the young hopefuls from Spain and Latin America; he recommended lodging in cheap hotels associated with the Symbolists; he probably introduced the Machado brothers to Oscar Wilde (and to Pío Baroja); and, in Antonio's case, during his second visit, he obtained for him the sinecure of Chancellor in the Guatemalan consulate.[16] Unswerving in his allegiance to French culture, he represented in his own prolific publications the most superficial and frivolous wing of *modernismo;* but his enthusiastic advocacy of Verlaine has considerable historical importance.[17] At the same time it seems clear to me that, despite their admiring subservience in many cases, Latin American writers, collectively dismissed as *rastacueros* [upstarts], were treated with thinly disguised disdain by the exclusive literary coteries, no less presumptuous and self-satisfied than the formal establishment. This scorn, which extended even to figures of the caliber of Darío and Gómez Carrillo,[18] applied no less strongly to Spaniards. Certainly there is little doubt that though the Machado brothers absorbed a great deal from their residence in Paris—a debt much more obvious in Manuel's case than in Antonio's—they themselves cut very little ice there.[19] I suspect that this may account to some extent at any rate for Antonio's distinctly unenthusiastic attitude towards France and especially Paris.

What specific consequences can we discern as a result of Antonio's two visits to Paris? By the time he produced his first volume of poetry, *Soledades* [Solitudes], at the end of 1902, written at least in part before his second visit, he had clearly been influenced by Verlaine, by far the most powerful inspiration of the time, perhaps by Baudelaire and indirectly by Poe, and possibly by some of the minor Symbolists like Samain and Régnier.[20] As far as Verlaine is concerned, it is evident that Machado knew the selection *Choix de poésies* [Selected poems] very well and some other poems besides;[21] he borrowed Juan Ramón Jiménez's copy and, much to the latter's annoyance, scribbled in the margins.[22] Yet as far as influence on his poetic practice goes, it is quite obvious that Antonio never attempts to do what Manuel accomplished so adroitly: to reflect the delicate, impressionistic technique of the French poet. What concerns Antonio are the melancholy *paysages d'âme* [mental landscapes] of *Poèmes saturniens* [Saturnine poems], the two most typical sections of which are entitled "Melancholia" and "Paysages tristes" [Sad landscapes], with their characteristic topics: the autumnal setting, the deserted garden, the fountain, the moon. About some of the early poems, nearly all of them discarded after 1903, there is a distinctly Parnassian descriptive quality, redolent of the early Verlaine. Moreover, a peculiar aspect of certain of these poems is a conscious urge to break away from Verlainian themes, using Spring scenes—"Salmodias de Abril" [April chants]—rather than autumnal ones: an interesting desire for independence which in fact betrays indebtedness.[23]

The influence of Edgar Allan Poe is significant and raises intriguing questions. At the time of *Soledades* the impact of the American poet seems to be confined to one aspect: the effect of fatality and doom conveyed by the refrain "Nevermore" of the poem *The Raven.* The word is used as the title, in English, of one of his early poems and in its Italian form, "Mai più", in another.[24] The related theme of the inexorable passing of time, personified as a fleeting female figure ("virgen esquiva y compañera" [aloof maiden and companion], "fugitiva ilusión de ojos guerreros" [fleeting illusion with warlike eyes], etc.) is present in many other poems.[25] The topic was, of course, in the air in both France and Spain, and a Colombian friend of the Machados, Viriato Díaz Pérez, published a commentary on *The Raven,* followed later by a translation, in *Helios* in 1904.[26] What is worth emphasizing is that, even at this stage, it is the temporal side of Poe which attracts Machado; there is no evidence yet that he knew the aesthetic theories which had so compelling an influence, in both a thematic and a formal direction, on Mallarmé. Amazingly enough, to me at least, Machado retained his admiration for *The Raven* all his life. In 1939, in his *Poética* [Poetic theory] for Gerardo Diego's anthology, he referred to "el siglo lírico, que acentuó con un adverbio temporal su mejor poema" (p. 150) [the lyrical century, which stressed its best poem with an adverb of time], while also attributing to Poe both the contemporary currents he discerned in poetry: "essentiality," which clearly springs from Poe's aestheticism and Mallarmé's derivations from it, and "temporality," from the "nevermore" theme.

Years later, in *Los complementarios* [Complementary notes], Machado makes a general remark about the early *Soledades* which runs as follows:

Lo anecdótico, lo documental humano, no es poético por sí mismo. Tal era exactamente mi parecer de hace veinte años. En mi composición "El canto de los niños" se proclama el derecho de la lírica ... a *contar* la pura emoción borrando la totalidad de la historia humana. El libro *Soledades* fue el primer libro español del cual estaba íntegramente proscrito lo anecdótico.[27]

[Storytelling, human documentation, is not in itself poetic. Such was exactly my view twenty years ago. In my composition "The children's song" the right of the lyric to *recount* pure emotion wiping out the whole of human history is proclaimed. *Solitudes* was the first Spanish book from which storytelling was completely banned.]

"El canto de los niños" establishes a parallel between the monotonous chanting of school children and the flowing water of a fountain. It concludes:

> Seguía su cuento
> la fuente serena:
> borrada la historia,
> contaba la pena. (VIII)

[The serene fountain continued its tale: with the story blotted out, it recounted the sorrow.]

The similarity with Juan Ramón's "todo verdad presente, sin historia"[28] [all truth present, without story] is evident, and it is not surprising that Machado proceeds to claim, not without pride, that "coincidía yo anticipadamente con la estética novísima" [I coincided in advance with the most recent aesthetics] only to separate himself radically in the next sentence from the poets of the twenties (and Juan Ramón): "la coincidencia de mi propósito de entonces no iba más allá de esta abolición de lo anecdótico. Disto mucho de estos poetas que pretenden manejar imágenes puras ... sin que intervenga para nada la emoción" (p. 69) [the coincidence in my aims at that time did not go beyond this abolition of storytelling. I differ greatly from those poets who claim to manipulate pure images ... without emotion being in any way involved]. These observations, though quite inexact as regards the collection as a whole, indicate clearly that Machado himself came as time passed to associate with all the poems of *Soledades* the poetic concentration characteristic of one aspect of Symbolism. In fact the statement applies only to the maturest and most Symbolist-orientated section of the book, *Del camino* [From the road].

In Machado's revised and expanded collection *Soledades. Galerías. Otros poemas* [Solitudes. Galleries. Other poems] of 1907, the *galerías* represent, quite clearly, the highwater mark of Machado's subjective vein and one of the peaks of European Symbolism.[29] It is not for nothing that Machado declared, as we have just seen, that he was the first to eliminate storytelling in Spain; however, Machado's symbolism does not imply the exclusion of human emotion, but rather the raising of it to a plane of generalization and dream in which emotions are, in intention at least, purified from their banal circumstances—in the words of Machado's review of Jiménez's *Arias tristes,* "sensaciones fundidas y acrisoladas al contraste de nuestra luz interna, más o menos turbia, y expresadas con una voz propia que dice: vivimos hacia la vida o hacia la muerte" (p. 762) [sensations fused or distilled in contrast with our internal light, more or less blurred, and expressed with a voice of our own which declares: we live orientated towards life or towards death]. In effect, the *galerías* are divided clearly into those expressing confidence and

reassurance and those full of foreboding and desolation: not a sign of
vacillation but of heartfelt questioning, the result of Machado's endemic
uncertainty which was with him all his life.

Beside certain *galerías* in which direct contact with natural or material
objects—be they churches, storks on the steeples, trees, the moon or the
stars—is tenuously maintained, and others (LXXXVIII, LXXXIX, etc.) which
have no clear natural context, some *galerías* show an evident Symbolist
displacement of the literal meaning of words. In such examples as "Llamó a
mi corazón un claro día" (LXVIII) [(the wind) called on my heart, one clear
day] and "Hoy buscarás en vano" (LXIX) [Today you will seek in vain] the
symbolization goes beyond an inner fusion or emotional identification with
nature such as we find in Verlaine or contemporary poems by Juan Ramón:
these flowers, perfumes, fountains, etc., simply do not exist as objects as such
but are components of the inner metaphorical garden or orchard of
Machado's soul. At the same time they are not abstracted away from an
individual human experience in the way which occurs in the famous passage
of Mallarmé's with which Machado's practice can evidently be connected: "Je
dis: une fleur! et, hors de l'oubli où ma voix relègue aucun contour, et tant
que quelque chose d'autre que les calices sus, musicalement se lève, idée
même et suave, l'absente de tous bouquets"[30] [I say: a flower! and beyond
the oblivion to which my voice relegates any real shape, inasmuch as I speak
of something else than known calyxes, there rises up musically the smooth
idea itself, the flower absent from all bouquets]. In Mallarmé the known
calyxes, the tangible flowers, are displaced by an abstract idea, an absent
musical impression of their beauty. Machado never goes to such extremes.

Any attempt at a full examination of the *galerías* would be inappropriate
here. I shall refer only to three facets: first, the extreme reduction, in a few
poems, of the area of experience encompassed by the poet:

> De toda la memoria sólo vale
> el don preclaro de evocar los sueños. (LXXXIX)

[Of the whole of memory only the supreme gift of evoking dreams is
worthwhile.]

Second, an apparent indulgence in the unfathomable quality of his dreams;
third, an evident satisfaction in an artistic achievement which appears at times
to offer an escape from the threat of death, in other poems accepted
realistically enough, and into an aesthetic paradise:

> Tú sabes las secretas galerías
> del alma, los caminos de los sueños
> y la tarde tranquila
> donde van a morir . . . Allí te aguardan
> las hadas silenciosas de la vida . . .
> y hacia un jardín de eterna primavera
> te llevarán un día.[31] (LXX)

[You know the secret galleries of the soul, the paths of dreams and the
tranquil evening where they go to die. There the silent fairies of life await you
and one day will take you to a garden of eternal Spring.]

Before the publication of the *galerías*, however, as early as the middle of
1903, Machado had started to demonstrate his dissatisfaction with some
features of Symbolism. First of all, he began to formulate a strongly critical

attitude towards France itself. In a letter to Miguel de Unamuno written shortly after his second visit to Paris, he implies that French literary circles are superficial, compromising and uninvolved compared with the quarrelsome, raw potentiality of Spain. Paris is a city, he goes on, which has made life into art, and not always good art, so that art itself has become redundant. By contrast, Machado himself now believes that "el artista debe amar la vida y odiar el arte. Lo contrario de lo que he pensado hasta aquí"[32] [the artist ought to love life and hate art. The opposite of what I have believed till now]. In making this contrast between art and life, Machado might well have been thinking of Axël's famous renunciation in Villiers de l'Isle-Adam's play: "Nous avons détruit, dans nos étranges coeurs, l'amour de la vie. . . . Accepter, désormais, de vivre, ne serait plus qu'un sacrilège envers nous-mêmes. Vivre? les serviteurs feront cela pour nous"[33] [We have destroyed, in our strange hearts, our love for life. To accept living, henceforth, would be nothing but a sacrilege towards ourselves. Live? Our servants can do that for us].

This strongly-held concept of France, though slightly attenuated during the First World War, is constant throughout his life, one of the harshest expressions of it being his review of Unamuno's *Contra esto y aquello* [Against this and that] in 1913. After exempting the defenders of Dreyfus and French protestants from his strictures, he declares:

Los que hemos vivido en Francia algún tiempo en estos últimos años sabemos que este gran pueblo no tiene hoy otra fuerza de cohesión que el miedo. . . . Y nosotros, que formamos un pueblo lleno de vitalidad, de barbarie y de porvenir, simpatizamos con este viejo verde, podrido hasta la médula, por su maestría en el arte cosmética. . . . Nuestras almas necesitan quien les enseñe a lavarse la cara, no a pintarse de colorete. ¿Qué absurda ceguedad nos lleva a imitar todo lo francés? (pp. 782-83)

[Those who have lived for some time in France know that this great people has no other cohesive force today but fear. . . . And we who form a people full of vitality, barbarity and future have friendly feelings towards this obscene old man, rotten to the marrow, because of his mastery of cosmetics. Our spirits need someone to teach them to wash their faces, not to use makeup. What absurd blindness makes us imitate everything French?]

These forthright statements, besides bearing a remarkable resemblance to Unamuno's own pronouncements, may be related to the type of poetry Machado had condemned some years earlier in "Retrato" [Portrait] :

Adoro la hermosura y en la moderna estética
corté las viejas rosas del huerto de Ronsard;
mas no amo los afeites de la actual cosmética,
ni soy un ave de esas del nuevo gay-trinar. (XCVII)

[I adore beauty and in modern aesthetics have cut the ancient roses in Ronsard's gardens; but I don't like the makeup used in today's cosmetics nor am I a bird to chirp in the present poetic crowd.]

It is very possible that in these criticisms of the artificial and the superficial, Machado is thinking, not just of Spanish *modernistas,* but of French-inspired poetry of the post-Verlainian type.

What is clear is that Machado's concept of France as sensual, passionless and essentially trivial is linked with some aspects of Symbolism. In one specific instance, Verlaine and Unamuno are confronted and opposed to each other. Unamuno had referred to Verlaine, in unexpectedly favorable terms, in his important review of Manuel Machado's *Alma* [Soul] :

[El poeta] vive al último soplo de viento, al minuto, abierta el alma a las más fugitivas impresiones. . . . Así fue Verlaine, y esta impersonalidad da personalidad a sus obras; fue arpa eólica vibrando a las brisas, vendavales y aquilones de la vida, eternizando lo momentáneo.[34]

[(The poet) lives in the last gust of wind, at the instant, his soul open to the most fleeting impressions. . . . Verlaine was like that, and this impersonality lends personality to his works; he was an Aeolian harp vibrating in the breezes, gales and north winds of life, making the momentary eternal.]

Machado comes back strongly in a poem dedicated to Unamuno entitled "Luz" [Light] :

¿Será tu corazón un arpa al viento,
que tañe el viento? Sopla el odio y suena
tu corazón; sopla el amor y vibra . . .
¡Lástima da tu corazón, poeta! (*SGOP*, pp. 247-48)

[Is your heart to be a harp in the wind, played by the wind? Hatred blows and your heart sounds; love blows and it vibrates . . . Poet, your heart is pitiful!]

It is evident that, under a more or less close influence of Unamuno, Machado is here reacting against a conception of poetry—fleeting, aetherial, impressionistic, impersonal—which he associates with Verlaine, and, more remotely, with France in general.

A second reaction is explicitly against the high priest of Symbolism, Mallarmé. In a letter of 1904 to Unamuno, Machado directly attacks a basic tenet of Mallarmé's conception of poetry:

Nada más disparatado que pensar, como algunos poetas franceses han pensado tal vez, que el misterio sea un elemento estético—Mallarmé lo afirma al censurar a los parnasianos por la claridad de sus formas—. La belleza no está en el misterio sino en el deseo de penetrarlo. Pero este camino es muy peligroso y puede llevarnos a hacer el caos en nosotros mismos si no caemos en la vanidad de crear sistemáticamente brumas que, en realidad, no existen, no deben existir.[35]

[There's nothing more non-sensical than to think, as some French poets have done on occasion, that mystery is an aesthetic element—Mallarmé asserts this when he censures the Parnassians for the clarity of their forms. Beauty lies not in mystery but in the desire to penetrate it. But this is a very dangerous road and can induce us to produce chaos in ourselves if we do not succumb to the vanity of creating systematically mists which in reality do not exist and ought not to exist.]

Mystery is of course central to Mallarmé's poetic theory,[36] and the word, or its synonym "enigma," crops up again and again in his writing. In the above quotation, Machado is clearly referring to Mallarmé's reply to the famous *Enquête* [Enquiry] of Jules Huret on Symbolism. In it Mallarmé criticizes the Parnassians, as Machado said, for treating their subject in a traditional manner, by presenting objects directly, with no use of allusion; and by so doing they lack mystery. Mallarmé then goes on to give one of the classic definitions of Symbolism: "*Nommer* un objet, c'est supprimer les trois-quarts de la jouissance du poème qui est faite de deviner peu à peu: le *suggérer,* voilà le rêve" (ed. cit., p. 60) [To *name* an object is to do away with three-quarters of the enjoyment of the poem, which is made up of guessing bit by bit: to *suggest* it, that's the dream]. This in turn is echoed by Machado many years later: "Silenciar el nombre directo de las cosas, cuando las cosas tienen nombres directos, ¡qué estupidez! " (p. 709) [To suppress the direct names of things, when things have direct names, what stupidity!]

The criticism of indulgence in mystery brings us to other aspects of Machado's dissatisfaction, aspects which are given a fuller expression in his review of Juan Ramón Jiménez' *Arias tristes.* After describing the book he turns to himself and his contemporaries: "De todos los cargos que se ha hecho a la juventud soñadora, en cuyas filas aunque indigno milito, yo no recojo más que dos. Se nos ha llamado egoístas y soñolientos. . . ." [Of all the charges leveled against young writers concerned with dream, in whose ranks I though unworthy count myself, I take up just two. We have been called self-centered and dreamridden . . .]. "Egoístas, soñolientos": Machado has chosen his words well, for each of them represents a complementary aspect of what is to be an enduring criticism of Symbolist attitudes. He goes on: "Yo no puedo aceptar que el poeta sea un hombre estéril que huya de la vida para forjarse quiméricamente una vida mejor en que gozar de la contemplación de sí mismo. . . ." [I cannot accept the idea that the poet should be a sterile man who flees from life to forge for himself in his phantasy a better life in which he can enjoy the contemplation of his own self . . .]. The danger for the poet lies in separating himself from life, in enveloping himself in a world of dreams; this is a form of self-centeredness and self-indulgence. He continues:

> Y he añadido: ¿no seríamos capaces de soñar con los ojos abiertos, en la vida activa, en la vida militante? Acaso, entonces, echáramos de menos en nuestros sueños muchas imágenes, y tal vez entonces comprendiéramos que éstas eran los fantasmas de nuestro egoísmo, quizás de nuestros remordimientos. (p. 763)
>
> [And I have added: may we not be capable of dreaming with our eyes open, in active, militant involvement with life? Then perhaps we should miss many images from our dreams and maybe then we would realize that they were the phantoms of our egoism, perhaps of our regrets.]

Although Machado goes on to declare explicitly that introspection is necessary—"lo más hondo es lo más universal" [the deepest values are the most universal ones] —he was clearly at pains to distinguish between "active life," "militant life" and an imaginary world of dreams a substitute life or artificial paradise, as advocated by the Symbolists or pursued by himself, at times, in the *galerías.* He also severely qualifies the role of dreams in favor of involvement in the material world: one should "dream with one's eyes open." What has gone before explains the otherwise rather surprising assertion at the beginning of the review that Juan Ramón Jiménez is not really sad. He is not sad because he is not involved in life. Instead, there is an absorption with feelings for their own sake which produces on the one hand an effect of anaesthesia, of narcotic intoxication, and on the other, the vagueness and imprecision Juan Ramón saw as a feature of Symbolism and which he himself assiduously cultivated.[37] What is needed to turn these amorphous, timeless impressions into true expressions of sadness or joy is for them to be "fused or distilled in the contrast with our inner light . . . and expressed with a voice of one's own," in the words already quoted.

We can accordingly see here the extent of the reaction against the implications of Symbolism and against those who, like Juan Ramón, reflected its fundamental criteria. It is seen as an escape from living into the cult of an autonomous, cocooned dream-world such as we may associate with Walter de la Mare or the early Yeats, cultivating the imprecision, blurring and fusing of sensation which is implied in the creation of an "état d'âme." It is revealing, I think, to take a comment by an early Symbolist critic, Arthur Symons, certainly unconnected with Machado, in order to bring out the sort of attitude Machado was reacting against:

> Our only chance, in this world, of a complete happiness lies in the measure of our success in shutting the eyes of the mind and deadening its sense of hearing, and dulling the keenness of its apprehension of the unknown. . . .[38]

Machado's insistence on "looking with his eyes open" is clearly at variance with this attitude. Incidentally, the opposition between objectivity and subjectivity implicit in this phrase recurs constantly in poets like Salinas, Guillén, Elouard and Octavio Paz who work within the ambit of the topics of Symbolism.[39] In Machado's case the emphasis on alert observation grows steadily stronger and accounts of course for much of the special strength of *Campos de Castilla* [Castilian lands].[40] The use of transferred or implicit language is entirely abandoned and neither of the two injunctions of a well-known poem by Mallarmé—the elimination of base reality and avoidance of the specific and precise—are followed:

> Exclus-en si tu commences
> Le réel parceque vil.
> Le sens trop précis rature
> Ta vague littérature. (ed. cit., p. 73)

[Exclude from it, if you start, the real because it is base. Too precise a sense erases your vague literature.]

At the same time it should be stressed that Machado remains capable of doubting the ultimate significance of objective reality. To give one example: under the emotional impact of his attachment to the landscape of Soria, he asks himself regarding the famous "álamos del río" [poplars of the river]:

> Me habéis llegado al alma,
> ¿o acaso estabais en el fondo de ella? (CXIII, ix)

[You have touched *my* soul, or perhaps you were already there in its depths?]

Schopenhauer's formulation "Die Welt ist meine Vorstellung" [The world is my representation][41] is still possible. What Machado does not now do is to pass over objects as objects and use their emotional impact as a facet of his own spirit.

The criticism of Symbolism as self-centered also has further implications, for its raises the whole question of communication, a notorious weak point of Symbolism. On several occasions Machado quotes Mallarmé's phrase "Parler n'a trait à la réalité des choses que commercialement" [Speech has only commercial dealings with reality] and approves it in part, since it appears to recognize the objective role of language as an instrument of exchange; but in fact Mallarmé is quite contemptuous of this commonplace function, as is made abundantly clear in the same piece of writing *Variations sur un sujet* [Variations on a theme]. There he declares that to narrate, describe, even to teach was all very well, and may be adequate for the exchange of human thoughts, or—to use his own metaphor—to take or put a coin silently in someone's hand, as a sort of universal reporting characteristic of all sorts of writing, but from all these activities literature is excepted.[42] This idea, which so unequivocally advocates the elimination of storytelling which Machado had declared to be characteristic of *Soledades,* is also clearly echoed, in a very different sense, in one of Machado's *cantares* or folk-songs:

> Moneda que está en la mano
> quizá se deba guardar;
> la monedita del alma
> se pierde si no se da. (LVII, ii)

[a coin which is in your hand should perhaps be kept; the small change of the soul is lost if it is not passed on.]

It is equally evident, too, that Machado reacts against an egotistical approach on the plane of human relations. As the importance of dialogue in his early poems shows, he was always concerned with a response from outside and hence reveals an incipient objectivation. Later he concedes greater individuality to persons, as he does to things, outside himself. His later philosophy, based on the "heterogeneidad del ser" [heterogeneity of being] and the recognition of the distinctive character of other people and the imperative need for them, is a logical culmination of his rebuttal of egocentricity.

So far I have been concerned principally with Machado's involvement with Symbolism as a young practising poet early in the century. He remains vitally concerned with the subject later in life when he is able to see the movement in its historical perspective. This aspect of his attitude now demands some attention. As is well known, he thinks of the turn of the century, his formative period and the age of Symbolism and *modernismo,* as essentially individualistic. One of the clearest expressions of this view is found in 1919 in the prologue to the second edition of *Soledades. Galerías. Otros poemas:*

> La ideología dominante era esencialmente subjetivista; el arte se atomizaba, y el poeta, en cantos más o menos enérgicos . . . , sólo pretendía cantarse a sí mismo, o cantar, cuando más, el humor de su raza. (p. 48)
>
> [The dominant ideology was essentially subjectivist; art was fragmented, and the poet, in more or less energetic songs, only claimed to sing his own feelings or, at most, the mood of his race.]

This corresponds in turn to an overall conception of the nineteenth century as grounded in subjectivity, with this subjective impulse deriving from Romanticism reaching its culmination in Symbolism. It is an idea he returns to time and time again, but which has its fullest treatment in the projected inaugural address to the Academy:

> . . . no vacilo en afirmar que el siglo XIX fue, entre otras cosas, propicio a la lírica y, en general, a las formas subjetivas del arte. En el movimiento pendular que va, en las artes como en el pensar especulativo, del objeto al sujeto, y viceversa, el ochocientos marca una extrema posición subjetiva. Casi todo milita contra el objeto. . . . Todo cuanto en el siglo ensalza o empequeñece al hombre, refuerza y afirma al sujeto. Individualismo se llama, en lo social y político, la nota específica del siglo XIX. La corriente individualista es un nuevo incremento de la subjetividad. (pp. 845-46)

[I do not hesitate to affirm that the nineteenth century was, among other
things, favorable toward lyric poetry and, in general, toward subjective forms
of art. In the pendular movement which, in the arts as in speculative thought,
goes from object to subject and viceversa, the eighteen-hundreds mark an
extreme subjective position. Almost everything is opposed to the object. . . .
Everything in the century which raises or diminishes man's stature, strengthens
and affirms the subject. The specific note of the nineteenth century, in the
social and political sphere, is called individualism. The individualistic current is
a further increase in subjectivity.]

This individualism led in turn to an emphasis on the lyrical, the dynamic and
the combative; it was what Machado called "struggle-for-lifista!"
Nineteenth-century man, he goes on, "fue el hombre menos clásico de todos
los siglos, el menos capaz de crear bajo normas objectivas, porque vive
encerrado en su conciencia individual" [was the most unclassical man of any
century, the least capable of creating under objective rules, because he lives
enclosed in his individual consciousness]. And, specifically on Symbolism,
after praising the coherence of the movement ("una escuela perfectamente
lograda") [a perfectly achieved school] with some immortal works to its
credit, he goes on to say: "Es evidente que en la poesía de los simbolistas el
largo radio de los sentimientos se ha acortado hasta coincidir con el radio,
mucho más breve, de la sensación y que las ideas propiamente dichas . . . se han
eclipsado" (p. 849) [It is clear that in the poetry of the Symbolists the wide
radius of feelings has been cut down until it coincides with the much shorter
radius of immediate sensation and that ideas, properly called, have been
eclipsed]. This criterion is obviously directly applicable to the *galerías*.

Nineteenth-century poetry thus despised intelligence and was what
Machado described in a vivid phrase in another essay as an "arte de ciegos
músicos" [an art of blind musicians] related to Wagner and Schopenhauer.
The Symbolist's concept of man was of "un ser sensible sentimental, volente
o ciegamente dinámico, y el poeta como un solitario atento a su melodía
interior" (p. 825) [a feeling, sentient being, willfully or blindly dynamic, and
the poet a lonely figure occupied with his inner melody]: the Machado, of
course, of his first book *Soledades*. This solitariness is apt to lead to a solipsist
attitude—compare with the question of egocentricity we have discussed
earlier—and to the cult of mystery and indirect expression associated with the
Symbolists.

After Symbolism, then, we learn from the Academy address, comes
disintegration, because of the extreme degree of subjectivity involved: "la
reducción al absurdo del subjetivismo romántico" [the *reductio ad absurdum*
of Romantic subjectivity]. In *Los complementarios* it is Rimbaud, otherwise
largely absent from Machado's meditations, who is mentioned in this
connection: "La poesía occidental tiene en Rimbaud su extrema expresión
dinámica. Después de Rimbaud la poesía francesa entra en un período de
desintegración" (p. 213) [Western poetry has its final dynamic expression in
Rimbaud. After Rimbaud French poetry enters a period of disintegration]. In
the Academy address Proust and James Joyce are seen as the final
monstrous results of extreme individuality and viewed, particularly in Joyce's
case, with very little sympathy. In "Reflexiones sobre la lírica" he
goes into further detail about the two "modos perversos" [perverse modes]
deriving from Symbolism: "dos sectas antagónicas: la de aquéllos que

pretenden hacer lírica al margen de toda emoción humana, por un juego mecánico de imágenes . . . y la de aquellos otros para quienes la lírica, al prescindir de toda estructura lógica, sería el producto de los estados semicomatosos del sueño" (pp. 823-24) [two antagonistic sects, those who claim to write lyrics leaving aside all human emotion, by means of a mechanical play of images . . . and those others for whom the lyric, doing without any logical structure, would be the product of the semicomatose states of dream]. The first direction is "pure poetry," while the second may be equated with Joyce and the surrealists. In the first case we have one example of Machado's frequent attempts, persistent but courteous, to wean the poets of the twenties away from the influence of Paul Valéry and Juan Ramón Jiménez. By contrast with the Symbolists whom he praises for their lack of triviality, he finds these poets intellectualized, conceptual and dehumanized. In his hostile and largely false images of Huidobro, Guillén and Diego, he associates them with his special *bête noire,* the Baroque; they are seen as frivolous and playing at poetry; according to Machado, they treat images as things, whereby things lose their relation to the individual, so that poetry becomes an idle pastime. Elsewhere, he links them again with the Symbolist tradition: his alter ego, Jorge de Meneses, suspects that their intellectualism may be "la hazaña de los epígonos del simbolismo francés" [the feat of the successors of French Symbolism]. And he adds that "Ya Mallarmé llevaba dentro el negro catedrático capaz de intentarlo" (p. 325) [Mallarmé already contained within him the dark professor capable of attempting it]. Similar is the phrase "obscura mazmorra simbolista" (p. 810) [dark Symbolist dungeon] used in another essay.

What hopes for the future of poetry did Machado have after the disintegration he postulated? Of the Romantic-Symbolist tradition the most attractive side, evidently, for him is its deep human involvement in time. "Sólo para él (el hombre del ochocientos)—y en ésto consiste su profunda originalidad—alcanza el tiempo un supremo valor emotivo. . . . Con Bergson y algunos de sus epígonos, ya en pleno siglo XX, el pensamiento del gran siglo romántico alcanza una conciencia total de sí mismo" (pp. 846-47) [For him alone (nineteenth-century man)—and this constitutes his deep originality—time achieves a supreme emotional value. With Bergson and some of his successors, now well into the twentieth century, the thought of the great Romantic century, gains a full awareness of itself]. In *Los complementarios,* he takes some pleasure in indicating parallels between his poetry and Proust's recall of past memories, and he is very concerned with Bergson,[43] but by no means uniform in his reaction. In fact it is in his comments on Bergson that Machado's ambivalent feelings come out more clearly. On the one hand, he has little doubt that Bergsonian intuitionism is the end of the anti-rationalist process: "en el camino hacia abajo del intelectualismo está Bergson, acaso, en el límite" (p. 826) [on the downhill slope from intellectualism Bergson is perhaps at the very limit]. In *Los complementarios* (p. 23) he calls him "el filósofo definitivo del siglo XIX" [the definitive philosopher of the nineteenth century], and in quite a few notes indicates certain limitations which are the result of his nineteenth-century ideology, as well as giving some personal recollections of him in 1910-11 (*Los complementarios,* p. 24). One of his jottings (p. 56), is particularly fascinating:

> La filosofía de Bergson será el herbario de la flora simbolista. De la musique
> avant toute chose. . . Suena a música vieja. Verlaine fue el poeta bergsoniano.
> Mallarmé fue un conceptista imaginativo.
>
> [Bergson's philosophy will be the showcase for the Symbolist flora. Music
> before everything . . . this sounds like out-of-date music. Verlaine was the
> Bergsonian poet. Mallarmé was a writer of conceits with imagination.]

In another note his speculations take off in a different, unexpected, direction
and he thinks of Bergson as the possible inspirer of a new rationalist
movement: "Cabe una ideología bergsoniana, marcadamente
intelectualista. . . . Será una reacción . . . contra toda la corriente filosófica
del siglo XIX. . . . Una filosofía antivoluntarista, antiactivista, antivitalista" (I,
p. 30 R; II, p. 57; the transcription mistakenly reads "idea" for "ideología")
[A Bergsonian ideology which is markedly intellectualist is possible. It will be
a reaction . . . against the whole philosophical current of the nineteenth
century . . . a philosophy opposed to voluntarism, activism and vitalism] . The
depth of his meditations, as well as his uncertainties about them, are thus
clearly demonstrated.

Yet in his *Poética* of 1931, no doubt as a result of his lack of sympathy
with the poets of the twenties, he comes back strongly in favor of a personal,
temporal and intuitive poetic program and a revindication of
nineteenth-century lyricism, though with a new slant: "ellos—los poetas de su
Antología—devolverán su honor a los románticos, sin serlo ellos mismos. El
poeta profesa más o menos conscientemente, una metafísica existencialista,
en la cual el tiempo alcanza un valor absoluto"[44] [They—the poets of his
(imagined) Anthology—will give their honor back to the Romantics, without
being Romantic themselves. The poet professes, more or less consciously, an
existentialist metaphysic, in which time achieves an absolute value]. It is the
first time, as far as I know, that the word "existentialist" is used in Spain.

In both *Reflexiones sobre la lírica* and the Academy Address Machado
does suggest the radically different solution, in direct opposition to the entire
Symbolist tradition and indeed to all post-Kantian philosophy, hinted at in
the notes quoted above. It is extremely tentative even for the cautious
relativist and pragmatist that Machado was; and it had little direct connection
with the poetry he was then writing, though it throws strong retrospective
light on *Campos de Castilla*. It may account too for his attempts at the
recreation of classical myths and his experiments with sonnet form; yet the
main impression we have of his verse at this time is of fragmentary inspiration
with the survival of subjects deriving from dream (the fascinating "Recuerdos
de sueño, fiebre y duermivela" [Memories of dream, fever and
sleeplessness] ) or memory (Proust) as its most prominent features, rather than
any new objective or rational vision.

Tentatively, then, Machado suggests that the future may be a return "a la
objetividad por un lado, y a la fraternidad, por el otro. . . . Comienza el
hombre nuevo a desconfiar de aquella soledad que fue causa de su
desesperanza y motivo de su orgullo . . . El yo egolátrico del ayer aparece hoy
más humilde ante las cosas" (pp. 856-57) [to objectivity on one side, and to
fraternity, on the other. . . . The new man is beginning to distrust that
solitude which was the cause of his despair and the motive of his pride. The

self-centered ego of yesterday today appears humbler in the presence of things]. In any new rationalism, which requires a return to Plato, the emphasis Machado placed long ago on observation will have to be reinforced and the incipient reaction against Symbolism carried much further. "El hombre actual no renuncia a ver . . . ha perdido la fe en su propia ceguera . . . empieza a creer en la realidad de cuanto ve y toca" [Present-day man will not give up seeing . . . he has lost faith in his own blindness . . . he is beginning to believe in the reality of everything he sees and touches]. Instead of dreaming he wakes up: "Su mundo se ilumina, quiere poblarse, no de fantasmas, sino de figuras reales. Este hombre no puede ya definirse por el sueño . . . sino por el despertar" (pp. 826-27) [His world lights up and wants to be filled, not with phantoms but with real figures. This man can no longer be defined by dream . . . but by awaking]. Thus the old doubts about introspective subjectivity persist, and the suggestions of the review of *Arias tristes* appear strengthened and consolidated, though, alas! with little further application to his own poetry:

> Si el soñador despierta, no ya entre fantasmas, sino firmemente anclado en un trozo de lo real, será el respeto cósmico a la ley que nos obliga y afinca en nuestro lugar y en nuestro tiempo, la fuente de una nueva y severa emoción, que podrá tener algún día madura expresión lírica." (p. 829)

> [If the dreamer wakes up, no longer among phantoms but firmly anchored in a patch of reality, the cosmic respect for the law which compels us to remain fixed in our place and in our time will become the source of a new, strict emotion which may find some day a mature lyrical expression.]

A new type of poetry akin to but not identical with social realism is thus hesitantly put forward, but not realized in poetic practice.

Machado was born at a time when he could hardly be other than a Symbolist, as he himself realized: "Yo amé con pasión y gusté hasta el empacho esta nueva sofística . . ." (p. 48)[45] [I passionately loved and enjoyed to satiety this new sophistry]. And his debt was deep and, in some respects at least, enduring. If he reacted very early against certain Symbolist attitudes, particularly the cult of dream, mystery and imprecision, still he retains, as his alter ego Juan de Mairena proves, a strong emotional attachment to the Romantic-Symbolist tradition. His attitude to the Symbolists in certain important respects, therefore, remains ambivalent. His historical sense enables him to set the Symbolist movement into its context, yet his views concerning the future of poetry are far from unequivocal, for at one moment he applauds the powerful lyrical temporality of the nineteenth century and at another he postulates developments inherent in his poetic and social attitudes which had been partly realized—and then decisively interrupted—in the poems of *Campos de Castilla*. For both directions Symbolism was the touchstone, and the issues he discussed with such depth, persistence and absence of dogmatism are still central, over a hundred years after his birth, to the problems of poetry today.

*Brown University*

## NOTES

[1] In Jules Huret, *Enquête sur l'évolution littéraire* (Paris: Bibliothèque Charpentier, 1901), p. 67.

[2] See, for example, Angelo P. Bertocci, *From Symbolism to Baudelaire* (Carbondale: Southern Illinois Press, 1964). It is because of the potential confusion inherent in the term that Lloyd Austin proposed a distinction between "la symbolique" (= transcendental symbolism, deriving from Baudelaire) and "le symbolisme" (= a more generalized symbolism of any period involving indirect expression): see *L'Univers poétique de Baudelaire* (Paris: Mercure de France, 1956). For a general discussion of the meaning of the word, see Anna Balakian, *The Symbolist Movement: A Critical Appraisal* (New York: N.Y. University Press, 2nd ed., 1977) and Henri Peyre, *Qu'est-ce que le symbolisme?* (Paris: Presses Universitaires de France, 1974).

[3] This is of course a Symbolist interpretation, exemplified particularly in Paul Valéry's famous phrase: "une volonté remarquable d'isoler définitivement la Poésie de toute autre essence qu'elle-méme" [a remarkable determination to isolate Poetry finally from all essence other than itself].

[4] For the development of French symbolism, see particularly, from the mass of work available, Guy Michaud, *Message poétique du symbolisme* (Paris: Nizet, 1947, 4 vols.), Kenneth Cornell, *The Symbolist Movement* (New Haven: Yale University Press, 1951), A. G. Lehmann, *The Symbolist Aesthetic in France* (Oxford: Blackwell. 1950), Svend Johansen, *Le Symbolisme: étude sur le style des symbolistes français* (Copenhagen: Munksgaard, 1945).

[5] René Wellek and Austin Warren, *Theory of Literature* (Harmondsworth: Penguin Books, 3rd ed., 1963), pp. 189-90.

[6] Edmund Wilson, *Axel's Castle* (London: Fontana Library, 1969), p. 24. For these wider repercussions, see also C. M. Bowra, *The Heritage of Symbolism* (London: MacMillan, 1943) and Peyre and Balakian. Professor William R. Risley has kindly drawn my attention to René Wellek's "The Term and Concept of Symbolism in Literary History," in *Discriminations* (New Haven: Yale University Press, 1970), pp. 90-121, which also argues forcefully for a wide interpretation of symbolism.

[7] Balakian, p. x.

[8] Charles Chadwick, *Symbolism* (London: Methuen, "The Critical Idiom," 1971), pp. 2-3.

[9] Quoted in Michaud, *La doctrine symboliste (Documents)* (4th vol. of *Message poétique . . .*), p. 47.

[10] J. M. Aguirre, *Antonio Machado, poeta simbolista* (Madrid: Taurus, 1973). Note in particular: "se mantiene aquí que cuando los poetas españoles del modernismo escriben del simbolismo francés se refieren con toda probabilidad a las tendencias poéticas representadas por los miembros de la tan mencionada generación de 1885" (p. 35) [it is here maintained that when Spanish poets of the *modernista* movement write about French Symbolism they are in all probability referring to the poetic tendencies represented by the members of the so much mentioned generation of 1885]. For an overall criticism of Aguirre's book, see my review in *Bulletin of Hispanic Studies*, 54 (1977), 75-77.

[11] See Allen Phillips' detailed study *Alejandro Sawa, Mito y realidad* (Madrid: Editorial Turner, 1976) and Luis S. Granjel, "Maestros y amigos del 98: Alejandro Sawa," *Cuadernos Hispanoamericanos*, 196 (March 1966), 430-44. An expatriate Frenchman named Albert Cornuty may also have had some impact.

[12] See Gordon Brotherston, *Manuel Machado: a Revaluation* (Cambridge: Cambridge University Press, 1968), pp. 14-15, and Gillian Gayton, *Manuel Machado y los poetas simbolistas franceses* (Valencia: Editorial Bello, 1975), pp. 15-16.

[13] In Gerardo Diego's famous Anthology of 1932; I quote from the "nueva edición completa," *Poesía española contemporánea (1901-1934)* (Madrid: Taurus, 1962), p. 150. See Antonio Machado, *Obras. Poesía y Prosa*, ed. Aurora de Albornoz y Guillermo de Torre (Buenos Aires: Losada, 1964), p. 51. All page references to Machado's works in the text are to this edition unless otherwise stated; poems are identified by the Roman numbers of *Poesías completas* as found in *Obras. Poesía y Prosa*. In a more extensive autobiographical note written in 1913 (see Francisco Vega Díaz's presentation of the text in *Papeles de Son Armadans*, XIV, liv, 160 [1969], 49-99), Machado states: "Tengo una gran aversión a todo lo francés, con excepción de algunos reformadores del ideal

francés, según Brunnetiére (*sic*). Recibí alguna influencia de los simbolistas franceses, pero ya hace tiempo que reacciono contra ella" [I have a great aversion for everything French, except for some who, according to Brunnetiére (*sic*), deform the French ideal. I received some influence from the French symbolists, but for a long time now I have reacted against it]. The autobiography is reproduced in my edition of *Soledades. Galerías. Otros poemas* (Barcelona: Labor, 1975), pp. 268-70; henceforth *SGOP.*

[14] See Jules Huret, p. 73, and Henri Mazel, *Aux beaux temps du Symbolisme, 1890-1895* (Paris: Mercure de France, 1943), p. 52.

[15] There is a recent edition of *Les premières armes* by Michael Packenham (University of Exeter, England, 1973). For Moréas, see the comprehensive study by R. A. Jouanny, *Jean Moréas, écrivain français* (Paris: Minard, 1969).

[16] See Miguel Pérez Ferrero, *Vida de Antonio Machado y Manuel* (Madrid: Rialp, 1947), pp. 86-87, 107.

[17] See John W. Kronik, "Enrique Gómez Carrillo, Francophile Propagandist," *Symposium,* 21 (1967), 50-60. For a full study of the introduction of Verlaine in Spain, see Rafael Ferreres, *Verlaine y los modernistas expañoles* (Madrid: Gredos, 1975).

[18] For one aspect of the relations between Latin-American and Spanish writers and the French literary world, see my article "Las primeras crónicas iberoamericanas del *Mercure de France,*" *Revista iberoamericana,* 42, Nos. 96-97 (1976), 381-409. The *Mercure de France* was without question the most outward-looking journal of the time. Darío often complained bitterly of French neglect. When Carrillo is referred to in passing, by Ernest Raynaud in *La Plume,* No. 336, 15 Apr. 1903, as attending the "Samedis" [Saturday discussion groups] hosted by the journal, he is called "le Portugais Gomez Carillo" (*sic*); the mistake is repeated in *La mêlée symboliste,* vol. I (1870-1890) (Paris: La Renaissance du Livre, 1918), p. 140. Carrillo is no doubt confused with Eugenio de Castro, but the confusion shows little acquaintance with or respect for either writer.

[19] See Gayton, pp. 27-42. As she notes judiciously, "no he encontrado ninguna referencia a Manuel Machado en las memorias de los escritores franceses que cita como amigos, y parece inverosímil que sin la ayuda de Carrillo, que era muy conocido, hubiera conseguido penetrar en ese mundo brillante y engreído" (p. 37) [I have found no reference to Manuel Machado in the memoirs of the French writers he lists as friends and it seems unlikely that without the help of Carrillo, who was very well known, he would have succeeded in penetrating that brilliant and conceited world].

[20] Note the explicit but immature symbolism of "La fuente" [The fountain], the first version of which dates from 1901: *SGOP,* pp. 223-26. See also Aguirre, pp. 215-369.

[21] See my "Nuevas precisiones sobre la influencia de Verlaine en Antonio Machado," *Filología* (Buenos Aires), 12 (1968-69), 295-305. Manuel possessed the Vanier edition of *Oeuvres complètes* (1899), though the first volume is missing from his library in Burgos: see Gayton, p. 41.

[22] See Ricardo Gullón, *Conversaciones con Juan Ramón Jiménez* (Madrid: Taurus, 1958), p. 94. Jiménez adds (p. 100) that both he and Antonio Machado knew the *Choix de poèmes* (*sic*) by heart.

[23] For a detailed study of Verlaine's influence see Chapter VII, "La influencia de Verlaine en Antonio Machado," of my *Niebla y Soledad: Aspectos de Unamuno y Machado* (Madrid: Gredos, 1971), pp. 255-87.

[24] "Nevermore," *SGOP,* pp. 240-41; "Mai più" becomes XLIII, *SGOP,* pp. 132-33.

[25] For an interesting interpretation of this apparition, see Michael P. Predmore, "The Nostalgia for Paradise and the Dilemma of Solipsism in the early poetry of Antonio Machado," *Revista Hispánica Moderna,* 38 (1974-75), 30-52.

[26] For further details, see my forthcoming article entitled "Antonio Machado y Mallarmé."

[27] See the facsimile edition of Domingo Yndurain, 2 vols. (Madrid: Taurus, 1971), II, 69.

[28] From "Quisiera que mi libro" [I should like my book], the last poem of the *Segunda antolojía poética, 1898-1918.* (I quote from the Austral edition, 1969, p. 258).

[29] See Ricardo Gullón, "Simbolismo y modernismo en Antonio Machado" in *Direcciones del Modernismo* (Madrid: Gredos, 2nd ed., 1971); Ramón de Zubiría, *La*

*poesía de Antonio Machado* (Madrid: Gredos, 3rd ed., 1973), especially pp. 62-102; Rafael Lapesa, "Sobre algunos símbolos en la poesía de Antonio Machado," *Cuadernos Hispanoamericanos*, 306-307 (Oct. 1975-Jan. 1976), 386-431; Alan S. Trueblood, "Apuntes sobre la metáfora en la poesía de Antonio Machado hasta 1907," *Homenaje a Rodrigo Molina* (Madrid: Insula, 1977), pp. 329-43; and *Niebla y Soledad*, pp. 192-205.

[30] *Oeuvres complètes*, ed. Henri Mondor and G. Jean-Aubry (Paris: La Pléiade, 1945), p. 368; and G. Michaud, *La doctrine symboliste*, p. 26. On Mallarmé's hermetic world, dehumanized and autonomous, see Hugo Friedrich, *Die Struktur der modernen Lyrik* (Hamburg: Rowohlt, 1956), pp. 95-139. (English translation: *The Structure of Modern Poetry*, trans. Joachim Neugroschel, Evanston: Northwestern University Press, 1974). For more details on Machado's reactions to Mallarmé, see my forthcoming study referred to in note 26.

[31] In a recent article, "Muerte y transmuerte en la poesía de Antonio Machado," *Revista de Occidente*, 3rd epoch, 5 and 6 (March-April 1976), 11-24, Dámaso Alonso has commented in a masterly fashion on the "paraísos quietos, en donde el gozo es muchas veces casi meramente intelectual ... la vaga descripción de una región de transmuerte bella, límpida, serena, en tres poemas de 1902 a 1903" [calm paradises, in which the pleasure is often almost entirely intellectual ... the vague description of a beautiful, transparent, serene region beyond death, in three poems from 1902 to 1903]. The poem quoted is one of these three. See also *Niebla y Soledad*, pp. 202-05.

[32] For this whole question, see "Unamuno y Antonio Machado," in *Niebla y Soledad*, pp. 288-322.

[33] *Axël*, IV, 2: "L'option suprême," p. 249. (I quote from the edition by Pierre Mariel, Paris: Le Courrier du Livre, 1969).

[34] *Obras completas*, ed. M. García Blanco (Madrid: Escelicer, 1968), III, 1083.

[35] Unamuno, "Almas de jóvenes," in *Obras completas*, ed. cit., I, 1157.

[36] See, in particular, his "Le mystère dans les lettres," in *Oeuvres complètes*, ed. cit., pp. 382-87, and examples in Michaud, *La doctrine symboliste*, pp. 15, 17, 74, 99, 100.

[37] For a contrast between the two poets, see my "Recaptured Memory in Juan Ramón Jiménez and Antonio Machado," in *Studies in Modern Spanish Literature and Art Presented to Helen F. Grant*, ed. Nigel Glendinning (London: Tamesis, 1972), pp. 149-61.

[38] *The Symbolist Movement in Literature* (1899; rpt. New York: Dutton, 1958), p. 93.

[39] See C. B. Morris, "*Visión* and *mirada* in the poetry of Salinas, Guillén and Dámaso Alonso," *Bulletin of Hispanic Studies*, 38 (1961), 103-12; J. González Muela, "Poesía y amistad: Jorge Guillén y Pedro Salinas," *BHS*, 35 (1958), 28-33; and Jason Wilson, "*Abrir/cerrar los ojos*: a recurrent theme in the poetry of Octavio Paz," *BHS*, 48 (1971), 44-56.

[40] See Arthur Terry's excellent Critical Guide: *Antonio Machado: "Campos de Castilla"* (London: Grant and Cutler, 1973) and my "The Unity of Antonio Machado's 'Campos de Soria,' " *Hispanic Review*, (1973), 285-96.

[41] Cf. Rémy de Gourmont: "... le monde, tout ce qui est extérieur à moi, n'existe que selon l'idée qu'il s'en fait. ... C'est ce que Schopenhauer a vulgarisé sous cette formule si simple et si claire: Le monde est ma représentation. Je ne vois pas ce qui est; ce qui est, c'est ce que je vois" (Michaud, *La doctrine symboliste*, p. 23) [the world, all that is outside me, exists only according to the idea that one conceives of it. ... It is what Schopenhauer has popularized in such a simple and clear formula: the world is my representation. I do not see what is; what is, is what I see].

[42] *Oeuvres complètes*, p. 368, and Michaud, *La doctrine symboliste*, p. 26.

[43] For a study of Bergson's influence on Machado's poetic practice, see Nigel Glendinning, "The Philosophy of Bergson in the Poetry of Machado," *Revue de littérature comparée* (1962), 50-70.

[44] *Obras: Poesía y Prosa*, p. 50; but it should be noted that in this edition a passage is missing, so that the sense is hopelessly garbled.

[45] See Aguirre, pp. 193-97.

# Symbol in the Poetics
# of Antonio Machado

## Ricardo Gullón

It is not possible to examine here the whole problem of the symbol and its meaning in poetry.[1] I shall limit myself to a study of its condensational value and function, without letting myself be seduced by questions that could only be poorly treated in the limits of this essay.

A symbol is, by nature, a figure that presents in tangible form an abstraction or a reality that cannot otherwise be grasped. St. John of the Cross remarked how the Holy Spirit, "no pudiendo . . . dar á entender la abundancia de su sentido por términos vulgares y vsados, habla misterios en estrañas figuras y semejanças"[2] [not being able . . . to make the abundance of His meaning understood through ordinary and commonly used terms, speaks mysteries in strange figures and similarities]. The singularity of those figures can be an obstacle to comprehension; the gentle saint recalled that this difficulty could arise because at times we want to show "lo que nosotros no podemos bien entender ni comprehender" (p. 4) [what we cannot well understand or comprehend]. For example, the *modernista* swan symbolizes beauty, but how many other things, clear or obscure, are insinuated by it?

Much of what I have noted elsewhere in relation to the image, as an instrument of condensation,[3] is applicable to the symbol. It is not indispensable to establish the differences between the one and the other since, essentially, with respect to this problem their affinities are more important. The differentiating element is that in a metaphorical image the two terms of comparison are precise, whereas what is symbolized by a symbol is imprecise. This is more easily understood if one looks at how they function. The same verbal object may function imagistically or symbolically, or imagistically *and* symbolically, with a duality that is in no way incompatible. The symbol, like the image, presents one thing in place of another, and not with the intention of hiding anything but, on the contrary, in order to facilitate the perception of something (the imprecise), which without the symbol could not be expressed as well. The symbol presents in concrete and tangible form what is in itself abstract and intangible: an abandoned harp serves to evoke the distant past; a train racing through the night is enough to suggest man's destiny.

Note the change in verbs: from "presenting" I have shifted to "evoking" and "suggesting." These verbs describe the ways in which a symbol operates: the figures are what they are and at the same time point to something else.

For example, the cats of the famous poem by Baudelaire, as symbol, point to the contemplative life and to contemplation itself. It can be assumed that there are zones so vast and unexplored that they cannot be encompassed by description; in view of this, one tries to incorporate them into the poem by means of the fascinating abbreviation, the symbol. Thanks to it, our reading carries us from one level to another, without effort, and without uprooting us either. Ultimately, one attempts to capture the music of the the spheres, an ideal harmony that, if it is not apprehended, at least can be evoked ("a veces enucia el vago viento/ un misterio" [at times the wandering wind enounces/ a mystery], said Rubén Darío in "El coloquio de los centauros" [The Colloquy of the Centaurs]). It is the height of ambition: to enclose the cosmos in a nutshell; to condense in a symbol—the sea, for example—the mystery of life, or in a figure—Helen—the attraction of beauty.

Symbolic function depends on the verbal construction in which the symbol appears—that is, on the weave of relationships and associations, evident or veiled, established by its terms. Upon entering and participating in that construction, the symbol multiplies its power, compensating for the word's limitations—so insufficient for expressing what is unlimited in the ideas, concepts, and sentiments that are to be expressed in them. The symbol functions as a changing mechanism: it evokes things that would be literally inexpressible, because of their number and because of their nature. Therefore, I say that it is an abbreviation, but a dynamic one: an abbreviation of different things, present or not, depending upon the level at which the reading is carried out.

To comprehend a symbol in its totality is to accede to a plurality of levels. The act of comprehension is, as always, a deciphering, which imposes a re-creation.[4] The reader repeats in reverse—in the inverse direction—the mental operations that led to the elaboration of the symbol. The author arrives at the symbol having started with an intuition. The reader arrives at the intuition having begun with the symbol and gone beyond it to the scattered notions that provoke the sudden triumph of consciousness that is the intuition.

The reader knows at least that the symbol has meaning, although he is not sure of what it means. To know that one does not know can be an incentive to a greater understanding; the brain, spurred on by an awareness of its limitations, passes from passivity to belligerent dynamism, changing and, if it is legitimate to put it this way, personalizing the conditions of receptivity. Amado Alonso stated the matter precisely with reference to language. Avoiding the risks of psychologism, this means that the reader should explore the context of the symbolic insertion in order to illuminate it in terms of what is said in adjacent passages. For one of the things that we cannot lose sight of is the symbol's ability to function in different ways in different contexts, and even to disguise itself, like the River Guadiana, and offer to our view a surface of complete literalness.

A symbol is the form of an idea and the formula of the equivalence between an idea and an image; it is also a sure means of rapid and permanent transference to a universe of plenitude which, thanks to it, is in the poem. Its wealth of possibilities does not mean it is capricious; it is limited by its need to be understood, and this requirement in no way lessens the freedom it attains in modern poetry. Even in the poetry of Rimbaud, or in that of the surrealists, the symbol responds to a system and has a logic of its own, even though it may be a logic of delirium.

Every symbol is legitimate and authentic if it carries out effectively its vicarious function. The use of personal symbols imposes difficulties, but these difficulties are overcome by the reader when he enters into the system and is capable of breaking the code. Thibaudet with the poetry of Mallarmé and Amado Alonso with Neruda's have shown how one can arrive at that in-depth reading, starting from an understanding of the nature of a given symbol and of the peculiar manner of its integration into the whole. For "freedom of symbol" please understand the enormous variety of its expressive possibilities, a variety which is not contradicted by constancy in its functioning. It always functions in the same way, and it always has the same relationship to what is symbolized: the relationship is constant in character and in purpose.

Lévi-Strauss has demonstrated that the magical practices of primitive peoples can be read as a manipulation whose invariable requirement is "qu'elle se fasse à l'aide de symboles, c'est-à-dire d'équivalents significatifs du signifié, relevant d'un autre ordre de réalité que ce dernier" ["that the manipulation must be carried out through symbols, that is, through meaningful equivalents of things meant which belong to another order of reality"], and that the cures, frequently achieved, are due to the fact that, thanks to these practices, "le chaman fournit à sa malade un *langage,* dans lequel peuvent s'exprimer immédiatement des états informulés, et autrement informulables"[5] ["the shaman provides the sick woman with a *language,* by means of which unexpressed, and otherwise inexpressible, psychic states can be immediately expressed"].[6] Poetic symbology operates in an analogous way. The poet finds in the symbol a possibility of expression, and of expression condensed to the utmost. Who could say how many things a rose can express? The ingenuous booklets on the language of flowers, still sold at fairs and markets, were intended to be a compendium and dictionary of an elemental symbology, but in their modesty and in their candor they did not fail to focus the symbol correctly: as language and, more precisely, as a part of *the* language.

The poetry of Machado is essentially symbolic. If in recent years some have thought otherwise, it was because of the temporary obfuscation of those who, wanting a committed Machado, considered political commitment incompatible with a poetic writing not abiding by the norms of prose. The defense of prosaic poetry, like that of the squared circle, is a historical curiosity confined to the cellars of an illiterate journalism. That Machado did not amuse himself by looking for difficulties, much less obscurities, no one will deny; but no less indisputable is his acceptance and use of the symbol as an expressive technique. The holm oak and the olive tree are in his poetry to symbolize his preferred regions, Castile and Andalusia; the autumnal park is a lackluster (intentionally lackluster) allusion to the paradise lost, to the place of illusions and dreams, to irreality dreamed more than reality lived. The old elm is a symbol of man and of his improbable hope; the galleries—as I have indicated elsewhere[7]—are the soul and its byways, the unconscious and its beckonings.

Underlying all these examples is the vastness of imagistic horizons. One might even observe among them a difference in substance: although holm oak and olive tree may not symbolize only particular geographic and historical realities, but much more—forms of life, attitudes, modes of existence—those realities are in what is symbolized, while they are not, nor can they be, in the old park and in the galleries. Perhaps it would be appropriate to call the first examples metonymical symbols and the second ones metaphorical symbols, thus introducing a new classifying principle and with it a new principle of order.

Another kind of division would be one that took into consideration the degree of familiarity of the reader with the tangible term of the symbol. We note immediately the difference between symbols like the noria or the flies, on the one hand, and the gardens of love in which Machado situates Guiomar, on the other. The symbol produces different effects depending on its degree of nearness to visible reality; distance determines different tones and atmospheres. Machado was aware of it, as he revealed when he titled the poems of familiar symbology *Humorismos* [Humorisms].

By this I do not mean that symbols like the spring, so impeccably studied by Dámaso Alonso that it seems unnecessary to add anything to his observations,[8] do not use as their point of departure an equally clear and simple sign, but that they operate in another way. Machado's springs, like his galleries, are interior:

> Anoche cuando dormía
> soñé, ¡bendita ilusión!,
> que una fontana fluía
> dentro de mi corazón.[9]

> [Last night when I was sleeping
> I dreamed, blessed illusion!,
> that a spring was flowing
> within my heart.]

The mule circles "outside"; the flies, before being substance and experience in the poem, were matter and annoyance in life; the spring is a form adequate for expressing metaphorically—like the beehive and the sun—the intuition of a deeply felt event. The degree of abstraction increases without changing the predominantly metaphorical nature of the device.

Since in these cases the equivalency image = symbol could lead to confusion, let us think of others that would be less equivocal. They might be, for example, the "Canciones a Guiomar" [Songs to Guiomar] that so effectively function as poetic condensation:

> No sabía
> si era un limón amarillo
> lo que tu mano tenía,
> o el hilo de un claro día,
> Guiomar, en dorado ovillo.
> Tu boca me sonreía.

> Yo pregunté: ¿Qué me ofreces?
> ¿Tiempo en fruto, que tu mano
> eligió entre madureces
> de tu huerta?

> ¿Tiempo vano
> de una bella tarde yerta?

¿Dorada ausencia encantada?
¿Copia en el agua dormida?
¿De monte en monte encendida,
la alborada
verdadera?
¿Rompe en sus turbios espejos
amor la devanadera
de sus crepúsculos viejos? (p. 339)

[I didn't know
if it was a yellow lemon
that your hand held,
or the yarn of a clear day,
Guiomar, in a golden ball.
Your mouth smiled at me.

I asked: What are you offering me?
Time in fruit, which your hand
selected among the ripeness
of your orchard?

Empty time
of a beautiful, stiff afternoon?
Golden, enchanted absence?
A copy in the sleeping water?
Burning from mountain to mountain,
the true
dawn?
Does love break in its turbid mirrors
the bobbin
of its old twilights?]

The symbol, if I am not mistaken, was built up through an accumulation of metaphors. The lemon is the real term of a first image in which the imaginary term, "dorado ovillo" [golden ball], functions in its turn as a real term of a duplicated imaginary term, "claro día" [clear day], which is at the same time the real term of another imaginary term, love, expressed by implication in the smiling mouth of the loved one.[10] Gradually, the imagistic duplication creates a series of distancing planes and includes in the poem possibilities that act as lyric stimulants. The following two stanzas expand further the field of suggestion; and, by casting in rhetorical form, as questions, what are really affirmations, they extend more and more the range of the image, which gradually rises to a superior hierarchy and reveals things that are abstract and imprecise. The lemon is time, full or empty, absence, dawn, again love. It is no longer an image but a symbol of hopeful life and of love, which in the next song will create for the lovers a secret place ("jardín de un tiempo cerrado" [garden of a closed time]), a symbol of the space invented for love, a space where "un ave insólita canta" [an unusual bird sings], a bird that is no less symbolic nor less capable of suggesting with its song the singularity of love.

These examples prove Saussure's affirmation that "el símbolo tiene por carácter no ser nunca completamente arbitrario; no está vacío" ["one characteristic of the symbol is that it is never wholly arbitrary; it is not empty"], a fact that is even clearer in poetry than in language, since in poetry we find not only "un rudimento de vínculo natural entre el significante y el significado"[11] ["the rudiment of a natural bond between the signifier and the signified"],[12] but also a complex network of relationships between the object that is functioning symbolically—analogous to the signifier—and the abstractions contained in it, which occupy in this relationship a situation similar to that of the signified. The symbol differs from the linguistic sign in that the second of the principles established by Saussure, that of the linearity of the signifier, can be applied to it only with restrictions. The symbol operates at different levels simultaneously, without need of being subjected to the law of succession; as Saussure recognized, it operates in a rational form, and that rationality makes it ultimately accessible and intelligible.

The correspondences, so sumptuously established by Baudelaire, between the visible and the invisible, are no less subtle in Machado, although they are stated in a minor key, with deceptive intimacy. If the cosmos stands reduced to the dimensions of the self, it is not to diminish it but rather to internalize it and allow the symbolic parallels to be captured in poems whose experiential character will bring them closer to the reader. Mallarmé and Neruda departed ostentatiously from the linguistic norms and from the symbology used in general or in their epoch; Machado did not. His break with the one or with the other is so subtle that it is hardly seen. No one uses greater discretion and naturalness with the words of prose to say what cannot be said in prose, and no one has made a more personal and more synthesizing use of the symbols his epoch offered him. Since he understood them as instruments of creation, it was in their manipulation and not in their novelty that he engaged with such constant elegance.

*The University of Chicago*

[English version by the editors in collaboration with the author]

## NOTES

[1] This essay is based on my *Una poética para Antonio Machado* (Madrid: Gredos, 1970), pp. 257-64.

[2] San Juan de la Cruz, *El cántico espiritual* (Madrid: Espasa-Calpe, 1962), p. 5.

[3] See my *Una poética para Antonio Machado*, pp. 238-40 and 247-56.

[4] Amado Alonso said in general terms: "Comprender—un poema o una frase coloquial—requiere cierto modo de recreación" (Prologue, *Curso de lingüística general*, by Fernando de Saussure [Buenos Aires: Losada, 1945], p. 25) [To comprehend—a poem or a colloquial expression—requires a certain kind of re-creation].

[5] Claude Lévi-Strauss, *Anthropologie Structurale*, I (Paris: Plon, 1958), 221 and 218.

[6] Claude Lévi-Strauss, *Structural Anthropology*, trans. Claire Jacobson and Brooke Grundfest Schoepf (New York: Basic Books, 1963), pp. 200 and 198.

[7] See my *Una poética para Antonio Machado*, pp. 247-51.

[8] Dámaso Alonso, *Poetas españoles contemporáneos*, 3rd ed. (Madrid: Gredos, 1965), pp. 130 ff.

[9] Antonio Machado, *Obras: poesía y prosa*, ed. Aurora de Albornoz and Guillermo de Torre (Buenos Aires: Losada, 1964), p. 101. Further references to this edition will be given in the text.

[10] The reading by Antonio Sánchez Barbudo also notes the symbolic element: " 'No sabía,' dice [Machado], y no sabemos desde luego nosotros, si era en verdad limón o simplemente luz lo que tenía en esa mano que el poeta, confuso, contemplaba. La confusión se explica por el verso que sigue: 'Tu boca me sonreía.' Lo importante, desconcertante para él, es que ella, sonriente, parecía ofrecerse. El limón–o la luz como amarillo limón–en la mano de Guiomar resultaba así simbólico" (*Los poemas de Antonio Machado* [Barcelona: Lumen, 1967], p. 421) ["I didn't know," says [Machado], and we ourselves do not know, of course, if it was in truth a lemon or simply light that she had in that hand which the poet, confused, contemplated. The confusion is explained by the line that follows: "Your mouth smiled at me." The important thing, disconcerting for him, is that she, smiling, seemed to offer herself. The lemon–or light like a yellow lemon–in Guiomar's hand thus turned out to be symbolic].

[11] Fernando de Saussure, *Curso de lingüística general* (see above, n. 4), p. 131.

[12] Ferdinand de Saussure, *Course in General Linguistics,* ed. Charles Bally and Albert Sechehaye, trans. Wade Baskin (New York: Philosophical Library, 1959), p. 68.

A vignette by Leandro Izaguirre. Reproduced from *Revista Moderna de México,* 6, No. 6 (Feb. 1905), 323.

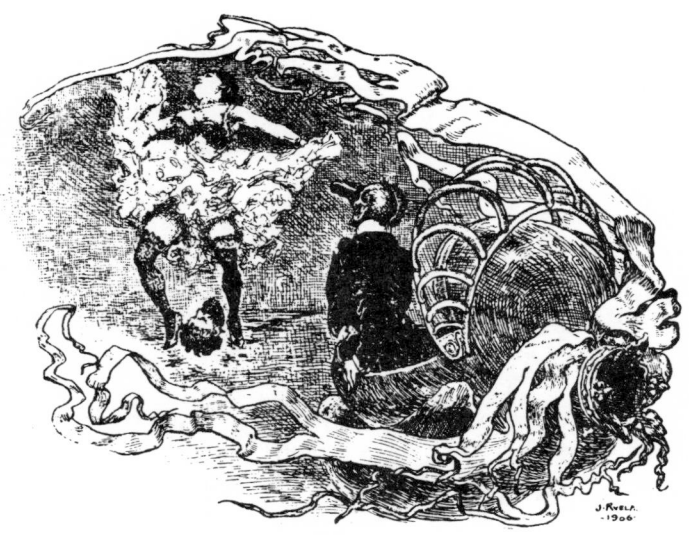

Eterna Salomé.

A vignette by Julio Ruelas, dated 1906. Reproduced from *Revista Moderna de México*, 12, No. 2 (Oct. 1907), 82.

# Decadent Elements in the Poetry of Manuel Machado

## Allen W. Phillips

In memory of Jorge de Sena (1919-1978),
friend and colleague

It is unfortunately a commonplace idea that Manuel Machado (1874-1947) has been overshadowed by the impressive poetry of his more famous younger brother Antonio with whom he maintained a deep and lasting friendship. My purpose here is not to dispute this accepted fact but to affirm that Manuel Machado was not a minor poet by any means, and his literary production, authentic and highly varied, gives clear evidence of a well defined lyric personality of original merit, which was a necessary antecedent of certain aspects of more contemporary Spanish poetry.[1] He was a master of the light and graceful, and, ever faithful to his native Seville, the melodic. However, my main interest here is to study a single aspect of his verse, a quality which he did not have in common with his brother, who was entirely free from certain literary decadent elements which characterized the poetry of the times, although they both did share for a short while, both in Madrid and Paris, the same bohemian life style so often associated with the decadent writers.

## Introduction to the Poetry of Manuel Machado

It seems appropriate here to point out first of all the wide range of poetic practice in Manuel Machado, whose variety of forms and inspiration lend to his literary interest. I am aware of the danger of excessive simplification, but one might without grave error reduce his poetry to four basic types, all present incidentally in his first book *Alma* (1901 or 1902).[2] First are the lyric songs of differing metre eminently influenced both by Verlaine in mood, setting, motifs and a suggestive musicality[3] and, to a lesser degree, by other French symbolists with whose work he was well acquainted even before his residence in Paris, as well as by Darío, who had arrived on the European literary scene by this time. Such songs are found in *Alma*, 1899-1900, and in *Caprichos,* 1900-1905.[4] Secondly, there are the many sonnets which so successfully recreate in the Parnassian manner famous paintings or portraits mainly to be found in the Prado which Machado knew so well (*Apolo. Teatro pictórico,* 1911). Third are the poems (*cantares*) of a popular vein inspired in his native Andalusia (*Cante hondo,* 1912).[5] Finally, there are compositions of an entirely different nature describing life in the city and embracing intentionally more prosaic subjects of daily life expressed in conversational language (*El mal poema,* 1909).

Machado was an exquisite poet, refined in the expression of sensations and nuances as was the master Verlaine. Other facets of his poetry are also singularly important and bear brief mention here: the constant use of masques and situations taken from the *commedia dell'arte,* surely following again the practice of Verlaine and Laforgue; a strong tendency to self-portraiture ("Retrato," "Prólogo-Epílogo," "Nuevo Auto-Retrato"); poems which offer sensitive and telling portraits of other writers and friends, among which those dedicated to Alejandro Sawa, José Palomo Anaya, Ricardo Fuente, and Ruelas (all decadent figures) are particularly outstanding (*Dedicatorias,* 1910-1922), and of special note are the poems scattered throughout his various collections of Castilian origin and theme, which reveal his deep preoccupation with Spain. He was not then indifferent to national concerns and the contemporary socio-political plight of his country. This fact, sometimes forgotten, again confirms the artificiality of trying to separate the writers of the period into two clearly defined and exclusive groups (*modernistas* and *noventayochistas*).[6] As we shall also see, love and death (*Ars moriendi,* 1921) are enduring themes in his verse, not to mention the typical subject of the bull fight (*La fiesta nacional,* 1906), which so fascinated the Sevillian poet.

I have left out of this rapid survey his long and fruitful theatrical collaboration with Antonio and also his final religious as well as political poetry. Some of his early religious verse is of excellent quality ("Se dice lentamente," "Kyrie Eleyson," "Es la mañana," "Domingo," which all belong to *Caprichos*). And in closing I should mention that *Phoenix* (1936), a later collection, contains various self-portraits and the reappearance of many familiar themes already mentioned.


### Machado's Poetics: A Brief Résumé

In reply to Gerardo Diego, who was compiling in the early thirties his indispensable anthology of contemporary Spanish poetry, Manuel Machado wrote:

> Ideas sobre la Poesía . . . Muchas y muy vagas y sutiles. Pero no las poseo, me poseen ellas. Nada puedo, pues, "decir" sobre eso que, para mí cae dentro de la indefinible, mejor: lo inefable.[7]

> [Ideas about Poetry . . . Many of them but vague and subtle ones. But I don't possess them, they possess me. I cannot affirm anything about that which in my opinion falls within the indefinable, better still the ineffable.]

Despite this disclaimer, in his miscellaneous prose (interviews, articles, reviews and occasional critical pages) can be found fragments which are useful in this context to complete the picture of the poet and his art. Of particular interest, of course, is the volume *La guerra literaria* (1913), in which he speaks as a witness and not as a literary historian at the turn of the century. In it the most significant text is the initial essay "Los poetas de hoy" (pp. 17-38). Of somewhat less importance is the already quoted *Unos versos, un alma y una época* (1940), although it, too, offers retrospective commentary on his life and writings.

First and foremost Manuel Machado was a *modernista* poet and a good one, but I hasten to add again that this does not mean he did not share the common concerns for Spain and its future that so preoccupied the writers of 1898.[8] However, he is much more than a mere imitator of Verlaine or Darío, both of whom were so admired by the Sevillian poet. No writer is accorded more praise than Verlaine, whose original personality he so admired from the point of view of both technique and sensibility.[9] Machado states ". . . the last great French poet was more than a Parnassian and more than a symbolist; he was supremely Verlaine," and elsewhere he reaffirms: ". . . he is paradoxically mystic and decadent. Decadent? Yes. Frequently sensuality dominates his will. Nevertheless there is no one like him, both spiritual and sensual at the same time . . . he is the most human and most divine of the poets."

In the essay "Los poetas de hoy" Machado recognized, of course, the lamentable state of Spanish poetry, which was clearly in crisis prior to the turn of the century; but *modernismo,* despite the general Spanish indifference to European styles, was finally imposed after a bitter struggle. He refers to all the familiar writers who contributed, each in his own way, to the renaissance of Spanish letters in the twentieth century. Machado then defines *modernismo,* a vague term at best without a precise meaning which he believed no longer existed at that time, in the following manner: a literary revolution principally formal in nature and characterized by an essential anarchy or individualism (p. 32). He stresses also that the new art was mainly a question of personality (p. 33), and Spain, by opening windows and doors, attained a new cosmopolitanism which it had previously lacked. Elsewhere Machado exalts the virtues of poetic music and its necessary appeal to the emotions. Receptive to innovation, and, although he tends to reject but respects classic rhetoric in his search for freedom, he nevertheless holds in great esteem the primitive poets of Castile. He also warns us: "Maximum respect for traditional rhetoric should not let us forget that rules are based on poetry, not poetry on rules." Machado also feels that authentic poetry blends the popular and the erudite; great art is transcendental and condenses the real and the fantastic. Be oneself and be original, he says. The poet ". . . must strive to reach a new creation of reality and, to do so, it is sufficient to filter it through his spirit or simply to see with his own eyes and not with borrowed ones."

A final word about technique. Machado intimates that he did bring to Spain the better qualities of Parnassianism and symbolism (he even refers to the colour of the vowels in the famous sonnet of Rimbaud), and, opening to us the doors of his workshop, he affirms with reference to internal form·

. . . Primeramente es de saber que desde que yo escribo conscientemente algo de que puedo declararme responsable, para mí escribir es . . . no escribir. Me explicaré. Así como otros confían inmediatamente a la cuartilla aquello que se les va ocurriendo, a reserva de corregirlo, modificarlo, perfeccionarlo luego, yo no consigno al papel sino aquello que habría de quedar en última instancia y todas aquellas operaciones de selección y acabamiento se obran en mi interior

de manera involuntaria y fatal . . . Esta dolorosa selección interna me hace
lento y poco fecundo, y me fatiga bastante, no por lo poco que escribo, sino
por lo mucho que dejo de escribir.

[First [with regard to the internal form of my verse] one should know that
from the moment when I consciously write something for which I consider
myself truly responsible, for me writing is . . . not writing. Let me explain. In
the case of others who put immediately on paper what is happening to them,
with the idea of correcting, modifying or perfecting it later on, I do not write
down anything except the final version and all those operations of selection
and polishing take place within me in an inevitable and fatal manner . . . This
painful internal selection slows me up and makes me less fecund. What tires
me is not the little that I write but rather the many things I fail to write.] [10]

## Manuel Machado and Decadentism

Both in his life style and his literature prior to 1910, the year when he
married and settled down to a much less bohemian existence, Manuel
Machado gives clear-cut evidence of being a decadent writer although he never
exclusively limited his art to its cult. I use the term decadentism here in its
broadest sense, considering it both as a style and an attitude. Machado's
poetry almost always gives off an aura which is both sensual and voluptuous,
elegant and aristocratic. He was a conscious writer who—under the spell
particularly of Verlaine, in whom he saw the paradoxical but typical fusion of
mysticism and sensuality—cultivated, as we have seen, exquisite themes
normally associated with *fin de siècle* motifs and *modernismo:* the courtly
scenes of Versailles, the playful or tragicomical themes taken from the
*commedia dell'arte,* and, above all, the pleasures of erotic love and his
amorous triumphs. Then there is also a studied pose of nonchalance and
indolence in Machado, which reaches a degree of apparent indifference or
frank disdain of life on the whole. This attitude—which, in making reference
to his poem "Adelfos," Pedro Salinas termed "derrotismo espiritual
enmarcado de exquisitez literaria"[11] [spiritual defeatism framed in an
exquisite literary mode]—is seen in other compositions as well. Machado tends
to react to life with a shrug of the shoulders and with ironic detachment
("Cantares"); and this cynical position is readily apparent in other works
which stress the hedonistic ("Encajes"), where he exclaims: " ¡No hay amor
en los placeres! / ¡No hay placer en el amor! " [There is no love in pleasures
and no pleasure in love!]. These disillusioned and nihilistic verses reveal a
posture which will reach its high point in *El mal poema* (1909), perhaps best
translated as *Song of Evil* since the influence of Baudelaire on the title seems
evident. It is Machado's most decadent collection and reflects, in a startling
new language, his *spleen* and his epicureanism. And how close is all this to
Jules Laforgue as well!

The poems just mentioned by title all belong to *Alma,* which is a
typically *modernista* volume showing the intense melancholy of a young poet.
Few motifs characteristic of the new poetry of the day are lacking. Some we
have mentioned already, others deserve brief notice: Wagner, Watteau, and
the page Gerinaldos, lover of the Queen. Machado bathes the old parks and
gardens in a distant and hazy grey, and fountains are also heard as part of the
general *mis-en-scène.* In "Antífona" the poet identifies his spirit with that of

a prostitute who suffers the same bittersweet passion. The following verses
are characteristic:

> Así, los dos: tú, amores; yo, poesía,
> damos por oro a un mundo que despreciamos . . .
> ¡ Tú, tu cuerpo de diosa; yo, el alma mía! . . .
> Ven y reiremos juntos mientras lloramos.
> [So, both of us: you, love, and I, poetry,
> we give for money to a world we scorn . . .
> You, your divine body; I, my soul! . . .
> Come and we shall laugh together while we weep.]

However, in "Inmoral," taken from the first book by Machado written with
Enrique Paradas, are to be found typical verses which affirm that the search
for beauty must naturally be placed far above any moral consideration: "Yo,
loco o delincuente,/ o delincuente y loco,/ busco lo bello donde quier se
asiente,/ en el bien o en el mal . . . Me importa poco" [I, mad or delinquent,/
or delinquent and mad,/ search for the beautiful wherever it may be found,/
in good and in evil. I couldn't care less]. He continues to evoke his passionate
but rapid love affairs, and he follows a vacillating course through life, tossed
hither and yon by the waves.

*Alma* is a good book, opening many paths for the author to follow. It is
not our intention to trace here the complex bibliographical history of the
aesthetic evolution of Manuel Machado, but the poems of *Caprichos*
(1900-1905) are in general terms a continuation of the preceding poems. In
addition to the religious compositions already mentioned, certainly one poem
of the volume deserves brief comment here because it seems to be, in more
than one sense, a farewell to Paris, to Machado's bohemian past, and it even
offers a slight note of repentance. Once a victim of sensual and passionate
love, Machado seems willing to abandon the adventures of a modern day
Harlequin. Moreover, in the same poem a new concept of nature and the
exterior world, full of light and no longer tinged in blacks and reds, is born.
In it Machado takes refuge and solace. He has momentarily found, it seems, a
new inner peace and spiritual direction. The final verses of *Caprichos* are as
much removed from decadentism as those that are inspired in the Andalusian
realities, however sensual and poignant, of the neopopular *Cante hondo*
(1912).[12]

Let us return now to *El mal poema* (1909) which contains some of the
most modern and certainly, in another sense, the most decadent of the lyrics
of Manuel Machado.[13] The complex book in question represents a significant
change in Machado's poetry both from the point of view of its subject matter
and its style. In addition to the sustained expression of his own personality,
basically empty and still in search of repose, he is now writing about the city
in its sordid but at the same time poetic aspects in a new colloquial language
and conversational tone. Without wishing to take anything away from
Machado, I feel everywhere, though it might be hard to pinpoint concrete
examples, the presence of Baudelaire and certainly of Laforgue.[14] He is the
bohemian who views through tired eyes the commonplace and the ordinary.
A new type of beauty, far removed from the traditional, has taken over for
the moment. In the well-known "Retrato," which opens the book and tells us
a great deal about the poet, several lines stand out. One case in this context is

the following: "Un destello de sol y una risa oportuna/ amo más que las languideces de la luna" [I like a ray of sunlight and an opportune laugh more than the languor of the moon]. In these two alexandrines a whole new aesthetic is formulated. The theme of poetry itself is central also in several other compositions of *El mal poema*. For example, Machado writes:

> Existe una poesía
> sin ritmo ni armonía,
> monótona, cansada,
> como una letanía . . .,
> de que está desterrada
> la pena y la alegría.
>
> Silvestre flor de cardo,
> poema gris o pardo
> de lo pobre y lo feo,
> sin nada de gallardo,
> sin gracia y sin deseo,
> agonioso y tardo.
>
> De las enfermedades
> y de las ansiedades
> prosaicas y penosas . . .;
> de negras soledades,
> de hazañas lastimosas
> y estúpidas verdades.
>
> ("Prosa")

[There is a poetry without rhythm nor harmony, so monotonous and dreary like a litany that even grief and joy have been banned from it. Wild thistle, grey drab poem which deals with the downtrodden and the ugly, without any saving grace, gallantry nor desire. Poetry about illnesses and anxieties, prosaic and hard to bear; about gloomy loneliness, pitiful exploits and stupid truths.]

And he continues to define his new poetry and state of mind in much the same way in "Nocturno madrileño" from which I copy a few stanzas:

> De un cantar canalla
> tengo el alma llena,
> de un cantar con notas monótonas, tristes,
> de horror y vergüenza.
>
> De un cantar que habla
> de vicio y de anemia,
> de sangre y de engaño, de miedo y de infamia,
> ¡y siempre de penas!
>
> De un cantar que dice
> mentiras perversas . . .
> De pálidas caras, de labios pintados
> y enormes ojeras.

[My soul is filled with a base song, whose notes are monotonous and sad, a song of horror and shame. A song which speaks of vice and anemia, of blood and deception, fear and infamy. And always of pain! A song which tells perverse lies and talks of pale faces, painted lips and enlarged rings under the eyes.]

He also tells us concretely of certain characteristic themes: ". . . que los toros he elogiado,/ y cantado/ las golfas y el aguardiente . . .,/ y la noche de Madrid,/ y los rincones impuros,/ y los vicios más oscuros/ de estos bisnietos del Cid" ("Yo, poeta decadente") [I have praised the art of the bull ring and sung of the street walkers and their drinks, of Madrid nights and tainted corners, and even the most obscure vices of these great-grandchildren of the

Cid.] Machado also laments that Art, which he here compares to a former mistress, now long abandoned and surrounded with ugly objects, has fled elsewhere with its music ("Prólogo-Epílogo"). In "Invierno" he talks of the implacable life of the poet: "Y esta ancestral pobreza/ española del vate . . ./ La tragedia ridícula/ de la bohemia . . . ¡El mártir/ que es un pobre poeta de sus sueños/ y de sus realidades!" [And this ancestral poverty of the Spanish writer. The ridiculous tragedy of the bohemian life . . . The poor poet who is the martyr of his dreams and his realities!]

Machado wants to capture the momentary. His love affairs are hurried and the objects of his amorous spirit more often than not are the prostitutes. "Mi Phriné," for example, recalls "Antífona" (*Alma*), already mentioned, and the delicious figure of "Mimí, la modelo" (*Caprichos*);[15] pleasure is brief and even pain is ephemeral ("Mutis"). His attitude of almost bored indifference is readily apparent, implying a type of resignation and lack of will to change anything. He goes through life seemingly not caring very much, vacillating, and represents this spirit in the following antithetical verses:

> Apenado, sin dolores;
> amoroso, sin mujeres;
> libertino, sin placeres,
> y rendido, sin reñir,
> ando, amante sin amores,
> con mi juventud podrida,
> por la feria de la vida
> sin llorar y sin reír.

("Ultima")

[Sorrowful, but without pain; amorous, lacking women; libertine, without dissolute pleasure, and defeated without having quarreled, lover without love affairs, I wander carrying my rotted youth through the farce of life without weeping nor laughing.]

On the whole, the poetry of *El mal poema* is not at all descriptive of the outer reality of the city, except for brief glimpses here and there. But there is one special poem which deserves mention; in it Machado evokes with prosaic but telling language the arrival of dawn after what we might suppose to have been a night of debauchery:

> El alba con las manos sucias
> y los ojos ribeteados.
> Y el acabarse las argucias
> para continuar encantados.
>
> Livideces y palideces,
> y monstruos de realidad.
> Y la terrible verdad
> mucho más clara que otras veces.

("La canción del alba")

[Dawn is like dirty hands and bloodshot eyes. And the ending of deceitful trickery although the trance-like spell continues. Deathly pale and ashen white, monstrous realities. And the horrible truth of it all seen even clearer than at other times.]

Up to now I have scarcely mentioned the initial poem of the volume, which is well known and often quoted, in any attempt to define the older Machado. The portrait is precise and frank:[16]

> Me acuso de no amar sino muy vagamente
> una porción de cosas que encantan a la gente . . .
> La agilidad, el tino, la gracia, la destreza;
> más que la voluntad, la fuerza y la grandeza . . .
> Mi elegancia es buscada, rebuscada. Prefiero,
> a lo helénico y puro, lo *chic* y lo torero.
> . . . . . . . . . . . . . . . . . . . . . . . . . . . . . . . . . . . . . .
> Medio gitano y medio parisién—dice el vulgo—,
> con Montmartre y con la Macarena comulgo . . .
> Y, antes que un tal poeta, mi deseo primero
> hubiera sido ser un buen banderillero.

[I admit to not caring very much about a bunch of things which delight ordinary people . . . (I prefer) quickness, knack, grace and skill more than I do will, strength or power . . . My elegance is showy, doubly contrived. I prefer the *chic* and all that relates to bullfighting over the Hellenic and pure. Half gypsy and half Parisian—so they say—I share the same feelings toward Montmartre as for the Virgin of La Macarena. And, before being a poet, my first desire would have been to be a good *banderillero*.]

Above all, elegant and distinguished, he adopts a pose of nonchalance which goes well with his epicurean attitude toward life. With another poet this might imply superficiality or triviality. We should bear in mind that this same writer wrote poems such as those contained in *Ars moriendi*—"Misterio," "Niños del parque," "Melancolía," "En la muerte de José Palomo Anaya"—and perhaps a half dozen more in this profound vein. This complex and variable attitude reaches a climax in the two brief strophes of "Rima" (*Phoenix*), which are typical of Machado's ambiguous and ironic attitude toward life:

> Sensual, epicúreo, decadente
> —amigo de gozar y "divertirse",
> como dice la gente—,
> he sabido poner en la alegría
> el ajenjo de la melancolía,
> y sé también sufrir alegremente.
>
> Y . . . nada más. En mi conciencia inquieta
> vigila el bien. Espero,
> sin saber qué. Y, en tanto,
> me anego en risa, disimulo el llanto . . .
> Y voy viviendo, mientras no me muero.

[Sensual, epicurean, decadent—given over to enjoying life and having a good time, as the saying goes—I have learned to immerse in joy the absinthe of melancholy, and I also know how to suffer in happiness.
And . . . that's all. In my restless conscience virtue is alert. I have hope, for what I do not know. And, in the meanwhile, I give way to mirth, as I conceal my grief. . . . I keep on living, as long as I don't die.]

In his classic essay on Manuel Machado the critic Dámaso Alonso speaks of a typical stylistic trait by means of which the poem is not finished, ending oftentimes on an intended note of indecision which does not bring the poem to a precise conclusion.[17] Probably the most famous example is that of "El príncipe de Orange" in *Apolo. Teatro pictórico*. Moreno Villa studies some years later the same technique typical of the Andalusian popular song and also of the intricacies of the art of bull fighting: *el cambio* or *el quiebro*.[18] He considers these at times surprising *changes* or *dodgings* as the result of corrections, repentances, parentheses or qualifications. Such a stylistic procedure implies dialogue within the poet himself, including the expression of the pro and the con of things. Moreno Villa and Alonso cite several examples, most of them from *El mal poema*. We content ourselves here with only one, the final verses of "Yo, poeta decadente," for in many ways it constitutes a good ending for the present essay on Manuel Machado and the decadent elements in his poetry:

> Porque ya
> una cosa es la Poesía
> y otra cosa lo que está
> grabado en el alma mía . . .
> Grabado, lugar común.
> Alma, palabra gastada.
> Mía . . . No sabemos nada.
> Todo es conforme y según.

[Because one thing is Poetry and another is what is engraved on my soul . . . Engraved, a commonplace. And soul, a hackneyed word. Mine . . . We know nothing for sure. It all depends, that may just be so!] 19

*University of California,*
*Santa Barbara*

## NOTES

I take full responsibility for the translations in this paper, but they are extremely free and only try to convey general meanings. I do owe thanks to my colleague David Bary for his much appreciated help in trying to get over some of the rougher spots.

1 Perhaps the poet himself had an inkling about his posterity. Late in life, in his acceptance speech before the Spanish Academy, he wrote: "Pero poeta yo menor, poeta 'di camera'; poeta del matiz, del siesnoés y del gesto inacabado—he aquí una de mis acepciones . . ." [As for my being a minor poet, a poet 'di camera'; poet of nuances, of the uncertain yes it is and no it isn't, of the unfinished gesture—this is one of my representative qualities] (*Unos versos, un alma y una época* [Madrid: Ediciones Españolas, 1940], p. 19).

Gerardo Diego's excellent book, *Manuel Machado, poeta* (Madrid: Editora Nacional, 1974), as well as his lecture read in June 1974 to commemorate the centenary of the poet's birth, *El poeta Manuel Machado* (Madrid: Fundación Universitaria Española, 1975), have dispelled all doubts about the authentic significance of the elder Machado as a poet and rectified many misconceptions about his so-called frivolity or superficiality.

Of course, the classic article about Manuel Machado is Dámaso Alonso's early study, "Ligereza y gravedad en la poesía de Manuel Machado," in *Poetas españoles contemporáneos* (Madrid: Gredos, 1952), pp. 50-102, in which he disproves any charge of frivolity, saying finally: "Manuel Machado es profundamente significativo, profundamente grave, profundamente triste: expresó la gravedad por medio de la ligereza" (p. 102) [Manuel Machado is profoundly significant, profoundly grave, profoundly sad: he expressed the grave by means of the light touch].

In a briefer note, "Recuerdo de Manuel Machado," *Peña Labra*, 11 (Spring 1974), 11-12, Ricardo Gullón, who knew Machado well in his later years and attended the *tertulia* at El Lyon, refers to the same questions and wonders if this so-called label of "minor poet" could be explained by the relatively scant quantity of his poetry, its intranscendency or decadence, or even perhaps the poet's apparent lack of concern with certain aspects of the literary program of 1898 (p. 12).

Further proof of the contemporary interest in the personality of Manuel Machado is confirmed by a series of recent publications: the excellent anthology *Alma. Apolo* (Madrid: Ediciones Alcalá, [1967] ), edited with exemplary care by Alfredo Carballo Picazo; Gordon Brotherston's well-prepared book, *Manuel Machado, a Revaluation* (London: Cambridge Univ. Press, 1968); and also the special issue of *Cuadernos Hispanoamericanos*, Nos. 304-307 (October-December 1975–January 1976), devoted to the two Machado brothers. As part of the centenary at least two further publications deserve mention here: Manuel Machado, *Prosa*, ed. José Luis Ortiz de Lanzagorta (Seville: Universidad de Sevilla, [1974]), and Francisco López Estrada, ed., *Doce comentarios a la poesía de Manuel Machado* (Seville: Universidad de Sevilla, 1975).

[2] Machado considered his poetic work to begin with his heterogeneous collection *Alma*, which incorporates poems written between roughly 1898 and 1900, but whose date of publication in a volume is in doubt despite the author's categorical statement that it was published in Madrid at the end of 1900 (*Unos versos, un alma y una época*, p. 75). Let us not forget, however, that in collaboration with Enrique Paradas, he had published *Tristes y alegres* (1894) and *Etcétera* (1895). There is also an important edition of *Alma*. *Museo*. *Los cantares* (Madrid: Librería de Pueyo, 1907), with a long prologue by Unamuno (pp. IX-XVII), who had also reviewed *Alma* in *Heraldo de Madrid*, 19 May 1901; and I mention the edition here inasmuch as José Moreno Villa in a particularly perceptive article, "Manuel Machado, la manolería y el cambio," in *Los autores como actores y otros intereses literarios de acá y de allá* (Mexico City: El Colegio de México, 1951), pp. 102-25, wrote the following: "Y este título nos dice que una de sus ramas sigue hacia la vida interior, otra hacia la vida externa o de los ojos, y la tercera hacia lo que percibe el sentido auditivo, la copla. Intimidad, visualidad y apego a la expresión del pueblo" (p. 109) [And this title tells us that one of its directions leads toward the inner life, another toward the exterior or the visual, and the third to what is perceived by the ear, the popular song. Intimacy, visuality and attachment to the popular expression].

[3] In his previously quoted discourse before the Spanish Academy, Machado evokes the distant days in Paris and refers to the French poets with whom he associated. Nor should we forget his early but close relationship with Darío, Gómez Carrillo, Nervo, and Alejandro Sawa. Jean Moréas was among those who, according to Machado, actually stimulated him to begin to write again; and so were born "Adelfos," "Castilla" (a poem which Unamuno liked so much), "Felipe IV," "Cantares," all among his best known lyrics, which would subsequently form part of *Alma* (*Unos versos, un alma y una época*, pp. 52-74). Machado also stresses in these retrospective pages the personal and intimate nature of his newly created compositions. He had, he said, abandoned the ingenious baroque style; and the elegant but cold Sevillian style had now been converted into an authentic poetic experience he felt to be really his own. The poet had found his own voice (pp. 58-59). Other references to his early Parisian experiences, including those of unquestionable decadent cast, are to be found in *El amor y la muerte* (Capítulos de novela), part of which is incorporated into the recent edition of *Prosa* (pp. 3-77), already cited.

[4] There is no doubt about the importance that Verlaine had in the formation of Manuel Machado, and in 1908 Machado was one of his best translators (into prose). The book was favorably reviewed by Alejandro Sawa, one of the master's closest friends among the Spaniards: "Ante un libro," *Los Lunes del Imparcial*, 23 Mar. 1908.

The topic of Verlaine's influence, complicated by Darío and his role, has been amply discussed by responsible critics (Alonso, Brotherston, Carballo Picazo, *et al.*), but it would be unjust not to cite also the excellent pages which Rafael Ferreres devotes to the subject: *Verlaine y los modernistas españoles* (Madrid: Gredos, 1975), pp. 156-76.

[5] In this respect the brief prologue to *Cante hondo*. *Sevilla* (Madrid: Editorial Mundo Latino, 1923), although written at a much earlier date and collected in *La guerra literaria (1898-1913)* (Madrid: Imprenta Hispano-Alemana, 1913), is a highly important document, indispensable for the study of the popular song in Andalusia.

[6] Darío, whom Machado served as secretary for a short time, in his answer to Gómez Carrillo's question about the general state of Spanish poetry wrote in 1905 the highest praise of both Machado brothers. With respect to Manuel, he made special allusion to his complete dominance of French art and called him a legitimate and skillful heir to Verlaine. And finally Darío applauds in him a verbal artist and a virtuoso of form (Rubén Darío, *Obras completas*, I [Madrid: Afrodisio Aguado, 1950], 414-15).

[7] Gerardo Diego, *Poesía española contemporánea*, 2nd ed. (Madrid: Taurus, 1958), p. 134.

[8] This is not the place to debate the exact classification of the poet, but I would like to call attention to the article of Manuel Muñoz Cortes, "Manuel Machado y el 98," *Cuadernos Hispanoamericanos*, cited commemorative issue (above, n.1), pp. 213-19, in which are reproduced the pertinent earlier texts by the author, Manuel Machado himself, and Pedro Laín Entralgo (pp. 219-28). Gerardo Diego also discusses the same subject in *Manuel Machado, poeta*, pp. 23-30. See also Dámaso Alonso, article cited (above, n. 1),

pp. 89-98. As for Machado himself, he again returns to history and his concept of Spain in the brief prologue to *Horas de oro; devocionario poético* (Valladolid: Imprenta Castellana, 1938).

[9] In addition to the sources to which I refer in the body of my essay, the anthology of Carballo Picazo collects a number of fragments upon which I shall draw heavily in this brief résumé of Machado's ideas about poetry inasmuch as some are not available in this country, particularly those taken from *El Liberal* (pp. 217-34).

[10] Machado repeats to Camilo José Cela the same ideas about slow and laborious artistic creations. He reaffirms that he works slowly but with surety, without correcting, and immediately after placing the final full stop to a poem begins to dislike it (ibid., p. 221).

[11] Pedro Salinas, "El problema del modernismo en España, o un conflicto entre dos espíritus," in *Literatura española, siglo XX*, 2nd ed. (Mexico City: Antigua Librería Robredo, 1949), p. 23.

[12] In the volume *Alma. Museo. Los cantares*, already mentioned, in which Machado includes the composition "Despedida a la luna," the two final sections which follow *Los cantares* are entitled respectively "Hablado" (pp. 131-38) and "La buena canción" (pp. 141-54). These two final sections are very different in mood and tone in that the note of repentance for the past is accentuated. The poet seems to have left behind his neurasthenia and libertinism. It is certainly a different Machado who writes these lyrics with religious overtones. Still later on he writes a quatrain in alexandrines entitled "El poeta de *Adelfos* dice, al fin . . ." in which he states that he has finally chosen his road and no longer will oscillate in the wind nor yield to the waves. He claims to know about love, renounces the impossible and no longer will succumb to Destiny (*Ars moriendi*, 1921).

[13] In 1908 Machado published a second edition of *Caprichos*. In this volume are included seven of the poems under the heading "El mal poema" (pp. 91-121), which stand out in the text, and also poems collected from elsewhere, grouped under different headings, because of their theme and language.

Manuel Machado, on reviewing *Rimas* of Juan Ramón Jiménez (*El País*, 3 April 1902), says that the author suffers from neurasthenia, ". . . that divine sickness which consists in having a sensitive soul, dreaming while awake, in seeing what the sun does not illuminate and in falling in love with the impossible." It is curious to note, as does Ricardo Gullón who also reproduces the text I have just quoted in part and for which I here indicate complete bibliographical data, that at a much later date (1913?) Machado—older and more influential than his younger friend and poet from Moguer—felt it necessary to publish the important text, "Autocrítica: Una carta al poeta Juan Ramón Jiménez," which dealt with *El mal poema*. Gullón reproduces these pages ("Relaciones amistosas y literarias entre Juan Ramón Jiménez y Manuel Machado," *Cuadernos Hispanoamericanos*, Nos. 128-129 [Aug.-Sept. 1960], pp. 115-39), and they also appear in *La guerra literaria*, pp. 117-20. It would seem more plausible to me to assign an earlier date to this "Autocrítica," perhaps 1910 or 1911. Also it is well to recall that, in a letter of 1911 written to Juan Ramón, Machado refers to *El mal poema*, calling it a work of his former bohemian life, broken and disjointed, far from his present attitude (ibid., p. 130).

This "Autocrítica" is exceptionally significant to understand the spiritual crisis Machado was undergoing at this period in his life, but above all because it sheds light on *El mal poema*. A rapid résumé or paraphrase of its most salient points will have to suffice here. Machado speaks of how difficult life is and even envies Juan Ramón's retreat from it. Speaking in direct terms of his book, he hopes not to have offended Juan Ramón's delicate sensiblities through certain trivialities and ugly voices heard in its poems. He defends his *malos poemas* by saying that a poet must also write about things he doesn't like. He confesses to having experienced "platonically or as a spectator" many of the unpleasant and bitter events portrayed in *El mal poema*. A definite family of writers ("adventurers in the ideal")—he mentions Poe, Heine, Verlaine, and Bécquer—have been with him, but he would have preferred the bucolic serenity of a Virgil and recognizes that he is far from the elegant madrigals of classic times. He states as well that he is ashamed of his book, which might seem to be "cinicismo de un libertino, no siendo en realidad más que impresiones de un enfermo muy sensible" [cynicism of a libertine, being actually only impressions of a sickly and overly sensitive nature]. Less remembered in this connection is Juan Ramón Jiménez's "Alma y capricho de Manuel Machado," in *La corriente infinita* (Madrid: Aguilar, 1961), pp. 41-44. In the text he refers directly to his decadence and to the sensual nature of the poet.

Luis Antonio de Villena has recently published a brief article, "Relectura de *El mal poema* de Manuel Machado (Notas sobre modernismo y bohemia)," *Insula*, No. 362 (Jan.

1977), pp. 1 and 11, in which he recognizes the decadent attitude of the poet and his bohemian sources. Villena points out, of course, the *antimodernista* qualities of these poems when comparing them with the more conventional ones of *Alma,* and refers to the *realism* of the book, no longer as traditionally literary, either in subject matter or in vocabulary. In this context, one waits in vain for mention of Lugones, whose *Lunario sentimental* was published also in 1909.

Even more recently and after the completion of the present essay, it has come to my attention that Luis Antonio de Villena has published another article entitled, "Simbolismo y decadentismo en *Alma* de Manuel Machado," *Insula,* No. 377 (Apr. 1978), pp. 1 and 12, a brief study of general nature which in no way influences my present contribution to the subject in question.

14 In the second poem of the volume, "Prólogo-Epílogo," Machado, in taking leave of poetry, writes that on the doctor's advice he is giving up being a Verlaine, a Musset, a D'Annunzio. He is, however, content because some women and quite a few Don Juans have found gentle solace in his poetry, which has given them pleasure in living and loving beauty. Although I think the formative influences in *El mal poema* are those of Baudelaire and Laforgue, the presence of Verlaine is never far away ("La mujer de Verlaine" and "Cordura").

Machado, of course, makes direct reference to *El mal poema* in *Unos versos, un alma y una época* (pp. 79-85), and of his book published in 1909 he says: "Siento hoy casi vergüenza de este libro en que se desnuda en público un alma lamentable y pecadora. Si bien es verdad que con una repulsión manifiesta a la contumacia en el mal" (p. 80) [Today I almost feel ashamed of this book in which a lamentable and sinful soul is laid bare. Although, it is true, with a marked reluctance to persevere in evil]. He quotes "Yo, poeta decadente" and "La canción del alba" and concludes: "Todo esto es agrio, duro, detestable. Pero no era mi vida mucho más amable entonces. . . . Afortunadamente todo lo cambió pronto la mano de una mujer santa . . . había sabido esperarme en nuestra Sevilla materna de vuelta de todas mis locuras" (p. 85) [All this is acrid, bitter and abominable. But, on the other hand, my life at that time was not much better. Fortunately the hand of a wonderful woman, who had waited for me in our native Seville to which I returned after all my follies, changed all that].

15 The miscellaneous chapters of *El amor y la muerte,* which can only be considered a novel by stretching the imagination, depict highly erotic and decadent scenes in the Latin Quarter, as well as the curious and often perverse types (including Oscar Wilde) who inhabit this world. My purpose here is merely to copy briefly from the vignette "Alma parisién" *(Prosa,* pp. 13-15; see n. 1, above) the initial description of Susana, who is another worthy candidate for the gallery of sensual women mentioned: "A ella me atrae su enfermedad, sus ojeras, la delgadez y palidez de sus labios, algo muy romántico y muy perverso que hay en sus ojos. Su hablar canalla, que me excita, en aquella voz dulce que me enternece, su mirar picaresco. Lo que tiene de rubia y de quebradiza, de viciosa y de mística, de virgen prerrafaélica y de gata parisiense" (p. 13) [I am attracted by her sickliness, the circles under her eyes, the thin and pale quality of her lips, as well as something very romantic and perverse lurking in her eyes. Her gross manner of speech, which excites me, in a sweet voice which moves me to pity, and even her saucy glance. Also I am not aloof to her blonde and brittle person, licentious and mystic, as well as her appearance of a Pre-Raphaelite virgin and a Parisian cat].

16 The chapters which Gerardo Diego devotes to the portraits in *Manuel Machado, poeta,* pp. 143-64, are particularly noteworthy.

17 Dámaso Alonso, pp. 68-75.

18 Moreno Villa, pp. 105-09.

19 An additional bibliographical note should be added here which has just come to my attention: Florencio Segura, "Manuel Machado, poeta decadentista," *Razón y Fe,* No. 927 (Apr. 1975), pp. 321-32.

# Symbolist Aesthetics in Spanish: the Concept of Language in Valle-Inclán's *La lámpara maravillosa*

## Carol S. Maier

As Octavio Paz has explained so well, twentieth-century Spanish literature must be studied as European literature written in the language of modern Europe.[1] Within that context, the formation of a national or personal aesthetics is a process of translation and the creation of an individual poetic tongue: Spain's true *modernista* poets were not Francisco Villaespesa and Salvador Rueda but Ramón de Valle-Inclán, Juan Ramón Jiménez, Antonio Machado and even Miguel de Unamuno, because they were able to translate contemporary Spanish American and European poetry into Peninsular—and personal—realities.[2] This transformation makes the study of influences at once more interesting and more difficult; apparent similarities can be misleading when not resemblance but change indicates response and appropriation. The paradox is especially complex when neither poet, period nor poetics can be defined simply.

Such is the case of Spain, symbolism and Ramón del Valle-Inclán (1866-1936) in the first decades of this century. *La lámpara maravillosa* (The Wonderful Lamp) Valle-Inclán's *ars poetica,* is often referred to as a clear example of Spanish symbolism,[3] yet the date of its publication, the climate of turn-of-the-century aesthetics in Spain, and the book's own multiplicity make that definition difficult. By the time *La lámpara maravillosa* was first published (1916), symbolism had become somewhat of an international cliché, a worn-out idiom rather than a fresh aesthetics.[4] Perhaps more important, even for poets who could read their French contemporaries in the original, is the fact that much of symbolism's influence in Spain occurred because of Spanish American *modernismo.*[5] Thus a movement already difficult to define precisely becomes an integral part of both a very synthetic—and very ambitious—aesthetic phenomenon and a very dense historical moment. As one voice in the chorus of *ismos* that characterizes early twentieth-century Spanish art and culture, *modernismo* blends well with what Ricardo Gullón terms the impulse to create a sense of universal and individual harmony.[6] For the poet, that impulse is most clearly embodied in language, and poetic idiom draws heavily on contemporary spiritual enthusiasms (Theosophy, Pythagoreanism, alchemy, occultism).

Nevertheless, not all poets make a thorough translation and truly possess both past aesthetics and the words of the present. Valle-Inclán is one of the few poets for whom the formation of a personal language is indeed the creation of a body; and that body is his primary work, a work Octavio Paz has described as a great tattoo of marvelous, fierce figures.[7] Within their very individual designs, some of those figures clearly suggest a relation to French Symbolism, especially when we examine the paradigm for poetic language presented in *La lámpara maravillosa* and the concept of symbol it exemplifies. For in *La lámpara maravillosa* Valle-Inclán explains his language in the words of that language itself: from the familiar allegories of Christianity and the worn-out images of *fin de siècle* poetry the synthesis of many different symbolisms creates a new symbol of the experience of beauty.

One further word of introduction: In spite of the importance attributed to *La lámpara maravillosa* by critics and by Valle-Inclán himself, the book has not been much studied, and its relation to other works of Valle-Inclán has not been fully investigated.[8] Nor has an English translation been published. The absence of those points of reference makes comparison particularly difficult. Given the scope of this essay, it seems most helpful to limit discussion to Valle-Inclán's concept of the poet and his language, suggesting almost incidentally some of the possible relations with French symbolism; the familiarity of English-speaking readers with the conventions of contemporary French poetry can be assumed, but few of them are aware of Valle-Inclán's aesthetics.

"Elige tus palabras siempre equivocándote un poco, aconsejaba un diá, en versos gentiles y burlones, aquel divino huésped de hospitales, de tabernas y de burdeles que se llamó Pablo Verlaine"[9] ["Always be slightly mistaken when you choose your words," advised one day in gentle and jesting verses that divine guest of hospitals, taverns and brothels named Paul Verlaine].The citation confirms Valle-Inclán's familiarity with Verlaine's "Art Poétique,"[10] but it also suggests a great deal about both his own poet-narrator and his own aesthetics. *La lámpara maravillosa* is a series of brief meditations or "Spiritual Exercises" grouped in five sections. Verlaine's words appear in the second section, "El milagro musical" [The Musical Miracle], where the poet-narrator explains the inexpressive nature of words, the impossibility of an entirely "new" verbal creation, and the possibility of a "miraculous" experience of beauty. The poet of *La lámpara maravillosa* is a person who knows words well, who has completed the spiritual journey or pilgrimage prerequisite to an intimate relation with language—described in parts one and five, "El anillo de Giges" [Gyges's Ring] and "La piedra del sabio" [The Philosopher's Stone], He has also followed a concurrent journey or apprenticeship with words; accepting rather than opposing their imprecision, he has learned to tap his perceptions and experiences allusively and suggest experiences that can never be communicated. He is thus able to follow Verlaine's instructions and work indirectly with language, as he explains in the first chapter of "El milagro musical":

> El poeta ha de confiar a la evocación musical de las palabras todo el secreto de esas ilusiones que están más allá del sentido humano apto para encarnar en el número y la pauta de las verdades demostradas. Las palabras son humildes como la vida. Pobres ánforas de barro, contienen la experiencia derivada de los

afanes cotidianos, nunca lo inefable de las alusiones eternas. El hombre que consigue romper alguna vez la cárcel de los sentidos, reviste las palabras de un nuevo significado como de una túnica de luz. (pp. 38-39)
[The poet has to entrust to the musical evocation of words the whole secret of those illusions which are beyond human perception's ability to embody them in the number and measure of proven truths. Words are humble like life. Simple clay amphorae, they contain the experience of daily endeavors, never the ineffability of eternal allusions, A man who succeeds once in shattering the prison of his senses clothes words in new meaning, as in a tunic of light.]

Consistent with his intention to provide an example as well as an aesthetic guideline, the narrator of *La lámpara maravillosa* introduces Verlaine and his poem in a non-erudite, rather ambiguous way. His apprenticeship with language has included a knowledge of the work and teaching of many other poets and spiritual figures. These figures are not competitors but teachers or brother pilgrims who appear in *La lámpara maravillosa.* Although the experience or mystery they share is achieved only through great effort and discipline, it is a spiritual rather than a scholarly enigma. Verlaine is not footnoted as an influential French symbolist, but quoted as an acquaintance, his words used in such a way that they seem to have been spoken rather than written. It is important that throughout *La lámpara maravillosa* the poet's magic does not occur because of a written text but because of his ability to use language orally (the spoken word) or musically (the sound and evocative power of words). The poet-narrator does cite instances of influence or discipleship which arise because of his reading, but those relationships are never presented in terms of books; teaching or communication occur as contact. When a text does exist it must be experienced, claimed by the reader; it is thus a link or bridge, not an end in itself.

It is also important that Verlaine's words are not quoted exactly as they are found in "Art Poétique." The source of the lines is not given; as a future poet or "brother pilgrim," the reader is no doubt expected to recognize them. By bringing to mind one of Verlaine's best-known poems, and specifically one that presents his aesthetics, the recognition will increase our understanding of Valle-Inclán's vision of the poet and provide the kind of knowledge intended by the poet of *La lámpara maravillosa.*[11] His reference to Verlaine is not precise in an academic way, but it is exactly the kind of allusion that precisely suggests the aesthetics of "Art Poétique." It is at once an explanation and an example: "Pero esta equivocación ha de ser tan sutil como lo fue el poeta al decir su consejo: Cabalmente el encanto estriba en el misterio con que se produce. Adonde no llegan las palabras con sus significados, van las ondas de sus músicas" (p. 43) [But this mistake must be as subtle as the poet when he gave his advice: The spell depends completely on the mystery that produces it. The waves of their music extend where words cannot reach with their meanings].

How does the poet of *La lámpara maravillosa* create—within language—that subtle balance of clarity and ambiguity, precision and error? Both an aesthetic theory and a particular example, the central concept or guiding principle of *La lámpara maravillosa* is the equation of light, love and understanding. As the poet explains in his introduction, entitled "Gnosis," knowledge is an illuminating experience of altered perception; instead of the usual barriers that define and separate us, we are given a sense of relation. Objects or situations themselves remain unchanged, but they suggest harmony and make possible the experience of beauty: "la belleza es la intuición de la unidad" (p. 26) [Beauty is the intuition of unity]. That intuition is the aesthetic miracle, worked in the case of language by the poet's words when they become Word in the theological sense of Logos, both thought and expression or representation. The poet is confined to the temporal and spatial limitations of language, but he is not confined *by* those limitations because he has learned to use language allusively. What he is unable to say he suggests, with the advantage that the reader is also able to glimpse meanings and implications masked in everyday conversation. The poet is thus a source of light—a center, sun, or lamp, as he explains in "La piedra del sabio": "Las [cosas] más espúreas estaban en mí con unidad de amor, allegadas por veredas iguales, que se abrían en círculo como los rayos de una lámpara" (p. 139) [The most spurious things converged in me with a unity of love; they approached on identical paths, which opened in a circle like the rays of a lamp].

The word "symbol" is not used in *La lámpara maravillosa;* instead the rather complex paradox of language and poetry (a phenomenon of the translation of light to illumination, insight to verbal image), is evoked and represented by the metaphor of the cipher. "Cipher," as Ernst Robert Curtius has explained, was traditionally used in Spain to indicate the "pictorial part of the *empresa* or emblem."[12] It occurs frequently in *La lámpara maravillosa* both as a noun (*cifra*) and a verb (*cifrar*), suggesting the visual expression of an ineffable experience that the poet must try to evoke in words. Indeed the metaphor is used in "Gnosis" to communicate that very impossibility: "La ciencia de las escuelas es vana, crasa y difusa como todo aquello que puede ser cifrado en voces y puesto en escrituras (pp. 15-16) [The science of schools is vain, crass and diffuse like everything that can be "ciphered" in voices and put in writing].[13] And in the same long paragraph it is equated with Augustinian love and understanding: "El amor de todas las cosas es la cifra de la suma belleza" [A love of all things is the "cipher" of supreme beauty]. The equation links the cipher indirectly but intimately with the poetic process, because later—in the first sentences of "Exégesis trina" [Three-Part Exegesis]—we will be reminded that the fact of Christ the Word is the same miracle of translation, or writing: "Cristo Señor Nuestro cifró en amor la suma perfección" (p. 67) [Christ Our Lord "ciphered" supreme perfection in love].

The poet of *La lámpara maravillosa* participates at least two ways in this ciphering. He learns to experience, discover or read the ciphers, as exemplified in "El anillo de Giges" in one of the first aesthetic ecstasies:"Aquel aprendizaje de las veredas diluido por mis pasos en tantos años, se me revelaba en una cifra, consumado en el regazo de los valles, cristalino por el sol, intenso por la altura, sagrado como un número pitagórico" (p. 24) [That apprenticeship of paths, diluted by my wandering during so many years, was being revealed to me in a cipher, consummated in the lap of the valleys, crystalline in the sun, intense through the height, sacred like a Pythagorean number]. By refining his own life, most particularly as that life is embodied in language, the poet himself becomes a cipher. As such, his words (the works or "deeds" of his aesthetic life) will evoke the experience for others:

> Yo he querido, bajo los místicos cielos de la belleza, convertir las normas estéticas en caminos de perfección, para alcanzar la mirada inefable que hace a las almas centros, y mi vida ha venido a cifrarse en un adoctrinamiento por donde acercar la conciencia a la suprema comprensión cíclica que se abre bajo el arco de la muerte. (pp. 129-30)

> [Beneath mystic skies of beauty, I have tried to convert aesthetic norms into ways of perfection, in order to attain ineffable sight which allows our souls to become centers; and my life has become a cipher, a teaching, an effort to guide consciousness toward the supreme cyclical comprehension that opens beneath the arch of death.]

That cipher, a representation in and through words, strives to be at once visual and verbal. It includes the pictorial *emblema* and its written explanation (the *letra* of the classic *cifra*).[14] But as the poet explains in "El milagro musical," the continual transformation of language makes this kind of simultaneous expression much more difficult for the literary arts than the plastic arts because words are inevitably linked to history (chronology and place). The plastic arts are more permanent and more accessible because their language is more constant: "... cifran en la luz el goce de su belleza" (p. 59) [. . . the enjoyment of their beauty is ciphered in the light]. By incorporating more the sound than the meaning of words, the poet of *La lámpara maravillosa* aspires to a very suggestive, far-reaching language which, like dance, will combine visual and auditory expression. As if he were trying to fuse the two elements of the emblem (words and picture) into one cipher, charging it, in addition, with the sound of oral language. Although he cannot change the nature of language and the aesthetic experience, although emotion can never be "ciphered" in words ("Esta emoción no puede ser cifrada en palabras," p. 26), the poet can fashion a cipher that will suggest his experience for the reader.

As a unity, *La lámpara maravillosa* itself exemplifies that concept of cipher or symbol: illumination and understanding. The nuance or absence of color required by Verlaine in "Art Poétique" becomes a deliberate obscurity, a delicate balance of light and darkness. It is an indefinite but precise use of words which indicates great care and control on the part of the poet. Because words, although inexpressive, can be overpowering. As Verlaine warns in "Art Poétique," rhyme very easily takes control. Valle-Inclán extends this warning to all language, reminding us that the use of words precedes our awareness of speech, that we must learn to speak not in words but in spite of them: "Las palabras imponen normas al pensamiento, lo encadenan, lo guían y le muestran caminos imprevistos, al modo de la rima. Los idiomas nos hacen, y nosotros los deshacemos" (p. 49) [Words impose norms on thought; they link it, guide it and show it unforeseen paths, as rhyme does. Languages make us, and we unmake them]. The poet-narrator of *La lámpara maravillosa* explains his own deconstruction and re-creation of language as an integral part of his spiritual preparation; multiple images of understanding and obscurity, vision and blindness both explain and initiate the aesthetic experience.

As partial reflections or rays of that experience, all of those images originate from the same center, a complete vision or understanding. In various ways they remind us that as human beings dependent on sensory perception (which is erroneous and at best partial) and on our own limited memories, we experience a very fragmented vision of the universe. We gauge eternity by things that seem old; time apparently unfolds as chronology; crystals are eternal, essentially more beautiful than the rose whose life is intense but short. Because the poet-narrator of *La lámpara maravillosa* learns to see Beauty ("erotic evocations") in both the crystal and the rose (to use his two most recurrent examples, both of which fuse visual knowledge and temporal duration), the aesthetic experience develops a perception beyond chronology, a glimpse—if not a vision—in the darkness. Paradox is inevitable; the poet is no more able to alter the limits of chronology or mortality than those of language, and even the experience of greatest illumination will take place in the total darkness of that impossibility. These considerations are well exemplified in the following passage from "El anillo de Giges," where the poet-narrator presents his first awareness of the aesthetic experience, in a mountainous area of Galicia he had known as a child:

> Mirando hacia abajo se descubrían tierras labradas con una geometría ingenua, y prados cristalinos entre mimbrales. El campo tenía una gracia inocente bajo la lluvia. Los senderos de color barcino ondulaban cortando el verde de los herberos y la geometría de las siembras. Cuando el sol rasgaba la boira, el campo se entonaba de oro con la emoción de una antigua pintura.... Ibamos tan cimeros, que los valles se aparecían lejanos, miniados, intensos, con el translúcido de los esmaltes. Eran regazos de gracia, y los ojos se santificaban en ellos. Pero nada me llenó de gozo como el ondular de los caminos a través de los herberos y las tierras labradas. Yo los reconocía de pronto.... Quedé cautivo, sellados los ojos por el sello de aquel valle hondísimo, quieto y verde, con llovizna y sol, que resumía en una comprensión cíclica todo mi conocimiento cronológico de la Tierra de Salnés. (pp. 23-24)

> [As we looked down, we could see lands cultivated with an ingenuous geometry and crystalline meadows between clumps of osiers. The countryside had an innocent charm beneath the rain. Undulant, ruddy-colored paths cut through the green of the grassy plots and the geometry of the sown fields. When the sun rent the mist, the countryside glowed with the emotion of an ancient painting. ... We had climbed so high the valley seemed distant, painted in miniature, intense with the translucence of enamels. They were laps of grace, and my eyes were sanctified in them. But nothing filled me with joy like those paths winding through the meadowlands and cultivated fields. Suddenly I began to recognize them. ... I was captive, my eyes stopped by the seal of that green, quiet and very deep valley, with mist and sun, that was summing up in a cyclical understanding all my chronological knowledge of Tierra de Salnés.]

The experience is a confluence of visual inclusiveness and complete memory. A newly expanded perspective facilitates the recovery of past experience. The time of day and physical setting are intimately related to the narrator's new awareness. Late afternoon occurs frequently in *La lámpara maravillosa* as a time of fusion, a moment of grace between night and day, the hour of the Word (*la hora verbo*) in "El anillo de Giges" (V). A time when, in mountainous Galicia, the sun can cut through the mist and create an extraordinary visual display. "Crystalline," here with the sense of outside of time, suggests the apparently timeless beauty of crystals. Although unchanged, the concept of time is challenged and, for an instant, for the poet-narrator, erased. Within that completeness, his past returns intact. As a gift of the sun, memory is a function and phenomenon of light, an experience of inner vision, whereby we can achieve wholeness, a plurality inaccessible at the moment of occurrence:

> ninguna cosa del mundo es como se nos muestra, y . . . todas acendran su belleza en los cristales del recuerdo, cuando se obra la metamorfosis de los sentidos en la visión interior del alma. Sólo la memoria alcanza a encender un cirio en las tinieblas del Tiempo. (p. 109)
>
> [Nothing in the world is exactly as it presents itself to us, and . . . all things refine their beauty in the crystals of memory when the metamorphosis of our senses is performed in the interior vision of the soul. Only memory is able to light a candle in the darkness of Time.]

The original, sensory vision is not so much repudiated as enlarged; and the recognition in Tierra de Salnés is a summation of all the previous experiences—all the paths—of that place.

In the final lines of the same chapter the poet-narrator indicates that his experience is the beginning of a new life. The very nature of his vision has changed, his eyes sealed or stopped by the newly cyclical perception. In other chapters Valle-Inclán will expand the relation of vision and rebirth as *alumbrar* opposed to *iluminar,* using *alumbrar* to suggest an inner vision, calling on its connotations of enlightenment (both perception and heretical movement) and giving birth. *Iluminar* has more historical connotations and suggests less an intuitive than an intellectual experience. The understanding achieved in *La lámpara maravillosa* is more *alumbramiento* than *iluminación;* knowledge is perception rather than fact, intuition rather than information. Knowledge comes through a bolt of lightning rather than an historical process of learning: "cual si de relámpago alumbrase mi memoria, una memoria de mil años" (p. 20) [As if a flash of lightning suddenly lit (or enlightened) my memory, a memory of a thousand years]. Vision is brilliant, but blind; it returns nothing but everything, and places the poet-narrator in the non-verbal instant that precedes and incites language: Valle-Inclán's *quietismo estético* [aesthetic quietism].

The term includes both experience and expression. Based on the Spanish sense of "quiet," an absence of motion rather than a silence, it represents the balance of searching and serenity, blindness and insight achieved by the poet-narrator. But even more importantly, the aesthetic paradox or oxymoron is also achieved by the reader. Because, in spite of its importance as the poet's central experience, it is presented allusively rather than defined explicitly. Consistent with the poet's realization that aesthetics affords an ineffable experience, his theory of beauty is not stated but suggested, worked out as a harmony of analogous conflicts and resolutions, exact impressions which gradually coalesce and become for the reader a chord or cipher of the aesthetic experience. The images are universal, but their combination, and thus their resonances, are translated, Hispanicized, seen in a new language: "El quietismo estético es la significación más expresiva de las cosas, en un nuevo entrever" (p. 121) [Aesthetic quietism is the most expressive meaning of things, glimpsed in a new way].

That new vision begins with the very first words of *La lámpara maravillosa,* in the poet-narrator's tone and the relationship he establishes with the reader (implicitly another, younger and aspiring poet). The words

are at once intimate and distanced. Speaking to the reader with the familiar
"tú" [thou] form, he shares some of his earliest memories, refers to the loss
of an arm at age thirty, and explains how that accident put an end to his
dreams of adventure and initiated an inner journey of aesthetic discipline and
creativity. It is a personal confession, but one that reveals nothing "personal"
about the poet-narrator. In spite of his complete self-portrait as a Poet, the
narrator will never become an individual poet. Certainly he is not limited to
Ramón del Valle-Inclán. For although several incidents of his aesthetic life
clearly suggest that of his author, their situation is quite different. They occur
in an aesthetic circumstance, a setting or reality drawn more from literature
than from a specific life. The first chapter of "El anillo de Giges," for
example, is situated—in spite of at least one very obvious allusion to
Valle-Inclán himself—in an emotional landscape of aesthetic and spiritual
confession, a synthesis of Saint Anthony's temptations, Saint Augustine's
conversion, Rubén Darío's poetic autobiography in "Yo soy aquel que ayer
no más decía," Bradomín's melancholy introspection in Valle-Inclán's
*Sonatas,* and others. The complexity of the portrait depends on the reader's
own receptivity. And even readers who are unable to identify all the allusions
will recognize the blend of openness and reserve that characterizes the
narrator's stance throughout *La lámpara maravillosa.*

That stance is also the essence of parabolic narrative, and each of the
incidents related by the narrator speaks for the aesthetic purpose shared by
all of them. It is not incidental that this parabolic narrator brings to mind
more brother pilgrims than the Verlaine of "Art Poétique." The continual
references to both a landscape and a language that are rural or simple as well
as arcane, common as well as enigmatic, suggest equally the life and works of
Christ and those of Saint Francis of Assisi. Both of those figures are present
in *La lámpara maravillosa* as persons whose words and lives are examples of
Words or links: love made visible. They inspire the poet because he aspires to
be an exemplary figure, one who—like Saint Francis—sees beauty in apparent
ugliness, who—like Christ—bridges the temporal, human limits of language
and manages to communicate a sense of mystery and eternity. Other figures
of mystery and magic are also suggested; the poet is a Renaissance magician, a
thaumaturge, an alchemist, somewhat like any figure who transcends the
limits of human understanding and attempts to share that experience with
others.

The reader only gradually becomes aware of this plurality. Although the
exercises record a chronological process of spiritual discipline and aesthetic
apprenticeship, the understanding to which they lead is circular, and the
structure of *La lámpara maravillosa* reflects that circularity. It is Book Three,
the    center,    that    offers    a    thorough—although    suggestive    and
obscure—explanation of aesthetic love and expression as an intensification of
love rather than a chronological increase. Books Two and Four record the
poet's struggle to use language evocatively and Books One and Five present
the expansion of his perception of beauty as well as an increased awareness of
the ethical implications in the possibility of experiencing eternity within
time. The reader is never permitted a sense of story or exposition. Although
many of the incidents bring him closer to that experience as he reads of
intuitive links or bridges between beauty and ugliness, he is held at a distance

by the complexity of some of the incidents and by the poet-narrator's restraint. Only after the book is read several times does the structure (pattern and process) of explanation and obscurity become clear; and only then does the reader realize to what extent that very ambiguity *is* the experience at the center of *La lámpara maravillosa, is* the achievement of the poet-narrator: "El quietismo estético tiene esta fuerza alucinadora. Inicia una visión más sutil de las cosas, y al mismo tiempo nubla su conocimiento porque presiente en ellas el misterio. Es la revelación del sentido oculto que duerme en todo lo creado, y que al ser advertido nos llena de perplejidad" (p. 105) [Aesthetic quietism has that dazzling strength. It initiates a more subtle vision of things, and at the same time clouds our understanding of them because it includes a presentiment of their mystery. It is the revelation of the hidden meaning asleep in all created things. and it fills us with perception and perplexity].

Perplexity is an essential aspect of aesthetic quietism because it is the catalyst necessary for the complete experience Valle-Inclán hopes to provide. At the close of the first reading, the balance of clarity and ambiguity must be intriguing; something must encourage the reader to intensify the experience, either by re-reading or through a further association of images and perceptions. The glimpse of unity confuses a reader, but it also creates desire. We want to know—or see—more, a circular continuation that Valle-Inclán presents as the movement of concentric circles which open and intensify simultaneously. Knowledge and love are creative, fertile phenomena, for they strengthen and multiply spontaneously: "Amor engendra amor" (p. 143) [Love engenders love]. It is an enlightening and energetic continuation that can initiate the reorientation of spiritual values and thereby influence our actions.

It is clear, then, that the poet's narrative takes place or takes form less as a book, an object, than an experience, a rose that opens within the reader. Its blossom synthesizes very well all of the aspects of symbolic language discussed in relation to *La lámpara maravillosa.* Most immediately, it is a flower whose brief but intense beauty is used to represent the way in which human actions can express or speak love. Christ, Saint Francis, the poet's *madrina* [godmother] are like rosebushes, and their deeds are flowers, ciphers, or symbols whose "fragrance" engenders and evokes love. The intensity of response will vary, as will the appearance of the individual flowers, but the experience is essentially the same. Even though, as we learn in "Exégesis trina," history has seen three basic conceptions of beauty, three different approaches to aesthetic expression, each expression is a rose, described in *La lámpara maravillosa* as an aesthetics rather than a particular period or genre. Each rose is distinct (corresponding to pagan, Christian or Gnostic love), but to some degree, each shares some of the characteristics of the other two. (For example, the striking appearance of the first, erotic or pagan rose is not without its sense of mystery or religion, while even the subtle, mystic rose has form, albeit deformation.) And each rose is timeless; as well as an awareness of eternity, each is formed in *La lámpara maravillosa* from very few references to contemporary aesthetics, creating a new flower from allusions to figures and works of Spanish and Christian history and literature. So that in a very subtle way the reader is made aware of aesthetics as a universal impulse, a response linked to history but outside of time, because the secret of beauty is the same for all periods: "En todos los momentos del mundo la belleza ha sido una cifra de amor y una clave teológica" (p. 83) [In all the world's moments beauty has been a cipher of love and a theological key].

In conclusion: Valle-Inclán's attempt to unify (even though allusively) all aesthetic expression exemplifies very well the Symbolist effort to transcend national, temporal and even mortal limits. His delicate yet very controlled balance of ambiguity and obscurity, as both theory and practice, also recalls contemporary European aesthetics, especially Verlaine's "Art Poétique." In addition to presenting Valle-Inclán's own language and his explicit desire to return to Castilian prose the vitality absent since the Conquest ("El milagro musical," VI), *La lámpara maravillosa* suggests the hope of all symbolist aesthetics and reminds us that the aesthetic experience celebrates and transcends the words from which it arises.

*Bradley University*

## NOTES

[1] Octavio Paz, "Una de cal. . . .," *Papeles de Son Armadans*, No. 140 (November 1967), pp. 174-97.

[2] Ibid., p. 194. See also José Angel Valente's comments about Valle-Inclán's linguistic originality in "Darío o la inovación," *Las palabras de la tribu* (Madrid: Siglo XXI, 1971), pp. 77-88.

[3] See, for example, the chapters Emilio González López dedicates to *La lámpara maravillosa* in *La poesía de Valle-Inclán: del simbolismo al expresionismo* (Río Piedras: Universidad de Puerto Rico, 1973); also Antonio Risco, *El demiurgo y su mundo: Hacia un nuevo enfoque de la obra de Valle-Inclán* (Madrid: Gredos, 1977), pp. 102-36, especially p. 102, and the *Introducción* to Gustavo Umpierre, *"Divinas palabras": Alusión y alegoría* (Chapel Hill: University of North Carolina, Estudios de *Hispanófila*, 1971), pp. 9-20.

[4] Anna Balakian, "The Conventions of Symbolism in European Literature" and "The Afterglow," in *The Symbolist Movement* (New York: Random House, 1967), pp. 101-21 and 156-93 and "The International Character of Symbolism," *Mosaic*, 2 (1969), 1-8.

[5] The intermediary role played by Spanish American poets and the relation between *modernismo* and Peninsular poetry has been much studied and debated. Although Rubén Darío and other *modernista* poets greatly influenced the course of Peninsular poetry at the beginning of the twentieth century, it is important to remember that Spaniards were reading French literature directly from France well before the advent of *modernismo*. See, for example, John W. Kronik, "Rubén Darío y la entrada del simbolismo en España," in *Poemas y ensayos para un homenaje [a Phyllis B. Turnbull]*(Madrid: Ed. Tecnos, 1976), pp. 95-106. Valle-Inclán had access in Pontevedra to the library of his friend Jesús Muruáis which had a large selection of French and European literature. See Eliane Lavaud, "Un prologue et un articule oubliés: Valle-Inclán, théoricien du modernisme," *Bulletin Hispanique*, 76 (1974), 364-65.

[6] Ricardo Gullón, "Pitagorismo y modernismo," *Mundo Nuevo*, 7 (1967), 22-32, rpt. in *Estudios críticos sobre el modernismo*, ed. Homero Castillo (Madrid: Gredos, 1968), pp. 358-83.

[7] Octavio Paz, p. 184.

[8] Since Valle-Inclán's centennial in 1966 there have been several studies of *La lámpara maravillosa*. In addition to the works cited above (notes 2 and 3), see: Guillermo Díaz-Plaja, *Las estéticas de Valle-Inclán* (Madrid: Gredos, 1965); Virginia Milner Garlitz, "El centro del círculo: *La lámpara maravillosa* de Valle-Inclán," Diss. Univ. of Chicago 1978, especially Chapter One which discusses *La lámpara maravillosa* and turn-of-the-century European aesthetics; Carol S. Maier, "Valle-Inclán y *La lámpara*

*maravillosa:* Una poética iluminada," Diss. Rutgers 1975; Ciriaco Morón Arroyo, "*La lámpara maravillosa* y la ecuación estética,*" in *Ramón del Valle-Inclán. An Appraisal of His Life and Works,* ed. Anthony N. Zahareas (New York: Las Americas, 1968), pp. 443-59; Emma Susana Sperrati-Piñero, *El ocultismo en Valle-Inclán* (London: Tamesis Books, 1974), especially pp. 163-80.

[9] Ramón del Valle-Inclán, *La lámpara maravillosa* (Buenos Aires: Espasa-Calpe, 1948), p. 43. All references are to this edition; henceforth page numbers will be given in parentheses in the text. English translations are mine.

[10] Rafael Ferreres also notes this passage in *Verlaine y los modernistas españoles* (Madrid: Gredos, 1975), pp. 235-36.

[11] As Raimundo Lida explains in "Darío, Lugones, Valle-Inclán," *Ramón del Valle-Inclán. An Appraisal . . .,* p. 436, this recognition is a question of neither parody nor burlesque but a common experience. On the basis of shared reading, Valle-Inclán can evoke a memory and work toward a new aesthetic awareness.

[12] Ernst Robert Curtius, *European Literature and the Latin Middle Ages,* trans. Willard R. Trask (1953; rpt. New York: Harper Torchbooks, 1953), pp. 363-64.

[13] Although "cipher" is not always the most appropriate English equivalent of *cifra* and *cifrar,* I have used that translation throughout this essay in order to indicate the development of the *cifra* in *La lámpara maravillosa.*

[14] Curtius, p. 364.

A vignette by Julio Ruelas, dated 1901. Reproduced from *Revista Moderna de México,* 6, No. 7 (Sept. 1904), 28.

*Las Marquesitas* by Roberto Montenegro. Reproduced from *Revista Moderna de México*, 6, No. 3 (Nov. 1904), 167.

# Flower Symbolism in
## *Jardines lejanos*

### Lily Litvak

At the end of the last century, various circumstances combined to make gardens an artistic and literary topos with strong erotic coloring. Lonely, isolated corners with winding paths, ancient trees, and silky shrubs represented a bit of ideal nature, within reach, that man transformed into a work of art with a very special message. The iconography of the period made them a proper frame for the amorous play of a couple, for the young man deep in erotic reverie, or for the maiden who waits for the one who will awaken her desires.

The erotic message of the gardens was possible thanks to the meaning that the end of the century imparted to nature, permitting it to be interpreted not merely with realistic aims but in a personal and subjective manner. The landscape painters had already prepared the sensibility for this new vision. The discovery of Japanese woodcuts[1] and the interest devoted to nature by the impressionists and later the symbolists allowed more profound meanings to be seen in landscapes. The influence was felt of painters like Whistler and Gauguin, who, under the aegis of Japanese models, showed the European artistic minority the way to new forms of sensibility. Gustave Moreau asked: "What importance does Nature have by Herself? She is nothing more than an excuse for the artist to express himself.... Art is the never-ending search for expression of internal feelings by means of plastic form."[2]

Thus, those stylized gardens, crossed by labyrinthine paths, carpeted with dry leaves, shaded by ancient chestnut trees, converted into modern paintings or glasswork, were sung by the poets—Verlaine, Samain, Maeterlinck, Rodenbach, Anton Neuf, Valle-Inclán, Antonio Machado, Villaespesa.... Santiago Rusiñol, in *Jardines de España,* wrote: "Ve pronto a ellos si quieres contagiarte por un momento de aquella tristeza de ensueño que hace palidecer el pensamiento· para poder soñar más tiempo; que te da deseos de hacer versos y borrarlos como se borran los versos hechos en los jardines, que te da deseos de abrazar las formas que se desvanecen y las estatuas que caen y las grandezas que mueren. Ve a ellos, poeta, si quieres escuchar la poesía un buen momento de la vida"[3] [Go to them right away if you want to catch for a moment that dreamy sadness that makes thought fade in order to be able to dream longer, that makes you want to write verses and erase them as one erases verses written in gardens, that makes you want to embrace the forms that vanish and the statues that fall and the grandeurs that die. Go to them, poet, if you wish to listen to poetry a good moment in your life]. There are also erotic gardens in painting. There are the Spanish ones of Rusiñol, the green and mysterious ones of Degouve de Nunques, those of Montald stylized by winter trees, the dark German gardens of Stratmann and Thomma.

Something of Wagner, the master of intellectual eroticism, reached the turn-of-the-century gardens. The ambiguous vegetal architecture of Klingsor's palace was described by Villiers de l'Isle Adam in *L'Ève future,* and the German composer inspired some of Gaudí's plant motifs in the Church of the Sagrada Familia. There, the plants extend from pedestals to capitals as roots and branches, achieving a vegetal animism that corresponds to Wagner's ambition to express the voice of nature and the glorification of the instincts.

Nor were the flowers of those gardens merely ornamental; they also came to be treated symbolically.[4] To archetypal and traditional flowers were joined the ones that the turn of the century rediscovered and popularized through the Gothic revival and the development of arts and crafts which caused artists and artisans to look for plant motifs, thus revitalizing forms desiccate from routine. Also important in this sense was the influence of Ruskin and the English Pre-Raphaelites, who adorned their paintings with a great variety of flowers bearing peculiar allegorical meanings.

Floral decoration departed from realism through an extreme stylization. Some of the most influential ideas in the new vegetal lyricism were those of Eugène Grasset, expounded in his book *La Plante et ses applications ornementales.*[5] There was a sensual floral invasion of irises, orchids, lilies, roses—often, as in the brooches of Lalique, associated or fused with a female figure—forming a forest of sexual symbols whose literary and artistic suggestions determined the modes of love and desire in *la belle époque.*

A preference was shown for flowers with long, curved stems, with elegant and sinuous shapes, and with corollas capable of bearing an erotic or exotic message. The promise of a closed bud about to burst into bloom was much appreciated. Some flowers, particularly certain lilies and irises, became popular in those years. The purple iris, made popular by Grasset, shined splendidly in the jewelry of Luis Masriera. It sprang up in the posters of Mucha, and in the poetry of Jean Lorrain it was converted into a phallic symbol. Swinburne's heroines press tiger lilies to their breasts, there are countless white lilies in the hands of dead women, and Valle-Inclán describes a woman in this way: "El cuello florecía de los hombros como un lirio enfermo, los senos eran dos rosas blancas aromando un altar . . ."[6] [Her neck bloomed from her shoulders like a sick lily, her breasts were two white roses perfuming an altar . . .]. The lily was popularized outside of literature; Sarah Bernhardt was frequently surrounded by lilies, a good symbol for *La Dame aux Camélias* since the lily also represents a recovered virginity.

Another flower that was in vogue was the Madonna lily, "lirio blanco" [white lily] in some Spanish poetry. Derived from the paintings of Rossetti, it represents the flower of the Annunciation, of purity and virginity. It was a nearly heraldic flower for the aesthetes. Puvis de Chavannes and the Rosicrucians displayed it as a symbol of the soul. Rachel, in Proust's work, recited fragments of Maeterlinck, in a dress inspired by the *Ecce Ancilla Domini* of Rossetti, while carrying a Madonna lily in her hand. The flower abounds in the poems of Darío, Villaespesa, and other *modernistas* as a symbol of virginity.[7]

Roses frequently alluded to the female sex organ, as in the novels of D'Annunzio.[8] They assumed various meanings according to their color: the red rose, a symbol of erotic love, the white rose, purity. They appeared on fabrics, tapestries, buttons, embroidered collars. . . . Beardsley and Mackintosh made use of them, the Catalan sculptor Lamberto Escaler employed them for his female figures, and the architect José María Barenys used them on his façades. Others found in them a more perverse pleasure, like the guests of Algabal, in the poem of Stephan George, smothered under a pile of roses. Some preferred withered roses. Juan María Guasch wrote:

> Aquest sospir d'olor
> aquest desmai d'amor
> es l'ànima fervent i adolorida
> de les roses colltortes i esfullades.[9]
> [This breath of odor
> this dismay of love
> is the fervent and sorrowful soul
> of the roses with necks twisted and petals fallen.]

The chrysanthemum, with its Oriental charm, shared the popularity of the lily. For Víctor Catalá, "Són les flors denses de les terres dels prínceps coberts de sederies que parlem una llengua inconeguda. Són les flors que res diuen als sentits i ho diuen tot a l'ànima"[10] [They are the dense flowers of the lands of princes covered with silks who speak an unknown language. They are the flowers that say nothing to the senses and say everything to the soul]. Chrysanthemums adorn Odette's apartment in Proust; and Maurice Maeterlinck, in a text published in 1904, in *Helios,* finds those of a copper color attractive: "el menos usual en el mundo de las flores, el más severamente prohibido, el color que únicamente lleva la corola de euphorbia venenosa en la ciudad de las umbelas, . . . es un amarillo envejecido y decrépito, que se ha posado en el azul fugitivo de los rayos de la luna"[11] [the least common in the world of the flowers, the most severely prohibited, the color that only the corolla of the poisonous euphorbia bears in the city of the umbels, . . . is an aged and decrepit yellow that has come to rest in the fugitive blue of the rays of the moon].

Other long-stemmed flowers were rich in phallic suggestions. In a painting by Thorn Prikker[12] there is a ground of menacing tulips. Before them is seen a chaste bride enveloped in a veil embroidered with white snapdragons that resemble skulls. Some flowers, on the contrary, like the lotus and the white water lily, alluded to the female sex organs. Only their corollas rise above the surface. Their hidden roots, in the form of long, flexible tubes, are rich in uterine suggestions. They abound in cover designs by Prouvé and by Schwabe and in drawings by Beardsley. A collection of poems by Juan Ramón Jiménez is called *Ninfeas* [Water Lilies]; and, in Pierre Louÿs, a woman ". . . tient dans ses doigts extatiques et beaux/ Au pli vièrge du sexe un lotus fabuleux"[13] [. . . holds in her ecstatic and beautiful fingers/ at the virgin crease of her sex a fabulous lotus].

Other flowers reveal erotic associations: orchids, which are found on vases by Gallé and in Odette's corsages (Cattleyas have a very special meaning for Proust); the blue hydrangea of the decadent Montesquiou, painted by Helleu and Le Sidanier, embodies sensuality and desire in a story by Jerónimo Zanné. Henri de Régnier and Juan Ramón Jiménez valued the velvety texture of lilacs and wistarias; there were countless narcissuses leaning over the sleeping waters of pools and lakes; foxgloves, violets, sunflowers, and magnolias were flowers that, following a symbology appropriate for the period, permitted the expression of a personal erotic attitude.

A thematic study of the first collections of poems by Juan Ramón Jiménez reveals that the poet had an erotology of his own, but in accordance with the general lines of the period. *Ninfeas, Almas de violeta, Jardines lejanos,* and *Pastorales* are fundamentally and primarily erotic, and failure to take this into account would hinder a full comprehension of the books. In those early works Juan Ramón expresses a personal erotic quandary. Sexual love has for the poet a vital attractiveness. Almost immediately, however, any idea of physical contact arouses in him a feeling of guilt; therefore, for him physical love is directly associated with evil. To that evil Juan Ramón opposes the absolute value of virginity; but that purity becomes so far removed from life that, rendered untouchable and cold, it is converted into sterility and death. Thus, his eroticism oscillates between a hope for the most absolute purity and a fascination with the flesh, between a nostalgia for life and the vertigo of nothingness.

In this study I shall try to show how Juan Ramón expresses these themes by means of floral motifs. For this purpose I have restricted myself almost exclusively to *Jardines lejanos*[14] (although at times I may have recourse to *Ninfeas, Rimas,* or *Almas de violeta*). In the former collection of poems an erotic and spiritual itinerary is developed. It is divided into three parts, and in each one of them we observe a phase of the drama. In the first part, "Jardines galantes" [Gallant Gardens], Juan Ramón reveals the erotic attraction and the nostalgia for pristine purity. "Jardines místicos" [Mystic Gardens], the second part, expresses the intention of eliminating from love the erotic and carnal element, an intention whose failure joins the symbols of purity to a series of images of sterility and death. In "Jardines dolientes" [Sorrowful Gardens] the poet attempts, without success, a reconciliation between the extremes. The book reveals this itinerary with the rigor of a thematic development, expressed coherently through form, light, sounds, colors, obsessive rhythms, and, of course, flowers. In the poetic weave the fluidity and plurivalence of the symbols are of capital importance. The symbols are characterized, as Ricardo Gullón has indicated, by their "plurivalencia" [plurivalence], their diversity of meanings, and by the peculiar development that the poet gives them, a "tipo continuado" [continuous sort], "que va desplegándose a lo largo del poema y lo llena de su fulgor"[15] [that gradually unfolds throughout the whole poem and fills it with its brilliance]. The symbols are dynamic, not immutable: they change according to the horizon against which they are projected and which makes them live.

The poems of "Jardines galantes" take place in the middle of spring. The garden has a ceiling of the green foliage of the trees and is enclosed by thick clumps of shrubbery. It is thus transformed into an enclosure that invites intimacy. The foliage forms one of the fundamental elements of the erotology of these poems; the plants watch, wait, are always receptive and sensual; at times their texture is like that of a woman's body: "mujer huyó hacia la umbría./ Todo era aroma de senos ..."[16] [woman fled toward the shade./ All was an aroma of breasts ...].

Among the flowers of these gardens the red rose predominates, with the meanings that the period gave it. The very form of this flower is suggestive, with its petals grouped in a converging intimacy. It is the symbol of feminimity: the rose of the mouth, the rose of the breast, and also, in Juan Ramón as in D'Annunzio, the rose of the female sex organ, the emblem of carnal love and the symbol of life. Juan Ramón writes: "Por esos labios de rosa" (p. 357) [Through those rose lips] ; "tarde de rosas con sol,/ ... el amor no es solitario/ ... sus flores son las rosas" (pp. 359-60) [afternoon of roses with sun,/ ... love is not solitary/ ... its flowers are the roses] ; "... Quise ver/ cómo estaban los rosales .../ y encontré rosas carnales" (p. 375) [I tried to see/ how the rosebushes were .../ and I found carnal roses].

It is necessary to note the association of this flower with the color red and with the sun. One of the erotic elements typical of the iconography of the *fin de siècle* was the sun and, through metonymy, fire, heat, and the color red. Recall the continuing influence of William Blake and his predilection for flame motifs.[17] The principal Spanish *modernista* journal was called *Helios.* Villaespesa wrote with reference to the sun:

> ¡Soñemos
> con nuestro nuevo amor!
> Arde en el campo
> la lujuria del sol.[18]
> [Let's dream
> of our new love!
> The lust of the sun
> burns on the field.]

Love is fundamentally torrid in Juan Ramón, and it appears frequently as a function of solar symbols. The sun illuminates strongly erotic scenes that culminate in intercourse:

> En un banco del sendero,
> cómo el cuerpo se abandona
> al cuerpo que va buscando
> la delicia más recóndita! ...
>
> Y cuando ya el sol es fuego,
> cómo todo se deshoja
> en una rosa de besos,
> de caricias y de rosas!
>
> [On a bench by the path,
> how the body abandons itself
> to the body that is searching for
> the most recondite delight! ...
>
> And when the sun is fire,
> how all sheds its leaves
> in a rose of kisses,
> of caresses and of roses!]

"Deshojarse" [to shed leaves] here refers to deflowering, the possession consummated in the final lines:

> Era un día dulce para
> los poetas y sus novias . . .
> Una novia y un poeta
> ensayaron en su lumbre
> la ternura de sus bodas. (p. 393)
>
> [It was a sweet day for
> the poets and their brides . . .
> One bride and one poet
> tested in its splendor
> the tenderness of their wedding.]

Metaphors that relate carnal pleasure to the sun abound: "tenía carne de aurora" (p. 396) [she had the flesh of dawn] ; "la carne llena de sol" (p. 393) [flesh filled with sun] .

Through association with the sun, the color red acquires paroxysmal erotic implications. Hours of love come to be ardent and red, which confers very precise meanings upon the sunset. In the following lines the sunset serves as a backdrop for the surrender:

> La tarde se irá muriendo
> sobre tus parques. . . .
>
> Vendrá frescura de fuentes,
> olor de lilas y acacias,
> tal vez alguna magnolia
> abrirá su carne blanca . . . (p. 377)
>
> [The afternoon will gradually die
> over your parks. . . .
>
> The freshness of fountains will come.
> odor of lilacs and acacias,
> perhaps some magnolia
> will open its white flesh. . . .]

The magnolia here can be taken as a symbol of the vulva.

The sunset appears often in the early poems of the author; the vision of the solar flame fighting with night communicates sentiments of disaster that are at once erotic and warlike, as in the poem, "La cremación del sol," in *Ninfeas.* At times the poet looks for the source of the incandescence of the love act in the woman, replacing solar fire with female fire: ". . . sus rojos/ labios mordían, quemaban/ lo que miraban sus ojos" (p. 394) [. . . her red/ lips bit, burned/ what her eyes were looking at] ; ". . . la niña se muere de deliquios de ardores" (p. 1494, *Ninfeas*) [. . . the girl is dying from ecstasies of ardor]. That internal female fire shows itself at times as a mysterious force rooted in the most secret place, in the blood that shines and burns beneath the skin of her nude body; it puts a blush on her whiteness, shows in her naked lips, in the nipples of her breasts: "senos tibios entre las rosas" (p. 349) [warm breasts among the roses] ; "Francina, en la primavera/ tienes la boca más roja?" (p. 382) [Francine, in the spring/ have you a redder mouth?] ; "tarde de rosas con sol,/ tarde de sangre en los labios" (p. 359) [afternoon of roses with sun,/ afternoon of blood in one's lips] .

It is characteristic of Juan Ramón that he uses color to transmit a sensual or spiritual perception and not necessarily to transmit a pictorial element. In those years artists began to realize that, in painting, color could express something by itself. Recall, for example, the analysis that Huysmans made of the colors in Gustave Moreau.[19] So for Juan Ramón, red and the whole gamut of shades and related colors represent sensations of pleasure and of sensuality, and the red flowers in "Jardines galantes" have a meaning that is nearly automatic. Sensuality is revealed in the red of the sunset, of lips, in the blush of cheeks, in the scarlet of a rose: "cada rosa me ofrece dos rojos/ labios llenos de besos ardientes" (p. 409) [each rose offers me two red/ lips full of ardent kisses]. The color red is explosive, sensual, insolent: "ríe, con los labios rojos,/ de las pobres azucenas" (p. 401) [laughs, with red lips,/ at the poor Madonna lilies]. The theme of blood and the color red appear in a much more obvious way in *Ninfeas*: "A la oliente sombra del rosal de sangre, del rosal florido,/ muerta su inocencia . . ." (p. 1498) [In the odorous shadow of the rosebush of blood, of the flowering rosebush,/ her innocence dead . . .]. Other flowers in "Jardines galantes" evoke love by their form or their texture; the wistaria reveals its intimacy in its velvety interior:

> Y el fresco verdor de abril
> está lleno de nostalgia:
> ayer tarde, las glicinas
> abrieron su seda malva. (p. 383)
>
> [And the fresh verdure of April
> is filled with nostalgia:
> yesterday afternoon, the wistarias
> opened their mauve silk.]

Compare this with the magnolia in the passage previously quoted: "tal vez alguna magnolia/ abrirá su carne blanca . . ." (p. 377) [perhaps some magnolia/ will open its white flesh . . .].

Along with flowers, the symbolists discovered the evocative power of perfumes. Ferdinand Brunetière spoke in that period of the "animalism" of the sense of smell, whose enjoyment is the least spiritual and the most sensual.[20] Baudelaire had given to these sensations a wealth of expression, and Juan Ramón expresses his erotic desires also in the perfume of flowers, as noted above in the reference to the odor of lilacs and acacias. At times the strong fragrance is converted into a caress: "Hubo flores y perfumes/ y caricias en mi sueño" (p. 179, *Rimas*) [There were flowers and perfumes/ and caresses in my dream]; "Hay caricias como rosas/ en la lívida mañana;/ la carne en flor da el perfume/ que han perdido las acacias" (p. 363) [There are caresses like roses/ in the livid morning;/ the flesh in flower gives off the perfume/ that the acacias have lost]. At other times, more concretely, the perfume becomes the woman herself: "Aroma de carne en gracia . . .,/ ¡olor de novias en flor! " (p. 370) [Aroma of flesh in grace . . .,/ odor of brides in flower!] Perfumes share the symbolic meaning of the flower from which they proceed. Thus, the odor of the rose has precisely the same meaning as the rose itself, as in the following lines in which the desire to break chastity is allegorized:

> Rosa turbadora, rosa
> que con tu dulce fragancia
> rompiste tanta oración,
> quebraste tanta ala blanca! (p. 388)
>
> [Disturbing rose, you rose
> who with your sweet fragrance
> broke so much prayer,
> fractured so much white wing!]

Already in "Jardines galantes" there appears alongside this erotic visualization of certain flowers another series that is usually linked to the spiritual values of chastity and purity. They are, in general, white or night-blooming flowers—the lily, jasmine, the Madonna lily, the white rose: "Tengo un altar blanco, lleno/ de divinas azucenas,/ con una Virgen de mayo,/ más brillante que una estrella" (p. 81, *Rimas*) [I have a white altar, full/ of divine Madonna lilies,/ with a Virgin of May,/ more brilliant than a star]; "De aquel lirio de mi infancia/ que murió con la inocencia" (*ibid.*) [Of that lily of my infancy/ that died with innocence]. Through these series of opposing symbols, the erotic conflict of Juan Ramón finds a means of expression. In the following poem there is a genuine struggle between eroticism and purity:

> —Madre, rojas son las rosas
> y blancas las azucenas;
> si las blancas son más buenas,
> las rojas son más piadosas.
> Madre, rojas son las rosas.
> . . . . . . . . . . . . . . . . . . . . . . . . . . . . . .
> Si hoy quiero tanto a esta flor
> de labios frescos y rojos,
> deja, virgen, que su amor
> ponga lascivia en mis ojos;
> hoy sus labios están rojos,
> mis labios están en flor. (p. 381)

> ["Mother, red are the roses
> and white the Madonna lilies;
> if the white ones have more goodness,
> the red ones are more devout.
> Mother, red are the roses.
> . . . . . . . . . . . . . . . . . . . . . . . . . . . . . .
> "If today I so much want this flower
> with lips fresh and red,
> Virgin, let its love
> put lechery in my eyes;
> today its lips are red,
> my lips are in flower."]

The poet here chooses the red rose since its erotic value, its ardor and its power to allude to the flesh and the vagina, provide him, along with the heat of desire, with the warmth of life.

Red flowers represent the female archetype dominant in "Jardines galantes," which is the dangerous woman. She was a commonplace figure of the *fin de siècle,* painted by Redon and Moreau, sung by Darío. Dangerous femininity appears, accompanied by the serpent, as one final temptation in the first poem of "Jardines místicos":

> Por las ramas en luz brillan ojos
> de lascivas y bellas serpientes;
> cada rosa me ofrece dos rojos
> labios llenos de besos ardientes. (p. 409)

> [Through the branches in the light shine eyes
> of lascivious and beautiful serpents;
> each rose offers me two red
> lips full of ardent kisses.]

At the side of the dangerous woman, as a contrast, one discerns another female figure: the spirit-woman, chaste, virgin, almost immaterial, whom the poet calls "novia de nieve" (p. 410) [bride of snow]. She also was a literary and artistic commonplace of the *fin de siècle,* whose distant ideal was Beatrice, the chaste loved one who would lead her beloved to a more transcendent reality. Juan Ramón describes her in floral terms: she has the "palidez de azucena y de claustro, y su sonrisa de santidad" (p. 407) [paleness of a Madonna lily and of a cloister, and her smile of sanctity]. In the Pre-Raphaelite pattern, her slender and diffuse silhouette distills chastity and frigidity, spirituality and death.

White is the color that Juan Ramón selected to translate his ideal of purity. His "Jardines místicos" blanch under the satiny light of the moon or beneath a blanket of snow. The gardens are pure and cold, chaste and dead. At times there does not appear "más flor que una calavera" [any flower but a skull]: "Y son blancos brazos/ que entreabren flores de muerte" (p. 448) [And they are white arms/ that half-open flowers of death]. The poet thus follows a symbolist topos adopted by the *modernistas.* Pedro Salinas has pointed out that "lo blanco . . . debe traducirse casi siempre en la poesía de Darío como aspiración a la pureza y místico anhelo de inocencia"[21] [whiteness . . . should nearly always be translated in the poetry of Darío as aspiration to purity and mystical yearning for innocence]. Ivan Schulman, in turn, affirms that for Manuel Gutiérrez Nájera whiteness "siempre simboliza lo perfecto, lo inmaculado e ideal"[22] [always symbolizes the perfect, the immaculate and ideal]. But the association between purity and death was also exploited by the *modernistas.* Jesús Urueta speaks of death as a white angel, and José Juan Tablada refers to the swans where "Tiembla y muere el fulgor blanco"[23] [The white brilliance trembles and dies]. In the same way, the French symbolists assigned similar meanings to this color. Mallarmé speaks of the sterile chastity of Hérodiade: "nuit blanche de glaçons et de neige cruelle"[24] [white night of icicles and cruel snow]. And white functions thus in exemplary paintings of the period as well—in the white maidens of Le Sidanier and in the ectoplasmic silhouettes of Alphonse Osbert.

Juan Ramón reserves the white flowers—white roses, jasmine, lilies, tuberoses—for the "novia de nieve" [bride of snow] of "Jardines místicos." The most abundant one, the Madonna lily, a symbol of virginity, is the flower of the Virgin Mary. It forms part of the language of the Annunciation, carried by the archangel Gabriel and indicating the purity of the Conception. It springs up in the typical iconography of symbolism. Rossetti's *Blessed Damozel* (in the Fogg Museum of Art, Harvard University) holds three Madonna lilies in her hands. It is the mystic flower of Gustave Moreau. Carlos Schwabe forms a path of Madonna lilies along which the Virgin walks, carrying the Child. And Juan Ramón writes: "viene un cándido olor de azucena . . ./ Aparece la novia de nieve . . ." (p. 410) [there comes a candid odor of Madonna lily. . . ./ The bride of snow appears]. This symbol is opposed to desire: "cómo matan las rosas/ la azucena y el incienso! " (p. 340, *Arias tristes*) [how the Madonna lily and incense kill the roses!] Other white flowers indicate the candor, frigid and velvety at the same time, of that woman: "Y me muestra sus dulces blancores . . ./ Tiene senos de nardo . . ." (p. 410) [And she shows me her sweet whiteness. . . ./ She has breasts of tuberose ...]. In one poem she is situated on a balcony, in an attitude that recalls the *Beata Beatrix* of Rossetti:

> ... En un balcón
> abierto, de otro palacio,
> está una mujer... No mira
> nada... Es blanca como un nardo... (p. 445)

> [... On an open
> balcony, of another palace,
> is a woman.... She looks at
> nothing.... She is white like a tuberose....]

The masculine "lirio" [lily or iris] corresponds to the feminine "azucena" [Madonna lily]. Often it represents the poet himself: "Estoy solo en mi jardín;/ .../ tengo un lirio como flor ..." (p. 359) [I am alone in my garden;/ .../ I have a lily as a flower ...]. White nocturnal flowers are associated with the coldness of the moon:

> Noche negra, yo te guardo
> el sueño de mi jardín...
> Tiene una luna de nardo
> y un aroma de jazmín. (p. 436)

> [Black night, I keep vigil for you over
> the sleep of my garden....
> It has a moon of tuberose
> and an aroma of jasmine.]

In these gardens the white rose takes the place of the red rose. Observe how it functions:

> **El corazón no es un sueño;**
> **hay corazones que sienten**
> **el enredo de las rosas**
> **de sus blancos floreceres;**

> **que sienten bien sus espinas**
> **que tienen sangre en la nieve**
> **perfumada de sus rosas,**
> **y que saben que la tienen...**

> **El corazón no es un sueño.**
> **Hoy el corazón me duele**
> **por esa flor que se ha ido**
> **a los parques de la muerte.**

> **Y he sentido deshojarse**
> **sus rosas blancas de nieve,**
> **esta tarde, tarde triste,**
> **¡ay!, tarde azul, tristemente....** (p. 437)

> [The heart is not a dream;
> there are hearts that feel
> the tangle of the roses
> of their white bloomings;

> that feel their thorns well,
> that have blood in the perfumed
> snow of their roses,
> and that know they have it....

> The heart is not a dream.
> Today my heart pains me
> for that flower that has gone
> to the parks of death.

> And I have felt the leaves fall from
> its white roses of snow,
> this evening, sad evening,
> oh!, blue evening, sadly. . . .]

The white rose alludes to spiritual values, but here the thorns link it with blood and the vital and erotic associations that this carries. The flower, nevertheless, dies of purity and loses its leaves sadly at the end of the poem in a blue mystic evening. In another poem the rose dematerializes progressively:

> Una rosa mate o rosa,
> o azul, o llorosa, o pálida;
> bruma, bancos fríos, flores
> que ya no son flores. . . Lánguidas
> músicas de otoño, llantos
> sin saber por qué, calladas
> tristezas que tienen nieve
> y espinas. . ., no sé . . ., fantasmas. (p. 433)

> [A rose, dull or rose,
> or blue, or weepy, or pale;
> mist, cold banks, flowers
> that are no longer flowers. . . . Languid
> musics of autumn, sobs
> without knowing why, hushed
> sadnesses that have snow
> and thorns . . ., I don't know . . ., phantoms.]

Initially, the rose had a dull coloration; for a moment it turns rose, but soon passes on to blue, pale, mist, sadness of snow and thorns. Materially, it exists only in a state of remorse—the thorns—for just a moment; and then the blurred scene of the garden evaporates.

In the last part of the book, "Jardines dolientes," the whole scenario changes as the sentiments of the poet also change. The garden becomes filled with dying, melancholic, and fragile refinements. The red of the gallant gardens and the white of the mystic gardens now give way to mauve, grey, and gold. They are soft, pearly and velvety tones with sentimental connotations: "tarde triste y malva" [evening sad and mauve], with "melodía en gris y rosa, en gris y amarillo, en gris y violeta, en gris y celeste; y verdes desteñidos, y blancos de oro y malvas de plata . . . Todo con un brillo trémulo de lágrimas . . ." [melody in grey and rose, in grey and yellow, in grey and violet, in grey and celeste; and faded greens and golden whites and silver mauves. . . . All with a tremulous shining of tears . . .]. Now one feels "la resignación doliente y casi cristiana de los jardines enfermos" (p. 469) [the suffering and almost Christian resignation of the sick gardens].

In this garden the itinerary of the poet reaches its final failure. It is a defeat which offers no opposition and forces a reconciliation of previously separate elements. The impressionistic brush employed here eliminates the definition of forms and the interweaving of planes; the symbols lose their weight and their counterweight and open themselves to a whole world of free recollections of sin. It is a mild atmosphere that offers no resistance, that neither imposes itself on nor opposes itself to the poet, but that offers him the richness of its melancholy:

Estoy envuelto en la tarde
como en un sueño violeta;
por todas partes se ven
las flores y las tristezas. (p. 496)

[I am wrapped in the evening
as in a violet dream;
everywhere are seen
flowers and sadnesses.]

Here only the fragrance of the flowers appears at times, but separated from its matter, as if it were merely the perfume of memory:

Tienen la fragancia de esos
jardines de los cariños . . .,
las palabras y los besos
de nuestras bocas de niños . . . (p. 506)

[They have the fragrance of those
gardens of affections . . .,
the words and the kisses
from our mouths as children. . . .]

The few flowers that exist here are faded and dull in color, deprived of conviction. The violet, strong in aroma, blooms and withers like the weak spark of memory:

A veces, una violeta,
en la más larga avenida,
es buena para la herida
de un corazón de poeta.

Es la fragancia, que envuelve
la pena del corazón. . . . (p. 510)

[At times, a violet,
on the longest avenue,
is good for the wound
of a poet's heart.

It is the fragrance that envelops
the pain of the heart.]

The violet appears also in the color that predominates in "Jardines dolientes"—mauve, mixed with greys, with whites, and even with blacks, and expressing the intensity of the memory of love, the fragility of that memory, the evanescence of an illusion: "¡Melancolía violeta/ sobre balcones dorados! (p. 480) [Violet melancholy/ on golden balconies!]

In the last poem of *Jardines lejanos* a yellow rose, an old rose, still speaks of love beside the fountain:

—Gime su viejo estribillo
una fuente melodiosa;
en un rosal amarillo
hay todavía una rosa. (p. 520)

["A melodious fountain
moans its old refrain;
on a yellow rosebush
there is still a rose."]

The poet will find it at the end of his road. How can one interpret the stanza that closes *Jardines lejanos,* if not as a failure?

¿ Volverá la primavera
con sus palabras de amor?
Ay! ¿No será una quimera
que vuelva la primavera
y que vuelva el ruiseñor? (p. 521)
[Will spring return
with its words of love?
Oh! Isn't it a chimera
that spring returns
and that the nightingale returns?]

*The University of Texas at Austin*

[Translated from the
Spanish by the editors]

# NOTES

[1] Toward the end of 1902 there was an exhibition in Bing's Art Nouveau salon of the works of Hokusai, Hiroshige, and Kuniyoshi. In 1903 a Japanese room was opened in the Louvre. On the new sense of nature, see L. Litvak, *A Dream of Arcadia* (Austin: Univ. of Texas Press, 1975), pp. 150-90.

[2] Quoted by Philippe Jullian, *The Symbolists* (London: Phaidon, 1973), p. 50.

[3] Santiago Rusiñol, "Jardines de España," *Pèl & Ploma*, 1903, p. 366. See also "El jardin abandonat," *Pèl & Ploma*, 3 (1 July 1900), 8-9; Pompeyo Gener, "Santiago Rusiñol," *Pèl & Ploma*, 13 (1 Dec. 1900), 7; A. Masera, "La nit en els jardins," *Joventut*, 322 (12 Apr. 1906); "Jardines de árboles en formas caprichosas," *La Ilustración Artística*, 2 Oct. 1905, pp. 646-47; Francisco de Bofarull, "El laberinto," *Pèl & Ploma*, 1903, pp. 213-19.

[4] See Émile Gallé, "Le Décor symbolique," a lecture delivered 17 May 1900 in the Académie de Stanislass, Nancy; printed in *Écrits pour l'art* ... (Paris: Librairie Renouard, 1908), pp. 219-25.

[5] *La Plante et ses applications ornementales* (Paris: E. Lévy, [1896]). Grasset conceived of stylization as a synthetic and nearly schematic interpretation of a flower. It was based on simplicity of line and careful attention to colors. On this subject, see also Roger Marx, *La Décoration et les industries d'art à l'Exposition de 1901* (Paris: Delagrave, 1902). Remy de Gourmont's review of this book, in the *Mercure de France*, Jan.-Mar. 1902, pp. 697-706, notes that the richness of decorative art in the period was due precisely to the numerous motifs that were stylized. Gourmont agrees with Marx on the appropriateness of the lily for this treatment. See also "Art Moderne," *Mercure de France*, Jan.-Mar. 1902, pp. 242-44, and the interesting book by A. E. V. Lilley and W. Midgley, *A Book of Studies in Plant Forms with Some Suggestions for Their Application to Design* (London: Chapman and Hall, 1895).

[6] Ramón del Valle-Inclán, *Sonata de otoño, Sonata de invierno: Memorias del Marqués de Bradomín*, 5th ed. (Madrid: Espasa-Calpe, 1966), p. 26.

[7] Other examples are found in the works of Bernewitz, frequently reproduced in Spanish publications. See a pitcher from which a nude woman entwined with Madonna lilies springs forth, in *La Ilustración Artística*, 9 May 1904, p. 329. This magazine also reproduced decorative works by Pickford Marriot which combined crystal, mother-of-pearl, and precious stones, and whose subjects were often flower-women. See *La Ilustración Artística*, 2 Oct. 1905, p. 638.

[8] The novels of the "Rose" cycle, which begins with *Il piacere* (1889, trans. *The Child of Pleasure*, 1898). D'Annunzio wanted to place his novels, impregnated with eroticism, under the sign of the female sex organ, which the poet called the rose. For works in a similar vein, see Enrique Sepúlveda, "Las rosas," *Blanco y Negro*, 322 (1897), and Manuel de Montoliu, "Cansó de les roses," from the *Llibre d'Amor*, in *Pèl & Ploma*, 1903, p. 137.

[9] "Les flors del Gerro Blau," *Joventut*, 1900, p. 365.

10 "Les crisantemes," *Joventut,* 1901, pp. 786-87.

11 Published originally in the Dec. issue of *Century Illustrated Magazine,* this trans. appeared in *Helios,* 10 (1904), 126.

12 Johan Thorn Prikker, *De Bruid* [The Bride] (1893), Rijksmuseum Kröller-Müller, Otterlo. On this painter, see Bettina Spaanstra-Polak, *Symbolism* (Amsterdam: Meulenhoff, 1967), pp. 19-20.

13 "Astarté," in *Poésies* (Paris: Éditions Montaigne, 1930), p. 75. Also interesting is a piece by Stéphane Mallarmé, "Le Nénuphar blanc," in *Oeuvres complètes,* ed. Henri Mondor and G. Jean-Aubry (Paris: Gallimard, 1956), pp. 283-86. In Oriental mythology the lotus had an erotic and vital symbolism. The nerve centers of the human body, called *chakras,* were represented by lotuses with different numbers of petals. The sex organs had six, the navel eight, the heart twelve, the forehead only two (Philip Rawson, *Erotic Art of the East* [New York: G. P. Putnam's Sons, 1968], p. 163). See also Thomas Freeman, "The Lotus and the Tigress," *Genre,* 7 (Mar. 1974), 91-111. Emilia Pardo Bazán tells "La leyenda del loto," *Almanaque Blanco y Negro para 1900.* There she refers to the symbolism of the petals that we have mentioned and to the story of Devi in the *Mahabarata.* She contrasts the Madonna lily, which represents virginity, with the lotus, which denotes erotic passion.

14 This book appeared in Madrid in 1904, published by Fernando Fe. It contains 84 poems. A subtitle suggests a tone for each part: "Jardines galantes" has at the beginning the music for a gavotte by Gluck and some lines by Verlaine and is dedicated to Vicente Pereda; "Jardines místicos" has some music by Schumann and some lines by Laforgue and is dedicated to Francisco de Icaza; "Jardines dolientes" has a melody by Mendelssohn and some lines by Rodenbach and is dedicated to Antonio Machado.

15 Ricardo Gullón, *Estudios sobre Juan Ramón Jiménez* (Buenos Aires: Losada, 1960), pp. 164-65.

16 Juan Ramón Jiménez, *Primeros libros de poesía,* ed. Francisco Garfias, 3rd ed. (Madrid: Aguilar, 1967), p. 375. All further page references to poems by Juan Ramón Jiménez, given in the text, will be to this edition. Unless otherwise indicated, poems are quoted from *Jardines lejanos.*

17 See Robert Schmutzler, *Art Nouveau* (New York: Abrams, 1962), pp. 109-14.

18 "Nuevas Rimas, III," in *Confidencias* (Madrid, 1899), p. 28.

19 It is necessary to recall also the influence of Whistler's paintings.

20 Ferdinand Brunetière, *Nouveaux Essais sur la littérature contemporaine* (Paris: Lévy, 1895), pp. 137-38.

21 "El cisne y el buho," *Revista Iberoamericana,* 2 (1940), 68.

22 "Función y sentido del color en la poesía de Manuel Gutiérrez Nájera," *Revista Hispánica Moderna,* 23 (1951), 19.

23 See Carole A. Holdsworth, "White Symbolism in Selected *Revista Moderna* Authors," *Revista de Estudios Hispánicos,* 2 (Nov. 1968), 1-12. The same symbolism appears in the following poems: Antón Benazet, "Nit de plata," *Joventut,* 213 (10 Mar. 1904), 157; Pedro Barrates, "Allá," *La Vida Galante,* 232 (1902); Ramón Pérez de Ayala, "Blanca," *Helios,* 5 (1903), 141; Joseph Maria Folch y Torres, "Tot blanch," *Joventut,* 56 (7 Mar. 1901), 174-75; Emanuel Alfonso, "La enamorada del cel," *Joventut,* 65 (7 May 1901), and "Maria Emanuel de Castell-Vila," *Joventut,* 73 (4 July 1901).

24 Mallarmé, *op. cit.* (above, n. 13), p. 47.

# The Window as Symbol in Spanish *Modernista* Poetry: Outline of a Model

## J. M. Aguirre

1

*Romeo.* But, soft! What light through yonder
          window breaks?

. . . . . . . . . . . . . . . . . . . . . . . . . . . . . . . . . .

*Juliet.*                             Ay me!

                      *Romeo and Juliet,* II, ii.

There are objects which, through the collective and unconscious efforts of several generations, and under certain conditions, may acquire a symbolic significance. Indeed, the "private" symbol is a contradiction in terms. "No genius," writes C. G. Jung, "has ever sat down with a pen or a brush in his hand and said: 'Now I am going to invent a symbol.' "[1] Man cannot invent symbols, but man invented the window, and it is modern man who has invented the window pane.[2] Literary windows can be found even in the Bible and in medieval Spanish poetry. Here, though, I am concerned with the window as an almost contemporary symbol: with its specific connotations in the literature of the European symbolist movement and after. It is my view that the window symbol was "invented" by just two or three generations of poets.[3] The fact that the window is a "hole" and, because of its shape, a mandala, and the additional fact that it is related to the mirror (and to the room and the door), must have helped subliminally in the creation of this symbol across Europe by so few artists in such a short period of time. As a necessary prelude to understanding the appearance and use of the window symbol in Spanish *modernista* poetry, then, I shall dedicate a large part of my essay to tracing its development in other literatures, especially that of France, where symbolism first became a movement.

2

All day till evening I watched the rain
Beat wearily upon the window pane.

I was not sorrowful, but only tired
Of everything that ever I desired.

    Ernest Dowson (1867-1900), "Spleen"

I cannot undertake here a definition of the symbol. Yet it must be stated categorically that any such definition ought *not* to be based on these well known sentences of Mallarmé:

*Nommer* un objet, c'est supprimer les trois quarts de la jouissance du poème qui est faite du bonheur de deviner peu à peu; le *suggérer,* voilà le rêve. C'est le parfait usage de ce mystère qui constitue le symbole: évoquer petit à petit un objet pour montrer un état d'âme, ou, inversement, choisir un objet et en dégager un état d'âme, par une série de déchiffrements.[4]

[To *name* an object is to suppress three-quarters of the enjoyment of the poem, which comes from the pleasure of guessing bit by bit; to *suggest* the object, that's the ideal. It is the perfect use of mystery which constitutes symbol: to evoke an object, little by little, in order to show a mood, or, conversely, to select an object and to elicit a mood from it by means of a series of decodings.]

This is a frivolous statement, worthy of a crossword-puzzle addict. Why should not the poet name an object when it is possible to do so? The essential function of the symbol is to evoke that which cannot be named. As Jung explains, "Symbols are not signs or allegories for something known; they seek rather to express something that is little known or completely unknown."[5] Tancrède de Visan observes: "là où l'expression directe est impossible doit intervenir la suggestion"[6] [Where direct expression is impossible, suggestion should intervene]. Symbols, according to D. H. Lawrence, "stand for units of human *feeling,* human experience" (p. 158). To which I add that they also stand for statements of the rational mind.[7]

But however we define the symbol, it would be misleading to regard the symbolic "object" as the main point of the poem. The main point is the dialectic in the "conversation" (interchange, exchange) between the object's shape or form that we all know and the connotations attached to that shape, which we can never be sure we know. If the symbol seeks to express "something that is little known or completely unknown," it follows that assigning a meaning to the window symbol must be nearly or completely impossible. Can we give meanings to a window? Does it mean anything beyond its *being* a window? Certainly in writing about symbols, we ought to eschew the categorical and the restrictive and not go beyond making vague enumerations of some of their likely metaphysical/emotional connotations within a given context. The moment we over-rationalize a symbol we run the risk of turning it into an emblem or an allegory. At this stage of my essay, the symbolic significances attached by Juan-Eduardo Cirlot to "room" and "window" will suffice:

*Room* A symbol of individuality—of private thoughts. The windows symbolize the possibility of understanding and of passing through to the external and the beyond, and are also an illustration of an idea of communication. Hence, a closed room lacking windows may be symbolic of virginity, according to Frazer, and also of other kinds of non-communication. . . .[8]

3

Shall I say, I have gone at dusk through
narrow streets
And watched the smoke that rises from the pipes
Of lonely men in shirt-sleeves, leaning out of
windows? . . .
T.S. Eliot (1888-1965), "The Love Song of
J. Alfred Prufrock"

Very tentatively, I wish to propose a model which I hope will facilitate the task of comparing and/or contrasting the values of the window symbol as used by a great number of modern poets. The window can be understood as a sort of dividing line between the inner and the outer worlds of human experience, or between the "room" and the "street" (or "road"). We can look at, or out of a window. In both instances the symbol will retain its value as "an illustration of any idea of communication" between the self and the "other." The basic situations are: (1) the "I" (self) in the street looks vainly at the person (the "other") behind the window panes of his room; and (2) the "I" (self) in the room may attempt to open the window, or decide to turn his back on it. When the "I" in the room chooses the second alternative, he is concentrating his gaze on what Henri Bergson calls "les couches profondes du moi"[9] [the deep layers of the self], or—to involve another key symbol—on the mirror.[10] The drama being enacted in the conscience of the "I" looking at, or out of the window alludes to the concepts of the self and of the "other" as formulated by idealist doctrines (see next section). Some symbolists conceived of themselves as the melancholy seekers of some kind of true communication with the "other," which they were doomed to fail to achieve in life (or art: the work of art is another "mirror").

Here is my model, based on the various possible situations of the "I" (self) to which I have just referred:

(self) Street⟶Window ("other")          (self) Room ⟨ Mirror
                                                      Window⟶Street ("other")

In general, the emotional connotations of the model range from melancholy hopelessness (the self in the street looking at the window of the "other") to *taedium vitae* (the self in the room), and from these to either despair (the self concentrating his gaze upon the mirror) or melancholy hope (the self looking out of his window at the "other" in the street).

4

Three blank walls, a barred window with no view,
A ceiling within reach of the raised hands,
A floor blank as the walls.
          Robert Graves (1895-), "The Philosopher"

The nature of the drama to which I have referred in the previous section is admirably and succinctly set out by Antonio Machado's apochryphal professor Juan de Mairena: "si nuestro prójimo no existe, mal podremos amarle"[11] [if our fellow man does not exist, it will be difficult for us to love him]. Machado's poem "El poeta cantaba su soledad porque creía en ella" (p. 856) [the poet was singing his solitude because he believed in it] offers both a clear indication of the type of metaphysics that structured European poetry at the turn of the century and an explanation of what Machado called its "carácter egolátrico"[12] [self-worshiping nature]. Certainly, if man is unable to believe in the real existence of the "other," he is doomed to solitude, to an existence confined within the strict limits of the room/conscience. Here the window allows the self to view an enticing outer reality; by contrast, the mirror will allow the only vision that the logic of idealism permits, that of the far-from-satisfactory reality of the self. "Apiadémonos," Gabriel Miró will

exhort, "de los que viven con las ventanas muy cerradas"[13] [Let us take pity
on those who live with their windows shut up tight].

The conflict between the logic of idealism and the wish to release man
from its straitening consequences was felt on aesthetic and/or moral grounds
by many symbolist artists. André Gide's *Le Traité du verbe* (1891),
meaningfully subtitled "Théorie du symbole" [Theory of the Symbol], is a
timid attempt to break Narcissus' mirror. Gide, perhaps echoing Mallarmé's
poetic theory, suggests that the mirror is in fact the work of art itself ("Car
l'oeuvre d'art est un cristal"[14] [For the work of the art is a crystal]) and as
such is more important than the "I" it reflects. Nevertheless, the *Traité* is still
a true symbolist document. When Gide describes Narcissus, "penché sur
l'apparence du Monde" (p. 11) [leaning over the appearance of the world],
he is doubtless painting a precise portrait of the idealist writer (see note 16
below). And in *Paludes* (1894), Gide really essays a serious, albeit
mischievous attack on the *fin de siècle* solipsism. In the "Postface pour la
deuxième édition" [Post-face to the twelfth edition], Gide tells his reader
that he wrote *Paludes* "pour me moquer des symboles" (p. 1477) [to make
fun of symbols]. It is obvious that this is exactly what he does, and the main
symbol at which he pokes fun is, quite fittingly, the window:
"J'étouffe! –Ah! par le fenêtre.–Je vais le refermer derrière moi; ... L'air
de la chambre m'entoura; je respirai avec méthode.–Fraîcheur–petit
matin–vitres pâles ... il faudra noter tout cela;–aquarium,–il se confond
avec le reste de la chambre ..." (p. 128) [I'm suffocating! – Ah! out
through the window.–I'm going to close it behind me; ... The air in the
room  surrounded  me;  I  breathed  methodically.–Coolness–early
morning–pale  window  panes  ...  I'll  have  to  take  note  of  all
that;–aquarium,–it's blending into the rest of the room ...].[15] It is on
moral and social grounds that Remy de Gourmont attempts to open a
window in the ironical fortress of idealism: "Ayant eu, ces derniers temps,
quelques doutes sur la valeur, non point philosophique, mais morale et
sociale, de l'idéalisme, je ne pus, malgré des méditations assidues, triompher
de mes hésitations par la méthode de la logique directe"[16] [Having had lately
some doubts about the value–*not* philosophical but moral and social–of
idealism, I was unable, in spite of assiduous meditations, to triumph over my
hesitations through the method of direct logic]. Antonio Machado
encounters similar difficulties: Sólo un pensamiento prágmático,
profundamente ilógico, puede afirmar la existencia de nuestro prójimo con el
mismo grado de certeza que la existencia propia" (p. 479) [Only a pragmatic
thought, profoundly illogical, can affirm the existence of our fellow man with
the same degree of certainty we have about our own existence].[17] In order
to achieve his objective, Gourmont observes that it will be enough to carry
out "la critique du néronisme mental, plus clairement appelé le
narcissisme" (p. 261) [the critique of mental Nero-ism, more clearly called
narcissism]. In other words, he tries to solve the problem by taking the
mirror away from Narcissus. As he cannot break it,[18] Gourmont, like Gide,
gives the mirror an ingenious one-hundred-and-eighty-degree turn and forces
it to become the "other"! : "La pensée d'autrui est le miroir même de
Narcisse, et sans lequel il serait ignoré éternellement" (pp. 267-68) [The
thought of others is the very mirror of Narcissus, without which he would be

eternally unknown]. Antonio Machado says it in verse:

> Los ojos por que suspiras,
> sábelo bien,
> los ojos en que te miras
> son ojos porque te ven.[19]

> [The eyes you sigh for,
> know it well,
> the eyes in which you look at yourself
> are eyes because they see you.]

Finally, what Arthur Symons called "this revolt against exteriority"[20] was the unavoidable consequence of the prevalent philosophy of the epoch. Yet we ought to speak of "drama" rather than "revolt" and of the symbolist artist as a Narcissus *malgré lui* [in spite of himself]. I can offer no more meaningful definition than this of the Janus-like figure, torn between the window and the mirror, in the closed and dimly lit room of so many symbolist poems.

5

> "O look, look in the mirror,
>     O look in your distress;
> Life remains a blessing
>     Although you cannot bless.
> "O stand, stand at the window
>     As the tears scald and start;
> You shall love your crooked neighbour
>     With your crooked heart."
>
>     W.H. Auden (1907-1973), "As I Walked Out
>                                 One Evening"

Renaissance painters seem to have been the first artists to discover the potential of the window as a formula for melancholy. Rembrandt's "A Young Girl on a Window Sill" (London, Dulwich College) and his disciple Nicolaes Maes' "Girl at a Window" (Amsterdam, Rijksmuseum)—often called "Dreaming"—are excellent proof of it. The appeal of these two girls, lost in the intimacy of their reflections, is irresistible. Both paintings illustrate well Cirlot's values for "room" and "window." Albrecht Dürer's famous "Melencolia" (1514) would appear to have been the starting point for an easily recognizable literary topos/symbol. Jean Lahor (pseudonym of Henry Cazalis, 1840-1909) may have forged the first link in the chain:

> *Devant la "Melancholia" d'Albert Dürer*
> La Melancholia médite solitaire,
> Le visage en sa main, cependant que le soir,
> Triste comme elle, étend son ombre sur la terre,
> Et qu'au loin le soleil s'éteint dans un ciel noir. (1868?)

> [*In the Presence of Albrecht Dürer's "Melancholia"*
> Melancholy mediates alone,
> Her face in her hand, while evening,
> Sad like her, spreads his shadow over the earth,
> And far away the sun dies out in a black sky.]

H. Delavelle, illustrator of Georges Rodenbach's *Bruges la morte* [Dead Bruges] (1892), offers a rough interpretation of Dürer's engraving. Hughes Viane, "Le veuf inconsolable" [the inconsolable widower] of the novel, "solitaire, il passait toute la journée dans sa chambre, une vaste pièce au premier étage, dont les fenêtres donnaient sur le quai du Rosaire, au long duquel s'alignait sa maison, mirée dans l'eau"[21] [solitary, would spend the whole day in his bedroom, a vast room on the ground floor, whose windows opened out onto the quai du Rosaire, with the length of which was aligned his house, reflected in the water]. In Delavelle's engraving the widower leans his bearded chin wearily on his hand; his thoughts seem to be dark and gloomy, like his face; his eyes look out of the window into emptiness, searching, meditating. Jules Barbey d'Aurevilly sees himself as a melancholy dreamer at his window:

> *La Haine du Soleil*
>
> Un soir, j'étais debout, auprés d'une fenêtre . . .
> Contre la vitre en feu j'avais mon front songeur,
> Et je voyais, là-bas, lentement disparaître
> Un soleil embrumé qui mourait sans splendeur! (*Poussières,* 1897)
>
> [*Hatred of the Sun*
>
> One evening, I was standing beside a window . . .
> Against the window pane on fire, I had my dreaming forehead,
> And I could see, down there, slowly disappearing
> A hazy sun that was dying without splendor!]

André Gide in the "Prelude" of his novel *Le Voyage d'Urien* (1892) [Urien's Voyage] had already used an analogous image: "Sans que je m'en fusse aperçu, ma lampe s'était éteinte; devant l'aube s'était ouverte ma croisée. Je mouillai mon front à la rosée des vitres, et repoussant dans le passé ma rêverie consumée, les yeux dirigés vers l'aurore, je m'aventurai dans le val étroit des metempsychoses" (p. 15) [Without my realizing it, my lamp had died out; in the presence of dawn my window had come open. I moistened my forehead in the dew on the window panes, and pushing back into the past my consummated reverie, with my eyes directed toward the dawn, I ventured forth into the narrow vale of metempsychoses]. The symbolist intention of the image is made clear in the "Envoi" [Envoy] which concludes this work (and which now should be read in conjunction with the quotation from Cirlot in Section 2 above):

> Ce voyage n'est que mon rêve,
> nous ne sommes jamais sortis
> de la chambre de nos pensées,—
> et nous avons passé la vie
> sans la voir. . . . (p. 66)
> [This journey is only my dream,
> we have never left
> the room of our thoughts—
> and we have spent our life
> without seeing it.]

Spanish literature of the early twentieth century is not without its moments of wistful contemplation. A picture similar to Delavelle's engraving is found in Azorín's prose work *Castilla* (1912): "En el primer balcón de la izquierda se ve sentado en un sillón un hombre; su cara está pálida, exangüe y remata en una barbita afilada y gris. Los ojos de este caballero están velados por una profunda tristeza; el codo lo tiene el caballero puesto en el brazo del sillón y su cabeza descansa en la palma de la mano . . ." [On the first balcony to the left is seen a man sitting in a chair; his face is pale, anemic, and it comes to an end in a pointed little gray beard. This gentleman's eyes are veiled by a deep sadness; the gentleman has his elbow placed upon the arm of his chair and his head is resting in the palm of his hand ...].[22] Juan Ramón Jiménez might have been thinking of Dürer's "Melencolia" while writing the following lines of "La elejía:" [The elegy] (1911):

> Tu sigues, mujer mustia, la orilla en flor, y mudamente
> vas a sentarte entre ruinas claras,
> ................................................
>     Y el mentón en la mano, y el codo en la rodilla,
> ceñudamente piensas en toda la belleza,
> mientras el sol que muere, exalta en su amarilla
> lumbre tu veste blanca, luto de tu pureza.[23]

> [You follow, withered woman, the river bank in flower, and
> silently you go to sit among clear ruins,
> ................................................
>     And with your chin in your hand, and your elbow on your knee,
> grimly you think about all the beauty
> while the sun that is dying exalts in its yellow
> light your white dress, mourning-clothes of your purity.]

And Antonio Machado writes in "Al gran pleno o conciencia integral" [To the great plenum or integral consciousnesss] :

> Que en su estatua el alto Cero
> —mármol frío,
> ceño austero
> y una mano en la mejilla—,
> del gran remanso del río,
> medite, eterno, en la orilla,
> y haya gloria eternamente. (p. 312)

> [Let the high Zero
> —cold marble,
> austere frown
> and one hand on his cheek—
> on the bank of the great backwater of the river,
> meditate, eternal,
> and let there be glory eternally.]

The series of connotations which all these quotations provide for the reader is worth noting: dream-like existence, fantasy, memories, loneliness, frustrated eroticism, meditation, etc., and, enveloping all, *melancholy*. Also, these connotations are good proof of the plasticity of the image: in fact, the more symbolic the poetic image, the easier it will be to represent it in concrete terms.[24]

6

> "You speak as though
> No sunlight ever surprised the mind
> Groping on its cloudy path."

> "Sunlight's a thing that needs a window
> Before it enter a dark room.
> Windows don't happen."

> R.S. Thomas (1913-), "Poetry for Supper"

To my knowledge the first literary works explicitly dedicated to the exploration of the room and the window as poetic images, are Baudelaire's poems in prose "La chambre double" [The double room] and "Les Fenêtres" [The Windows].[25] Baudelaire's "chambre" is like "une rêverie" [a reverie], a room "véritablement *spirituelle*" [truly *spiritual*]. It houses the soul at dusk, when "l'esprit sommeillant est bercé par des sensations de serre-chaude" [when the drowsing mind is lulled by hothouse sensations].[26] In this room the poem's *persona* is unaware of the passing of time, experiencing the mystery and the silence of the "vie suprême [supreme life]. It is "La chambre paradisiaque" [the Paradise-like room], "la souveraine des rêves" [the sovereign of dreams]. But the room is "double"; it is also "real," the "séjour de l'éternel ennui" [sojourn of eternal ennui], and its windows are "tristes" [sad]. In this second room time makes its appearance, and the clock says: "Je suis la Vie, l'insupportable, l'implacable Vie!" [I am Life, unbearable, implacable Life!]. The exit is not by way of the window but through "la fiole de laudanum" [the vial of laudanum]. Baudelaire believed in the objectivity of the world, and at the same time he abhorred it. That is why the "I" of "Les Fenêtres" prefers to look at another person's closed window: "Celui qui regarde du dehors à travers une fenêtre ouverte, ne voit jamais autant de choses que celui qui regarde une fenêtre fermée. . . . Ce qu'on peut voir au soleil est toujours moins intéressant que ce qui passe derrière une vitre. Dans ce trou noir ou lumineux vit la vie, rêve la vie, souffre la vie" [The one who looks from outside through an open window, never sees as many things as the one who looks at a closed window. . . . What one can see in the sunlight is always less interesting than what is going on behind a window pane. In this black or luminous hole life lives, life dreams, life suffers]. Therefore: "Qu'importe ce que peut être la réalité placée hors de moi" [What does it matter what reality that is placed outside of myself may be?].[27]

Philosophically speaking, Baudelaire was not truly an idealist. As Henri de Régnier has argued, Baudelaire was both a romantic and a realist.[28] And there is no contradiction in this. Baudelaire dreams because he does not like reality. The symbolist poet dreams because he does not believe in reality. Baudelaire's poems contain some of the emotional values normally attached to the room and the window. The melancholy atmosphere of "La Chambre double" and the attitude of the *persona* of "Les Fenêtres" *vis-à-vis* external reality were perhaps the most important factors in the evolution of both these objects from poetic images to symbols. Two decades after the publication of *Le Spleen de Paris* the window had become a topos/symbol throughout European poetry.[29]

7

I swim like a minnow
behind my studio window.
          Robert Lowell (1917-1977), "Fall 1961"

Though I have no space to offer a detailed account of the evolution of the window from poetic image to symbol, I think it wrong to ignore the question completely. I wish to mention very briefly the work of three poets who, in my opinion, were of paramount importance in the invention of a symbolic role for the window. They are: Georges Rodenbach (1855-1898), Henri de Régnier (1864-1936) and Charles Guérin (1873-1907).

Rodenbach's reflective lyric poems work almost as the emotional counterpoint to the idealist philosophy of Henri Bergson. A book like *Les Vies encloses* (1896) [Enclosed Lives] could be understood as a poetic exploration of what Bergson terms "le moi fondamental" [the basic self] in his *Essai sur les données immédiates de la conscience* (1889) [The immediate data of consciousness]. Yet already in Rodenbach's *La Jeunesse blanche* (1886) we find an intuitive approach to the consciousness of the self very similar to that of his later books. According to Cirlot, "a closed room lacking windows may be symbolic of virginity." Rodenbach situates his Beguines "dans l'exil de leurs chambres" [in the exile of their rooms] with the windows closed. At the end of the poem "Béguinage flamand" [Flemish Beguinage] (in *La Jeunesse blanche*), Rodenbach suggests the emotional tensions that such enclosure creates in the conscience of the Beguine, who is seen at night "Debout à sa fenêtre au vent joyeux" [Standing at her window in the joyful wind]. (As a symbol, the wind is credited with the power of fecundation). Elsewhere, in an untitled poem of *Le Règne du silence* (1891) [The Reign of Silence], he evokes the mystery of the room (the self) in conjunction with the window and the mirror:

> Les chambres vraiment sont de vieilles gens
> Sachant des secrets, sachant des histoires,
> —Ah! quels confidents toujours indulgents!—
> Qu'elles ont cachés dans les vitres noires,
> Qu'elles ont cachés au fond des miroirs.
>
> [Rooms truly are old people
> Knowing secrets, knowing stories,
> —Ah! What ever-indulgent confidants!—
> Which they have hidden in black window panes,
> Which they have hidden in the bottom of mirrors.]

Rodenbach's preoccupation with these symbols culminates in a section of *Les Vies encloses* entitled "Les Malades aux fenêtres" [The Sick People at the Windows]. I know of no other set of poems so powerfully evocative of the emotional/metaphysical content of *la maladie du siècle*, of the melancholy of "l'éternel ennui" [eternal ennui].[30]

According to some critics and young poets of the time, the most important poet of the symbolist movement was Henri de Régnier.[31] This poet's melancholy-nostalgic style together with his exquisite sense of rhythm greatly contributed to the acceptance of symbolist aesthetics in France. While space limitations prevent me from quoting and commenting extensively on his work, it is worth mentioning that his books of poetry contain abundant examples of the points made so far in this essay.[32]

Charles Guérin is the third link in the chain. He has been considered one of the three or four authentic poets of French Symbolism's second generation.[33] What he calls "the passionate melancholy," doubtless derived from his avowed admiration for Rodenbach, informs the whole of his poetry. "Fenêtres sur la vie" [Windows on Life] is the title of one section of his book *Le Coeur solitaire* (1898) [The Solitary Heart]. Guérin, like Régnier and Machado, believed in his own solitude and detested Narcissus' mirror:

> O rêveur, tu dormis trop longtemps, lève-toi!
> Range ta lampe éteinte et rouvre la fenétre.
> . . . . . . . . . . . . . . . . . . . . . . . . . . . . . . . . . . . . .
> Ah! lève-toi, Lazare, et romps tes bandelettes!
> Que, miroirs élargis, tes prunelles reflètent.
> . . . . . . . . . . . . . . . . . . . . . . . . . . . . . . . . . . . . .
> Avec un grand frisson plonge-toi dans la vie! (XXXV, *Le Coeur solitaire*)
>
> [O dreamer, you slept too long, arise!
> Put away your extinguished lamp and reopen the window.
> . . . . . . . . . . . . . . . . . . . . . . . . . . . . . . . . . . . . .
> Ah! Arise, Lazarus, and break your wrappings,
> which your pupils, enlarged mirrors, reflect.
> . . . . . . . . . . . . . . . . . . . . . . . . . . . . . . . . . . . . .
> With a great shudder, plunge into life!]

Gourmont is justified in claiming that Guérin represents well the ideal type of the young poets who proclaim their faith in life but do not know how to live (p. 232). The start of the first poem of *Le Semeur de cendres* (1901) [The Sower of Ashes] should remind the reader of André Gide's gibe at the symbolist window (section 4 above):

> J'étouffe dans la chambre où mon áme est murée,
> . . . . . . . . . . . . . . . . . . . . . . . . . . . . . . . . . . . . .
> Et j'ouvre au clair de lune immense la fenétre.
> [I am suffocating in the room where my soul is walled in
> . . . . . . . . . . . . . . . . . . . . . . . . . . . . . . . . . . . . .
> And I open the window to the immense moonlight.]

However:

> Va, ferme la croisée, et quitte ton espoir.
> . . . . . . . . . . . . . . . . . . . . . . . . . . . . . . . . . . . . .
> Ouvre ton lit désert comme un sépulcre, et dors
> Du sommeil des vaincus et du sommeil des morts.[34]
> [Go, close the window, and leave your hope.
> . . . . . . . . . . . . . . . . . . . . . . . . . . . . . . . . . . . . .
> Open your bed, empty like a sepulcher, and sleep
> The sleep of the vanquished and the sleep of the dead.]

In general, the symbolists saw themselves as the explorers of "le moi fondamental." Their conception of the poem as the "objective correlative" (T.S. Eliot) or "l'équivalent émotionnel" (Bergson, *Essai*) [the emotional equivalent] of the experience of the solitary "I" inevitably led them to introspection and, consequently, to the symbols which I have begun to outline.

8

> Seduction fantasies of the public mind,
> or Dilthey's dream from which he roused to see
> the cosmos glaring through his windowpane?
> Prisoners of what we think occurred,
> or dreamers dreaming toward a final word?
>     Adrienne Cecile Rich (1929-), "Readings of
>                                     History"

The foregoing sections are not intended as an essay on the history, nature and drama of the window symbol; as such they would be quite inadequate.

They are intended to offer an oversimplified model of an important aspect of symbolist poetry, a model which I believe can be put to good use in the study of post-symbolist Western literature. Rilke's novel *Malte Laurids Brigge* (1910), for instance, includes windows as meaningful as the one which follows: "O Nacht ohne Gegenstände. O stumpfes Fenster hinaus, o sorgsam verschlossene Türen; Einrichtungen von alters her, übernommen, beglaubigt, nie ganz verstanden" ["O night without objects. O obtuse window outward, o carefully closed doors; arrangements from long ago, taken over, accredited, never quite understood"].[35] The application of the model to the first section of the second part of Eliot's *The Waste Land,* "A Game of Chess," should be rewarding.[36] Italian poets who made use of the window as a symbol are, among others, Umberto Saba (1883-1957), Clemente Rebora (1885-1957), Aldo Palazzeschi (1885-?) and Dino Campara (1885-1932). One of the greatest poets of this century, the Portuguese Fernando Pessoa, seems to have been obsessed with this symbol.[37] A survey of the poetry written in other European languages should yield interesting results. I cannot resist the temptation to give here an English translation of a composition by the Greek poet Constantine Cavafy (1868-1933):

> *The Windows*
> In these dark rooms I live out empty days,
> I wander round and round
> Trying to find the windows.
> It will be a great relief when a window opens.
> But the windows aren't there to be found—
> Or at least I can't find them. And perhaps
> It's better if I don't find them.
> Perhaps the light will prove another tyranny.
> Who knows what new things it will expose?[38]

> 9
> There are no windows, so I can't see what is in
>      there.
> There is only a little grid, no exit.
>      Sylvia Plath (1932-1963), "The Arrival of the
>      Bee Box"

Hitherto I have been following the "story" of a symbol, or something as near a symbol as we are likely to find in the history of non-popular poetry. Now I turn to the heart of my "story," the presence of the window as symbol in Spanish *modernista* poetry. Of the many poets that could be considered in this section, five will suffice: Antonio Machado, Francisco Villaespesa, Juan Ramón Jiménez, José Ortiz de Pinedo and Enrique de Leguina y Juárez.[39]

The first poem of Machado's *Soledades, galerías y otros poemas* (1907) [Solitudes, Galleries and Other Poems] memorably illustrates the *modernista* use of the window symbol:

> Deshójanse las copas otoñales
> del parque mustio y viejo.
> La tarde, tras los húmedos cristales,
> se pinta, y en el fondo del espejo. ("El viajero")
> [The autumn treetops shed their leaves
> in the withered old park.
> The afternoon, behind the moist window panes,
> begins to turn red, and in the depths of the mirror.]

The two sentences of the passage come right from the heart and reveal in a flash the real genesis of the poem. They evoke the melancholy ("l'éternel ennui") of the situation and also the implicit drama between the window and the mirror. Moreover they show both symbols in intimate relation with other objects much favoured by symbolist and *modernista* poets alike: the evening, the park, the rain, the autumn leaves. Time and silence were part of Baudelaire's "chambres"; both appear at the end of Machado's poem:

> En la tristeza del hogar golpea
> el tictac del reloj. Todos callamos.[40]
> [On the sadness of the home
> knocks the tick-tock of the clock. We all keep silent.]

The amorous and unhappy character of the *modernista* "inscape" is aptly evoked by Juan Ramón Jiménez. He begins one of his poems by striking the genuine Spring-morning note of former poets:

> El sol entra en mi vida por la ventana abierta,
> de modo que el rosal se ilumina de flores;
> y las rosas de oro, en la casa desierta,
> cantan no sé qué anjélicas sonatillas de amores.
> [The sun comes into my life through the open window,
> in such a way that the rosebush lights up with flowers;
> and the golden roses, in the deserted house,
> sing unknown angelic little love-sonatas.]

From this we pass, in the poem that follows the one just quoted, to a confession of failure, already implicit in the expression "la casa desierta":

> ¡Oh soledad sonora! Mi corazón sereno
> se abre, como un tesoro, al soplo de tu brisa.
> Y esta aventura eterna de un amor sin amores . . .[41]
> [O sonorous solitude! My serene heart
> opens, like a treasure, in the gust of your breeze.
> And this eternal adventure of a loveless love . . .]

In a piece from *Poemas májicos y dolientes* (1907) [Magic and Sorrowful Poems] we find a similar wording of the experience: "Todo el campo de abril entra por mi ventana" [The whole April countryside comes in through my window]; but the heart of the poem's "I" is like "un cementerio cerrado" [a closed cemetery]. In the light of such lines we can easily understand the following poem in which Jiménez describes the bewildering experience of the man in the closed room:

> ¿Soy yo quien anda, esta noche,
> por mi cuarto, o el mendigo
> que rondaba mi jardín,
> al caer la tarde?. . .
>                    Miro
> en torno y hallo que todo
> es lo mismo y no es lo mismo . . .
> ¿La ventana estaba abierta?     (*Jardines lejanos,* 1903-04)
> [Am I the one who is walking, tonight,
> about my room, or the beggar
> who was prowling around my garden,
> at dusk?. . .

I look
around and find that everything
is the same and is not the same . . .
Was the window open?

Whether the window is open or closed, the tonality of the symbol changes little. The fusion of its multiple connotations is apparent in the work of Villaespesa, whose unhappy *persona,* torn between the window and the mirror, can only give a picture of his drama in the following "Nocturno" [Nocturne]:

La noche se desliza
por la abierta ventana.
. . . . . . . . . . . . . . . .
y en las sombras se duerme
de silencio la casa . . .
En el péndulo sueña
el tiempo.
. . . . . . . . . . . . . . . . . . . .
Se abren las temblorosas
pupilas asustadas,
mirando entre las sombras
que envuelven a la estancia,
como en una laguna
de silenciosas aguas,
temblar en los espejos
las estrellas lejanas! . . . (*Las horas que pasan,* 1909)

[Night slips in
through the open window.
. . . . . . . . . . . . . . . . . .
and in the shadows the house
falls asleep from silence . . .
In the pendulum
time dreams.
. . . . . . . . . . . . . . . . . .
The trembling,
frightened pupils open,
watching—among the shadows
that swaddle the room,
as in a lagoon
of silent waters—
tremble in the mirrors
the distant stars! . . .]

The poem's *persona* in the "laguna" is reminiscent of Rodenbach's "I" in the "aquarium" of his conscience. In another "Nocturno," Villaespesa, alone with himself in "este pobre cuarto" [this poor room], confesses his narcissism: "Yo soy el soberano de mi propio egoísmo" [I am the sovereign of my own egoism].[42]

Enrique de Leguina, in a poem entitled "Melancólicamente" [Melancholically], headed by the first line of Barbey d'Aurevilly's "La Haine du soleil" (see section 5 above), writes of the "ilusión del cristal, frente al jardín florido" [illusion of the window pane, facing the flowering garden]; but alone in the room, when "so many caresses" are mocking his weariness, he discovers the deep-seated loneliness of the idealist poet: "y miro, y la penumbra me dice: ¡soledad! . . ." (*Poemas simbólicos,* 1914) [and I look, and the penumbra tells me: solitude!]

The poems quoted are rooted in a heartfelt quest or pursuit of the objective reality of the "other." The failure of such a quest inevitably leads to the traditional alternative of all amorous poetry, that is to say, to the consideration of death, very often to a genuinely experienced death wish. In his poem "Paz" [Peace] (*Tristitiae rerum,* 1906), Villaespesa searches vainly for peace in a "cuarto pequeño y misterioso" [small, mysterious room] whose windows are closed "a piedra y lodo" [tight-shut] ; by the end of the composition "peace" is equated with "dormir eternamente" [to sleep forever]. Poetically this means no less than these lines by Machado:

> Sonaba el reloj la una,
> dentro de mi cuarto.
> . . . . . . . . . . . . . . . . .
> Por la entreabierta ventana
> llegaban a mis oídos
> metálicos alaridos
> de una música lejana.
> . . . . . . . . . . . . . . . . . . . . .
> y . . . morirse es lo mejor. (LVI)
>
> [The clock was striking one
> inside my room.
> . . . . . . . . . . . . . . . . . . . . .
> Through the half-open window
> were reaching my ears
> metallic squeals
> of a distant music.
> . . . . . . . . . . . . . . . . . . . . . . .
> and . . . to die is the best thing.]

In a composition by Ortiz de Pinedo, a grandmother meditates in "los salones/ de la casa en calma" [the rooms/ of the house in tranquillity], whose windows have lost "la visión riente/ de las dos hermanas" [the laughing vision/ of the two sisters]. This grandmother is, in fact, the self of the poem's *persona:*[43]

> Contempla los viejos
> retratos queridos
> que aún tienen reflejos
> de amores perdidos.    ("La abuela," *Dolorosas,* 1903)
>
> [She contemplates the old
> beloved portraits
> that still have reflections
> of loves lost.]

The two sisters who had disappeared from the window can be seen in another composition by the same poet:

> En un rincón de la estancia
> las dos hermanas, unidas,
> lloraban . . . Llena de encanto
> la rosa tarde moría.    ("Pena," ibid.)
>
> [In a corner of the room
> the two sisters, united,
> were crying. . . . Full of charm
> the rose afternoon was dying.]

Very often these two sisters are allegorizations of the two faces of the "other": of Woman ("ella") and of Death ("Ella"), the two mistresses of the symbolist/*modernista* poet. Both haunt the room/conscience of the poem's *persona.* Their company, always unattainable, is both desired and/or feared. At times, the intuition of their presence is obtained through the open window; other times it is felt knocking at the panes of the closed window. When the "I" of the poem is objectified as the "viajero" [traveler], no less conscious of his essential solitude for being "outside," "ella" and "Ella" appear at the window of the room of the elusive "other."

Let us see a few examples of these possibilities. It must be understood that frequently, the two sisters, instead of being introduced allegorically, are alluded to symbolically. The following fragment of a poem by Machado constitutes a clear instance of the latter technique; in it "ella" and "Ella" are suggested respectively by "perfumes de rosas" and "doblar de campanas":

> Fue una clara tarde de melancolía.
> Abril sonreía. Yo abrí las ventanas
> de mi casa al viento . . . El viento traía
> perfumes de rosas, doblar de campanas. (XLIII)

> [It was a clear afternoon of melancholy.
> April was smiling. I opened the windows
> of my house to the wind . . . The wind carried
> perfumes of roses, tolling of bells.]

The intutition of death becomes visible in a poem by Villaespesa entitled "En la sombra" [In the shade] :

> ¡Responde, misteriosa
> negra sombra encubierta,
> que tras de los cristales
> de mi ventana acechas
> a que el postrer reflejo
> de mi lámpara muera!    (*Tristitiae rerum*)

> [Answer, mysterious
> hidden black shadow,
> who, behind the panes
> of my window waits in ambush
> for the last reflection
> from my lamp to die out!]

A parallel vision is found in Leguina's poem "La voz interior" [The inner voice] . It is not difficult to know how the poet intended us to be affected by such lines as the following:

> La sombra de la muerta
> reflejóse en el cristal . . . estaba
> en las tinieblas exteriores . . . Desierta
> la calle y lóbrega la noche, era
> el eco misterioso de la "intrusa",
> esa nocturna sombra de la amada
> amiga y pasajera,
> adivinada y pálida y difusa
> y sonriendo siempre enamorada . . .    (*Poemas simbólicos*)[44]

> [The shadow of the dead woman
> was reflected in the glass . . . it was
> in the outer darkness . . . With the street
> deserted and the night gloomy, it was
> the mysterious echo of the "Intruder,"
> that nocturnal shadow of my dear

and fleeting beloved,
intuited and pale and diffuse
and smiling lovingly forever . . .]

In his poem "Eros" (*Idealismos*, 1913), Leguina has a premonition of the arrival of "ella," "con el mágico encanto de su aljaba de oro" [with the magic spell of her golden quiver] , and he exclaims: " ¡Abre bien las ventanas! [Open the windows wide!] . As Stephen Reckert has shown, Pessoa's female face behind the window is as elusive as Baudelaire's "passante": both are the "other". The *modernista* "passionate pilgrim" sees behind the window panes little more than shadows. Here are two evocative examples from the poetry of Antonio Machado:

| | |
|---|---|
| (*ella*) | ¿No ves, en el encanto del mirador florido, el óvalo rosado de un rostro conocido? (XV) |
| (*Ella*) | La tarde está cayendo frente a los caserones de la ancha plaza en sueños. Relucen las vidrieras con ecos mortecinos de sol. En los balcones hay formas que parecen confusas calaveras. (XCIV) |
| [(she) | Don't you see, in the charm of the flowery bay window the rose-colored oval of a familiar face? |
| (She) | Evening is falling in front of the big houses on the broad, dreaming plaza. Their window panes shine with dying echoes of the sun. On their balconies are forms which seem to be confused skulls.] |

My final examples, which I give without commentary, are taken from works by Jiménez, Villaespesa and Ortiz de Pinedo, respectively:

En los balcones, a las altas horas, siguen
blancas mujeres mudas, que parecen fantasmas.   (*Laberinto*)
[On the balconies, in the late hours, there are still
white mute women, who seem ghosts.]

"¿en dónde estás . . .? ¿En qué país lejano
aún esperas mi amor a tu ventana?"
. . . . . . . . . . . . . . . . . . . . . . . . . . . .
       —No llores por tu hermana . . .
Nunca existió, ni existirá ni existe . . .
Fue tan sólo un ensueño de tu alma.   (*Tristitiae rerum*)
["Where are you . . .? In what distant land
do you still wait for my love at your window?"
. . . . . . . . . . . . . . . . . . . . . . . . . . . .
       "Don't weep for your sister . . .
She never existed, nor will she exist nor does she exist . . .
She was only a daydream of your soul."]

Se abre una ventana silenciosamente:
poco a poco un rostro se asoma por ella;
. . . . . . . . . . . . . . . . . . . . . . . . . . . .
       La carita blanca, blanca y sonriente,
desapareciendo brilla en la negrura . . .
La ventana luego silenciosamente
se cierra . . . Una estrella se apaga en la altura.   (*Dolorosas*)
       A window opens silently:
little by little a face peers out through it;
. . . . . . . . . . . . . . . . . . . . . . . . . . . .
       The little white face, white and smiling,

> while disappearing shines in the blackness . . .
> The window then silently
> closes . . . A star goes out in the heavens.]

The exploration I have undertaken has been selective; what emerges from it is hardly more than an outline of some of the features that characterize the symbolism of the window. As literary criticism, my essay has little value. Only a detailed examination of the way in which each poet makes use of the symbols, followed by a comparison of their respective achievements, would yield a valid basis on which to judge the merits or demerits of those achievements. Nevertheless, I have provided a starting point for future investigations by documenting the existence of the particular symbolic objects and situations which revolve around the window in symbolist/*modernista* poetry.

### 10

> The etymology of "window"
> very quickly becomes an emotional threat—
> we bang our heads against the mirror as if
> it were us who turned the current,
> as if we didn't anyway have a yearly increasing
> price to pay for keeping warm indoors.
> Peter Riley (1940-), "The Quarters"

"Influence" is perhaps too strong a word for the relation which exists between the French symbolist movement and twentieth-century Western poetry. And yet it can hardly be denied that the contemporary poet is still exploring some of the territories of emotional experience mapped out by his nineteenth-century predecessors. I have tried to explain the legacy which those writers bequeathed to our own epoch. It has not been my purpose to follow in detail the history of that legacy, but rather to provide some understanding of the roots—understanding necessary for appreciating at least one major branch of the rich symbolist tree. I can add, perhaps gratuitously, that even if a symbol derived from man-made objects cannot always retain all its original numinosity or "spell," the symbolism of the window has lost little of its peculiar energy at the hands of twentieth-century poets. Apollinaire and Eluard wrote poems bearing the titles of, respectively, "Les Fenêtres" (1913) [Windows] and "A la fenêtre" (1925) [At the Window] which are in the tradition I have outlined.[45] The quotations heading the sections of my essay show the uninterrupted presence of the window symbol in the poetry of the English-speaking world. The window is an integral part of the poetry of Pedro Salinas, Jorge Guillén, Federico García Lorca, Rafael Alberti, Luis Cernuda and Vicente Aleixandre, to mention only some of the main poets of Spain's Generation of 1927. Quite obviously, the symbol lost some of its importance in Spain during the period 1940-1965, which was dominated by the prosaic verse of the so-called "social poets." But it is still with us. The latest example I am aware of is the following composition by Angel Guinda, a young Spanish poet (b.1948) of—perhaps paradoxically—Marxist tendencies:

> *Ventana*
> Zona de vidrio. Fisura
> fragilísima que avisa

los volúmenes; la altura
del sol, del árbol; la prisa
del viento; la inclinación
del ave; la consunción
del tumulto callejero.
Piel que la lluvia acaricia.
Testigo de mi avaricia
de asomarme al mundo entero.   (*Entre el amor y el odio*, 1977)

[*Window*          [*Window*
Zone of glass. Fissure
so very fragile that informs about
volumes; the height
of the sun, of the tree; the haste
of the wind; the glide
of the bird; the consumption
of the tumult in the streets.
Skin that rain caresses.
Witness to my avarice
to look out onto the whole world.]

No man can invent symbols. Windows don't happen. We cannot assign meanings to a window. And yet the window, as I have tried to show, has become an important structural feature in the edifice of modern Western poetry.

*University of Wales, Cardiff*


# NOTES

The translations of quotations from foreign languages throughout this essay have been added by the editors.

[1] "Approaching the Unconscious," in C. G. Jung et al., *Man and His Symbols* (London: Aldus Books, 1964), p. 55. D. H. Lawrence had put the same idea thusly: "No man can invent symbols" ("The Dragon of the Apocalypse," 1930, in D. H. Lawrence, *Selected Literary Criticism,* ed. Anthony Beal [London: W. Heinemann, 1955] p. 158). Further references to this last source will appear in the text.

[2] In the third century A.D. the Romans produced the first window panes, but the glazing of windows did not become widespread over Europe until approximately the sixteenth century.

[3] Perhaps the first modern poet who used the window, charging it with sentimental connotations, was Leopardi (1798-1837). See for instance his poem "Le Ricordanze" (1829) [The Remembrances], "Ispirato da un ritorno alla casa paterna dopo una lunga assenza e dall'onda dei ricordi che questo gli ha suscitato" [Inspired by a return to the paternal home after a long absence and by the wave of memories that this has provoked in him] (Giacomo Leopardi, *Opere,* I, ed. Sergio Solmi [Milan: R. Ricciardi, 1956] p. 56, note). The revisiting of the paternal home seems to have been a frequent experience of symbolist poets. See, among other relevant instances, Georges Rodenbach, "La Maison paternelle," *La Jeunesse blanche* (1886) [White Youth], Henri de Régnier, "Le Seuil" [The Threshold] and "La Gardienne" [The Guardian-Lady], *Tel qu'un songe* (1892) [Like a Dream], and Charles Guérin, "C'était un soir au coucher du soleil" [It was another evening at sunset], *Le Semeur de cendres* (1901) [The Sower of Ashes]. Antonio Machado's poem VII of *Soledades* (1907) [Solitudes] was first published under the title of "El poeta visita el patio de la casa en que nació" [The poet visits the patio of the house in which he was born]. Enrique de Leguina wrote a poem entitled "La casa solariega" [The ancestral home], *Idealismos* (1913) [Idealisms].

[4] Answer to Jules Huret's *Enquête sur l'évolution littéraire* (1891). In Stéphane Mallarmé, *Oeuvres complètes,* ed. Henri Mondor et G. Jean-Aubry, Bibliothèque de la Pléiade (Paris: Gallimard, 1965), the expression "du bonheur" is omitted (p. 869).

[5] C. G. Jung, *Symbols of Transformation* (vol. V of his English *Collected Works*), trans. R. F. C. Hull (London: Routledge and Paul, 1956), p. 222.

[6] *Paysages introspectifs. Avec un Essai sur le symbolisme* (Paris, n.p., 1911), p. XLIX.

[7] See Jean-Baptiste Landriot, *Le Symbolisme* (Paris: V. Palme, 1886), Ferdinand Brunetière, *L'Evolution de la poésie lyrique en France au XIX$^e$ siècle* (Paris: Hachette, 1894), and Tancrède de Visan, op. cit. and *L'Attitude du Lyrisme contemporain* (Paris, n.p., 1911).

[8] Juan Eduardo Cirlot, *A Dictionary of Symbols*, trans. Jack Sage (London: Routledge and Paul, 1962), from the article "Room," p. 262.

[9] Henri Bergson, *Essai sur les données immediates de la conscience* (1889), in *Oeuvres* (Paris: Presses Universitaires de France, 1959), p. 90. The following is a very apt definition of symbolism, to be understood in conjunction with Bergson's own branch of idealism: "Le symbolisme est l'affirmation d'une analogie essentielle entre un moment de la durée du moi et un moment de la durée des choses" [Symbolism is the affirmation of an essential analogy between a moment of the duration of the self and a moment of the duration of things] (Georges Bonneau, *Le Symbolisme dans la poésie française contemporaine* [Paris: Boivin, 1930] p. 84).

[10] As a symbol the mirror "is the instrument of self-contemplation as well as the reflection of the universe. This links mirror-symbolism with water as a reflector and with the Narcissus myth . . ." (Cirlot, "Mirror," p. 201). The door should be taken as forming part of the model: "A feminine symbol which, notwithstanding, contains all the implications of the symbolic hole, since it is the door which gives access to the hole; its significance is therefore the antithesis of the wall. . . ." (Cirlot, "Door," p. 81). See also the articles "Hole," pp. 142-43, and "Wall," p. 343.

[11] Antonio Machado, *Juan de Mairena*, in *Obras. Poesía y prosa.*, ed. Aurora de Albornoz y Guillermo de Torre (Buenos Aires: Losada, 1964), p. 478. All page references for Machado are to this edition and henceforth will be given in the text wherever possible.

[12] "Proyecto de discurso de ingreso en la Academia de La Lengua," p. 856. See my article, "Don Juan. A la manera de Juan de Mairena y Abel Martín," in *Cuadernos Hispanoamericanos* (forthcoming).

[13] Gabriel Miró, "De los balcones y portales," *Libro de Sigüenza* (1903; rpt. Buenos Aires: Losada, 5th ed., 1957), p. 126.

[14] André Gide, *Romans, Récits et Soties; Oeuvres Lyriques,* introduction par Maurice Nadeau, ed. Yvonne Davet et Jean-Jacques Thierry, Bibliothèque de la Pléiade (Paris: Gallimard, 1969), p. 10. All page references for Gide are to this edition.

[15] I suggest that, when writing *Paludes,* Gide probably had in mind the work of poets like Maurice Maeterlinck and, above all, Rodenbach. See the section of Rodenbach's *Les Vies encloses* (1896) entitled "Aquarium mental."

[16] Remy de Gourmont, "Dernière Conséquence de l'idéalisme" (1894) [Final Consequence of Idealism], in *La Culture des idées* (Paris: Mercure de France, 1916). Further page references to this edition will appear in the text. According to Gourmont, idealism "est une conception philosophique du monde. Schopenhauer, qui ne l'a pas inventé, en a donné la meillure formule: le monde est ma représentation, c'est-à-dire le monde est tel qu'il me paraît; s'il a une existence en soi, réelle, elle m'est inaccessible. . . . La formule de Schopenhauer brave toute critique. Elle est irréfutable" [is a philosophical conception of the world. Schopenhauer, who did not invent it, gave the best formulation of it: the world is my representation, which is to say, the world is such as it seems to me; if it has an existence in itself, a real one, this existence is inaccessible to me. . . . Schopenhauer's phrase defies all criticism. It is irrefutable] ("Les Racines de l'idéalisme," 1904, in *Promenades philosophiques* [Paris: Mercure de France, 1913], p. 80. Obviously, the "other" of my model forms part of Gourmont's "monde" and consequently is also inaccessible.

[17] See also Machado's letter to Miguel de Unamuno (pp. 922-25).

[18] Compare Antonio Machado: "Y esta esperanza vana/de romper el encanto del espejo" (p. 219) [And this vain hope/ of breaking the spell of the mirror].

[19] CLXI, "Proverbios y cantares," xl, p. 259. See also "Don Nadie en la Corte," pp. 379-80.

[20] Arthur Symons, *The Symbolist Movement in Literature* (London, 1899; rpt. New York: Dutton, 1958), p. 5.

[21] Georges Rodenbach, *Bruges la morte* (Paris: Flammarion, n.d. [1896?]), p. 1. Also: "il appuya son front brûlant aux vitres, fraîcheur d'eau où délayer tout sa peine" (p. 252) [he pressed his burning forehead to the window panes, coolness of water in which to dilute all his sorrow].

[22] Azorín (José Martínez Ruiz), "Una ciudad y un balcón" [A City and A Balcony], *Castilla* (Buenos Aires: Losada, 4th ed., 1952), p. 61. This portrait is the first of three parallel ones in this long lyrical sketch (pp. 61, 64, 67) which present a sad-eyed man seated on a balcony, contemplating. The piece concludes by explicitly linking these melancholy meditators to Garcilaso de la Vega's famous phrase "No me podrán quitar el dolorido/ sentir, . . ." [They shall not be able to deprive me of my feeling of grief] which serves as its epigraph and thus emphasizing the "insondable eternidad de dolor" (p. 67) [unfathomable eternity of grief]: although mankind's progress will surely be wondrous, nevertheless "Junto a un balcón, en una cuidad, en una casa, siempre habrá un hombre con la cabeza, meditadora y triste, reclinada en la mano. No le podrán quitar el dolorido sentir" (pp. 67-68) [Beside a balcony, in a city, in a house, there will always be a man with his head, meditative and sad, leaning on his hand. They'll never be able to take away his feeling of grief].

[23] In *Segunda antolojía poética* (1898-1918), Colección Austral (Madrid: Espasa-Calpe, 1969), pp. 130-31. Further references are to this work and will be given in the text.

[24] The plasticity of the "unconscious image" should be evident to any one familiar with Jung's works. Of course, this does not mean that all descriptive poems must of necessity be symbolic. See Aniela Jaffé, "Symbolism in the Visual Arts," in *Man and His Symbols,* pp. 230-71.

[25] Respectively published in *La Presse* (1862) and *Revue nationale* (1863), later in *Le Spleen de Paris* (1869). Quotations from these poems refer to the Pléiade edition of Baudelaire's complete works: *Oeuvres complètes,* ed. Y.-G. le Dantec et Claude Pichois (Paris: Gallimard, 1966), pp. 233-35 and 288.

[26] Recall that Maeterlinck published his famous book of poems *Serres chaudes* [Hothouses] in 1889.

[27] In the light of this composition I am inclined to believe that the poems "Un jour de pluie" (pp. 214-15) [A Rainy Day] and "Je me disais: Pourquoi son front est-il si pâle?" (p. 218) [I was saying to myself: Why is his forehead so pale?] have been wrongly attributed to Baudelaire.

[28] See Régnier's introduction to *Les Fleurs du mal*, ed. La Renaissance du livre (Paris, 1919).

[29] In my opinion, Mallarmé's "Les Fenêtres" (dated "London, May 1863" but published in 1866 in *Le Parnasse contemporain*) had no really meaningful part in the invention of the symbol. For him the window is little else than an emblematic image of the work of art. My contention is that the poetry of Mallarmé does not include true symbols, but analogies, "selon la formule de la comparaison parnassiene" [according to the formula of the Parnassian comparison]. See Albert Thibaudet, *La poésie de Stéphane Mallarmé* (Paris: Gallimard, 1926), pp. 37-49, 92-96, 218-37; A. R. Chisholm, *Mallarmé's "Grande Oeuvre"* (Manchester, Eng.: Manchester University Press, 1962), pp. 122-29; Robert Greer Cohn, "Mallarmé's Windows," *Yale French Studies*, 54 (1977), 23-31. Adolphe Racot wrote that "Mallarmé peut résumer le type du Parnassien a sa dernière puissance" [Mallarmé can sum up the type of the Parnassian to the *n*th power] (In *Petits memoires d'un Parnassien* par Louis Zavier de Ricard. *Les Parnassiens* par Adolphe Racot, ed. M. Pakenham [Paris: Minard, 1967]). Yet it would be an error to attribute the spreading of the image entirely to the influence of Baudelaire's poems. Mallarmé's "Les Fenêtres," too, helped, by means of its anecdotal first part (the doomed patient at the windows of the "triste hôpital" [dreary hospital] rather than through the aesthetic narcissism of its second part ("Que la vitre soit l'art" [Let the glass be art]).

[30] The importance of Rodenbach has been ignored by the modern critic, though it is a well established fact that Rilke admired his work. I suggest that he exerted some influence on Valéry (*Le Cimetière marin*), and perhaps on T. S. Eliot. The "fog that rubs its back upon the window-panes" in "The Love Song of J. Alfred Prufrock" has clear affinities with "Le brouillard indolent" [The lazy fog] that "se déplie et se replie" [unfurls and folds up again] and "dort comme du linge sur les remparts" [sleeps like a

piece of laundry on the ramparts] of the poem "Les Femmes en mante" [The women wearing mantles], XII, *Le Miroir du ciel natal* (1898).

[31] For Adolphe van Bever and Paul Léautaud, Régnier was "Le premier et le plus célèbre des 'poètes d'aujourd'hui' " [The leading and the most celebrated of the "poets of today"] (*Poètes d'Aujourd'hui. Morceaux choisis.*, vol. II [Paris: Mercure de France, 1917], p. 113). See Paul Fort, *Mes Memoires: toute la vie d'un poète, 1872-1943* (Paris: Flammarion, 1944), p. 154. If we trust present-day panegyrics of the symbolist movement we should be misled to believe that Baudelaire, Rimbaud, Mallarmé, Verlaine and Valéry were its chief poets.

[32] See especially the references to windows and mirrors in the following poems: "Scènes au crépuscule" [Twilight scenes], IV, *Poèmes anciens et romanesques* (1890); "Le Seuil" [The Threshold], *Tel qu'un songe* (1892); "Reveil" [Awakening], *Les Medailles d'argile* (1900); "Un homme parle" [A man is speaking] and "L'Adieu" [The Goodbye], *Vestigia flammae* (1921).

[33] Remy de Gourmont, "Charles Guérin" (1898), in *Promenades littéraires* (Paris: Mercure de France, 1929), p. 236. All further quotations from Gourmont will refer to this work and this edition.

[34] Compare with these lines by Antonio Machado: "Con negra llave el aposento frío/ de su tiempo abrirá. ¡Desierta cama/ y turbio espejo y corazón vacío" (CLXV, v, *Nuevas canciones*, p. 290) [With black key the cold room/ of his time he shall open. Deserted bed/ and cloudy mirror and empty heart!].

[35] Rainer Maria Rilke, *Die Aufzeichnungen des Malte Laurids Brigge* (Frankfurt am Main: Insel Verlag, 1910, rpt. 1973), pp. 72-73. The English translation here is from Rilke, *The Notebooks of Malte Laurids Brigge,* trans. M. D. Herter Norton (New York: W. W. Norton and Co., 1964), p. 69.

[36] In fact, if the model is extended to the author's reference, in his notes to 1. 412 of "What the Thunder Said," to Dante's Count Hugolino (*Inferno, XXXIII, 46*), then Eliot's quotation of F.H. Bradley (about the inevitable privacy of each ego's experience) becomes almost redundant. See Remy de Gourmont's "Interpretation" of Dante's passage, in "Dernière Conséquence de l'idéalisme," p. 267, note. Did Eliot know Gourmont's essay?

[37] See Stephen Reckert's important essay, "Fortuna e metamorfosi di un 'topos' nella poesia di Pessoa," in *Quaderni portoghesi* (Spring 1977), pp. 55-94. The topos examined by Reckert is one derived from Baudelaire's poem "La Passante" [The Lady Passer-by]; yet by now we should not be surprised by the close relationship found by the critic between "la passante" and the window as a symbol. "Questa finestra o porta vetrata," writes Reckert, "diventera nella poesia di Pessoa, un simbolo costante dell'isolamento dell'uomo, non solo dal mondo exteriore ..., ma anche, in esso, da quello interiore degli 'altri' " (p. 66) [This window or glass door will become in the poetry of Pessoa a constant symbol of the isolation of man, not only from the external world ... but also, within it, from that interior world of others]. Curiously, though, the mirror does not seem to form part of Pessoa's symbolic world.

[38] C. P. Cavafy, *Collected Poems,* trans. Edmund Keeley and Philip Sherrard, ed. George Savidis (Princeton: Princeton University Press, 1975), pp. 24-25. I am grateful to Professor Reckert for his kindness in sending me this text. I also wish to thank Dr. S. Gamberini for having rendered me a similar service regarding the Italian poets mentioned in this essay.

[39] Though I have already studied at some length the symbolism of Antonio Machado (see my book *Antonio Machado, poeta simbolista* [Madrid: Taurus, 1973]), I cannot avoid reference to his poetry in this essay. I have chosen to include obscure or unknown poets like Ortiz de Pinedo and Leguina precisely because they are obscure and unknown, and their poems are wholly relevant to my intentions.

[40] For the possible influence of Baudelaire on Machado, see Bernard Sesé, "Résonance baudelairienne dans la poésie d'Antonio Machado," in *Les Langues néo-latines,* No. 203 (1972), pp. 37-44.

[41] "Elejías puras" (*1* and *2*), *Elejías* (Madrid: Revista de Archivos, 1908), p. 75.

[42] In *Poesías escogidas* (Madrid, n.p. [Biblioteca universal?], 1917), p. 51.

[43] We must not forget that for Rodenbach "Les chambres sont de bons vieillards/ Et sont aussi de bonnes aïeules" [Rooms truly are good old folks/ And they are also good grandmothers]. See section 7 above.

[44] The "Intrusa" in this poem is a direct reference to Maeterlinck's play *L'Intruse* (1891)[The Intruder]. Something similar appears in Villaespesa's "Canción nocturna" [Night Song] (*Tristitiae rerum*): "De la Intrusa las manos temblorosas/ no hilaron tu sudario todavía" [The Intruder's trembling hands/ have not yet spun your shroud].

[45] It is opportune to quote part of what P. Emmanuel had to say about Eluard's poem: "Comme toujours dans cette poésie, le Je déborde infiniment le moi. Quand le second déserte le premier, il souffre, et se débat en aveugle dans la nuit (nuit de la vie sociale, nuit des rêves). Quand il se réintègre, il devient principe de vie, règle du monde: ce n'est pas lui qui vit, c'est le Je sans bornes qui vit en lui" [As always in this poetry, the "I" infinitely overflows the self. When the latter deserts the former, it suffers, and it struggles like a blind man in the night (night of social life, night of dreams). When it is reintegrated, it becomes a principle of life: it does not live itself, but rather the unlimited "I" lives in it] (Paul Eluard, *Oeuvres complètes,* vol. I, ed. Marcelle Dumas et Lucien Scheler, Bibliothèque de la Pléiade [Paris: Gallimard, 1968], p. 1395). The Bergsonian terminology of these statements is most revealing.

*Una Ventana* by F. Martín. Reproduced from *Revista Moderna,* 2, No. 10 (Oct. 1899), 311.

# The Impact of Symbolism in Portugal and Brazil

## Raymond S. Sayers

If during the nineteenth century the influence of French culture was paramount throughout the western world, in no country was it stronger than in Portugal and Brazil, where the intellectual and social elites prized themselves on their knowledge of French literature and their fluency in the French language. All Portuguese and Brazilian artists and writers who could do so flocked to Paris to join colonies of their compatriots, and the Portuguese poet Mário de Sá-Carneiro, who was among those who lived and died there, called Paris the capital of the Latin world. This situation continued through the beginning of this century and after the period of the First World War, and even those who could not get to Paris were often more familiar with recent French literature than with their own. French culture has never been more truly international than in those years in which symbolism was taking the world by storm. Verlaine, Mallarmé, Maeterlinck and Claudel found their equals in Yeats, Eliot, Synge, George and D'Annunzio, and in poetry, at least, among Portuguese and Brazilians of genius.

The Portuguese and Brazilians had, of course, read Baudelaire and Poe. Long before the name symbolism had been invented they were familiar with the *Parnasse contemporain,* which had published the work of two future leaders of the Symbolist movement, Mallarmé and Verlaine, and they knew Remy de Gourmont and other critics of symbolism. They absorbed the basic tenets: the idea of the independence and superior truth of poetry and the right of the artist to live according to his own desires, free from the restraints of society. In this second respect they were like the romantics, but they differed from them in that, while they wanted to withdraw, the romantics were eager to participate in the life of their country and world. Even the greatest Brazilian symbolist, João Cruz e Sousa, wrote his powerful pages of social criticism against racial discrimination not so much because of an intellectual conviction that society must be reformed, but because as an Afro-Brazilian, the son of slaves and a black writer without any trace of European ancestry, he realized that he himself could never be accepted and understood by a society that believed in white superiority, by a society that attributed the talent of mulatto writers like Machado de Assis to the white blood that flowed in their veins. In the case of Cruz e Sousa, it was not he who rejected society but society that rejected him.

The poets of Brazil and Portugal took avidly to the doctrines adopted by Baudelaire and his followers: the theory of *correspondances,* the value of the metaphor as a vehicle for extending the realms of human thought and emotion, the power of the music of words to deepen the poet's meaning in his lyrics, the contemplation of the beauty of organic corruption and decay, the beauty of ecclesiastical imagery and language, Satanism, and the importance of the world of dreams and of the subconscious as worthy subjects of poetry. Some sought inspiration in the occult sciences, Rosicrucianism, theosophy and other Oriental religions and philosophy. They turned resolutely away from the Parnassians, whom some had first accepted as their masters, for they wanted fluidity and freedom rather than sculptural rigidity. Although not all Brazilian and Portuguese symbolists paid homage to all these points of doctrine, all seem to have accepted the need for a new literary aesthetic; and, following the example of Baudelaire, many wrote about literary theory in magazine articles and the prefaces to volumes of their poetry. There were few who were not deeply pessimistic.

Because of Portugal's geographic position, it was not very difficult for writers to travel to Paris and many did so, sometimes to study at the Sorbonne, sometimes to drink in inspiration from the atmosphere of the wonderful city. Among them were António Nobre (1867-1900), who was an important precursor of symbolism and one of the finest Portuguese poets of the time, Dom João de Castro (1871-1955), whose *Alma Póstuma* (1891) helped to shape the style of Portuguese symbolism, and Eugénio de Castro (1869-1944), the guiding spirit of its early phase. Rio de Janeiro was three or four times further away from Paris than Lisbon, and few Brazilian poets were able to reach the French capital; yet some poets and novelists who entered the diplomatic corps were able to do so, notably Magalhães de Azeredo (1872-1963), a poet and prose writer and friend of Machado de Assis, Domício da Gama (1862-1925), who was a friend of both Machado and Eça de Queiroz and a short story writer, and the much more famous Graça Aranha (1868-1931), whose interest in symbolism is seen in his novel *Canaã* (1902) and his play *Malazarte* (1911) and who was also the friend of Machado de Assis.

Symbolism made its appearance in Brazil before it got to Portugal. A prominent critic of the end of the century, Araripe Júnior (1848-1911), writes that as early as 1887 Medeiros e Albuquerque (1867-1934), a poet and novelist, was receiving from a friend in Paris the works of such French Symbolists as Mallarmé, Ghil, Stuart Merrill and Jean Moréas, and the literary reviews in which Viélé-Griffin and others of the school were being published. Araripe shared his new books and articles with Gama Rosa (1852-1918), a critic and sociologist who had become interested in and wrote on symbolism, which Araripe called *decadismo*.[1] The poems that Medeiros e Albuquerque wrote in the new manner in 1887 were collected into a volume, *Canções da Decadência,* which was published in 1889, the same year as his second symbolist collection, *Pecados* [Sins]. Although Araripe was too discerning a critic to be enthusiastic about the poetry of Medeiros e Albuquerque, a less than second rate poet, he studied it and indicated its *decadence* and pointed out the influence of René Ghil's *Traité du verbe*. An example of the poet's symbolism may be seen in his poem "Proclamação Decadente." It begins with an epigraph which is his declaration of allegiance to the new movement:

> Carta escrita por um poeta
> a 20 de Floréal,
> sendo Verlaine profeta
> e Mallarmé—deus real.
>
> [A letter written by a poet
> the 20th day of Floréal:
> Verlaine is the prophet,
> Mallarmé the true god.]

The "Proclamação," which is written in lines with an odd number of syllables as Verlaine recommended, states that the idea of the poem can only be expressed by music of an uncertain, indecisive tone, and declares the supremacy of form over idea: "Que importa a Idéia, contanto/ que vibre a Forma sonora . . .?" [What matters the Idea/ as long as Form vibrates sonorous?]

Meanwhile, by 1889 symbolism was sweeping into Portugal from Paris. In that year a new, short-lived magazine called *Boémia Nova* made its appearance in the university of Coimbra, which for a while was to be the Portuguese center of the movement. It contained poems by António Nobre and his friend Alberto de Oliveira (1873-1940), whose *Poesias* (1891) was one of the first books to reflect the new doctrines, and an essay by Alberto Osório de Castro (1868-1946), the friend of the greatest symbolist, Camilo Pessanha (1867-1926), in which he spoke of the need to study the new literature of France from Baudelaire to Mallarmé so that Portuguese literature might take on new vigor and a new spirit. In 1889 also there appeared another literary review, *Os Insubmissos* [The Unbowed], which is more completely committed to symbolism and in which Eugénio de Castro began his new career as a symbolist and the Portuguese leader of the movement—a position which he assumed on his return from Paris where he had been overwhelmed by the movement, and in which he was aided by the intellectual position of his family and his considerable wealth.

Castro's first symbolist collection, published in 1890, was *Oaristos* or "conversations," a word he had found in Verlaine. Verlaine, though not the greatest poet connected with the movement, was the most popular in both Portugal and Brazil, a subject that is studied by Maria de Lourdes Belchior Pontes in an article entitled "Verlaine e o Simbolismo em Portugal."[2] Before the decade had elapsed, Eugénio de Castro had lost his enthusiasm for the movement and had abandoned it, but before doing so he had published other symbolist volumes—*Horas* (1891), *Interlúnio* (1894) and the play *Belkiss* (1894), which could hardly have been written if Wilde had not written his *Salomé* (1893). Later, the poet followed the example of Jean Moréas and wrote in a more classical, chastened vein. *Oaristos* begins with a preface which struck his fellow poets as novel and daring although it had already been preceded by similar manifestos by French symbolists. In it he defends the use of neologisms on the ground that words have a beauty of their own and says that the art of *decadence* (symbolism) is the result of research that can push back the frontiers of language. At the end he says that his book was conceived "far from the barbarians and with the proud disdain of a *nefelibata* or cloud watcher." Unamuno must have come across this preface, for in an essay he wrote on the poet in 1907, he expresses the belief that the word was first used in Portuguese by the Portuguese scholar and poet, Teófilo Braga, an attribution denied by Castro, who claims the credit for having enriched Portuguese with it, saying that he had found it in Plowert's *Glossaire*.[3] It may be mentioned here that Castro was known in other lands, that his poems had been translated into French, Italian and other languages, and of course all students of Rubén Darío are familiar with the essay on Castro in *Los raros.*

Castro made many technical innovations such as writing alexandrines without fixed caesuras and with alternating rhymes and using alliteration as a basic poetic resource. He freshened the metaphor with new vitality and strained for greater originality in its use with effects that at times were appealing, as when he speaks of "O sol esfarrapando o incenso dos espaços" [The sun, tearing to tatters the incense of space], in the first poem, but which may also be unpleasantly surprising, like one from the second poem, "A sua boca é um sorvete de morangos" [Her mouth is a strawberry sherbet]. Physical decay is the subject of many poems, as for example "Podridão" [Putrefaction] from *Interlúnio* and "Tísicos" from *Oaristos,* in which he speaks of a tubercular person spitting "Poppies on the pure snow." He is often irreverent or even blasphemous, as in his parody on the *Ave Maria.* Still he is to be admired for his great technical prowess, which is evident in the alliteration and the free caesuras of the alexandrines of the eleventh poem of *Oaristos*:

> Na messe, que enlourece, estremece a quermesse . . .
> O sol, o celestial girassol, esmorece . . .
> E as cantilenas de serenos sons amenos
> Fogem fluidas, fluindo à fina flor dos fenos . . .

In a lame attempt to keep alliteration and rhyme, this may be rendered:

> In the golden gleaming wheatfield, a carnival's begun
> With the fading of heaven's flower, the setting of the sun,
> And songs sounding sweet, subtle and serene,
> Flee flowing to fair flowers of grasses gleaming green.

Before giving symbolism up, he gave it more support, not the least of which was the founding of *Arte: Revista Internacional* with his friend Manuel da Silva Gaio. The journal lasted only from November 1895 to June 1896, but during that time it presented the whole world of symbolism to its public. It printed contributions in Portuguese, French, German and English and translations from other languages, and in its pages appeared a host of writers: Verlaine, Gustave Kahn, Stuart Merrill, Pierre Louÿs, Laurence Binyon, Arthur Symons, and others. Castro was a great propagandist for the movement, and he showed the Portuguese to what extent they could enrich their literature by embarking on technical adventures and testing the possibilities of subject matter that till then had been eschewed. He was the master of the opulent, musical style and the decorative metaphor.

It remained for others to develop possibilities of symbolism of which Castro had been aware but which he did not pursue; from the preface to *Oaristos* and its long quotation from Gautier it becomes evident that he knew that the world of dreams and the subconscious could be explored through symbols and expressed through metaphors so as to present a little-known aspect of man's existence, to enlarge the world of communication and to express what had never before been said. Castro's influence was great and even affected older poets, one of whom, Guerra Junqueiro (1850-1923), was the most popular of his time. Yet António Nobre, who is usually not considered a symbolist, seems closer to what the greater symbolists were trying to do: to probe the mystery of man's psyche and fathom the melancholy of his existence, using the tools of synesthesia, unusual images, music, and, less frequently, personal symbols. In his poetry he returns to his childhood and recalls fairy tales, visions and legends that belong to a vanished part of his existence. So he says in "Cantai" [Sing] from his volume *Só* [Alone] (1892):

> Cantai! cantai as límpidas cantigas!
> Das ruínas do meu Lar desaterrai
> Tôdas aquelas ilusões antigas
> Que eu vi morrer num sonho, como um ai.
> [Sing! sing the limpid ballads!
> Search in the ruins of my lost home
> For all those old illusions
> That died in dreams, in sighs.]

There are critics who would limit the number of true symbolists among the Portuguese poets to three or four, and the late Jorge de Sena, one of the great modern poets and critics, accepts only Camilo Pessanha.[4] However, most people say that there are more symbolists than one; there are Mário de Sá-Carneiro (1890-1916) and Fernando Pessoa (1888-1935), at least in his early phases, António Patrício (1878-1930), Roberto de Mesquita (1871-1923) and his brother Carlos (1870-1916), Augusto Gil (1873-1929), and some others including a few who have been mentioned in this article. There is no question about Jorge de Sena's authority, but not all will agree with his definition of symbolism, which excluded even Jean Moréas, a coryphaeus of the movement in France, Gustave Kahn, René Ghil and other similar French poets. For Jorge de Sena symbolism was much more than a question of verbal novelty, new metrical techniques or decorative metaphors. Nor was it a question of the use of novel subject matter or imagery, as in António Nobre's famous lines about the beggars in a church procession in "Lusitânia no Bairro Latino" [Portugal in the Latin Quarter]:

> E êsses, acolá, todo o corpinho numa chaga,
> Labareda de cancros em fogueira,
> Que o sol atiça e que a gangrena apaga.
> [And those over there, their bodies one festering sore,
> A flame of cankers in a bonfire
> Kindled by the sun, soothed by gangrene.]

Sena did not accept Augusto Gil's sentimental symbolism, so Verlainean in manner, in the poem "Luar de Janeiro" [January Moonlight] (from the volume of the same title published in 1910). However, the true note seems to exist in the verse of Patrício and the Mesquitas, a note that is struck in the last tercet of Roberto Mesquita's "Almas Penadas" [Wandering Souls] from *Almas Cativas*:

> Oh! tenho mêdo do meu íntimo onde tendes
> Habitação, velhos avós, onde elevais
> A voz misteriosa de duendes!

[Ah, I fear my inner self, in which you have
Your dwelling, ancient forebears, in which you speak
In mysterious spirit verses.]

Roberto de Mesquita spent all his life as a civil servant in his native Azores, and that existence on the tiny islands of the archipelago must have been at the root of the melancholy, vague longings and nostalgia of his verse. His brother, on the other hand, spent the larger part of his life in Coimbra, where he was a professor of French and English literature and where he distinguished himself as the foremost contemporary critic of symbolism. Patrício was a diplomat and he traveled widely. His symbolism infuses his dramas and his short stories as well as his poetry, especially in the posthumous collection *Poesias* (1942), which is largely pantheistic in philosophy.

Camilo Pessanha's life, like his verse, falls well within the tradition for symbolist poets. The illegitimate son of a Coimbra law student and his housekeeper (Camilo was legitimized in his adolescence), he studied law at the University when Eugénio de Castro and António Nobre were there, though he does not seem to have been the friend of either. Like his friend Alberto Osório de Castro, his associate Wenceslau de Morais, and the Brazilian diplomat, Oliveira Lima, he was sent by his government to the Orient; and, after being assigned to a teaching position in the lycée in Macau, he made that small Chinese peninsula his home. There he succumbed completely to the spell of Chinese life: he studied Chinese civilization, became an opium addict, and lived with a Chinese mistress who bore him a son. In spite of his official position as a teacher and as a Portuguese civil servant, he lived in a state of schizophrenic squalor of which he seems to have been unaware, imagining and composing his lyrics (he composed them completely before writing them) in what one critic calls a state of "hiperlucidez, lucidez não da inteligência, mas dó instinto, que lhe proporcionava o uso habitual do ópio"[5] [hyperlucidity, a lucidity that was not mental but instinctive and came from his habitual use of opium]. However, he was not only an inspired but also a careful artist who constantly revised his poems, some of which exist in several versions. He had studied Chinese literature and translated Chinese poems, and he must have learned much of his symbolism through that preparation. All his poetry is contained in a small volume, *Clepsidra* (1920), the title of which recalls Baudelaire's "Le gouffre a toujours soif; la clepsidre se vide" [The abyss is always thirsty; the clepsydra empties]. His lyrics, which include many sonnets, present in an intensely dramatic form emotional states usually suggestive of unsatisfactory or broken personal relations and sometimes of deep sexual anguish. At one time he said that three of the foreign poets he most admired were Verlaine, Darío and Samain. Though Pessanha seems to have absorbed little from the latter two, from Verlaine he learned the capacity for drawing from words a music capable of transmitting feelings of tragic deprivation too vague for purely intellectual or even suggestive expression, and the capacity for evoking moods that no previous Portuguese poet had ever been able to record. His verse was as musical as Verlaine's but more highly concentrated. He had learned Mallarmé's power of transposing associations, but he was less abstract and more emotive than Mallarmé. He was startling in his ability to invent metaphors that were suggestive in both idea and sound. The extraordinary power of his symbols and the absoluteness of his metaphors are exhibited in all his great poems, one of which is the following sonnet:

> Quem poluiu, quem rasgou os meus lençóis de linho,
> Onde esperei morrer,—meus tão castos lençóis?
> Do meu jardim exíguo os altos girassóis
> Quem foi que os arrancou e lançou no caminho?
>
> Quem quebrou (que furor cruel e simiesco!)
> A mesa de eu cear,—tábua tósca de pinho?
> E me espalhou a lenha? E me entornou o vinho?
> —Da minha vinha o vinho acidulado e fresco . . .
>
> O minha pobre mãe! . . . Não te ergas mais da cova.
> Olha a noite, olha o vento. Em ruína a casa nova . . .
> Dos meus ossos o lume a extinguir-se breve.
>
> Não venhas mais ao lar. Não vagabundes mais.
> Alma de minha mãe . . . Não andes mais à neve,
> De noite a mendigar às portas dos casais.

The translation, unfortunately, cannot convey the musical imagery:

> Who polluted, who tore my sheets of linen?
> The sheets I was to die in, my own chaste sheets?
> And the tall sunflowers in my narrow garden,
> Who tore them out, who flung them in my road?
>
> And who, in what cruel, simian rage, broke
> My supper table, my board of rough pine?
> Who scattered my firewood, who spilled my wine?
> My own vineyard's wine, biting and cool. . . .
>
> Oh, my poor mother! Do not rise from the grave again.
> Observe the night, observe the wind. The new house a ruin. . . .
> And in my eyes the dying flame.
>
> Come home no more. Wander no more.
> Oh, soul of my mother. . . . Roam in the snow no more
> At night, begging at farmhouse doors.

The first small collection of Pessanha's poems, sixteen in all, was not published until 1916. They appeared in a literary review, *Centauro*, founded by Luís de Montalvor (1891-1947), a Portuguese critic and poet who had spent some time in Brazil, and Ronald de Carvalho (1893-1935), a Brazilian who was also a poet and critic. One year earlier they had collaborated in the founding of the most important Portuguese *modernista* review, *Orpheu*. The later magazine, *Centauro*, is the last explosive effort of Portuguese symbolism. It brings together Fernando Pessoa, who at that time was passing from his symbolist phase to *modernismo*, of which he was to be the great exponent; Pessanha, whose sixteen sonnets have been mentioned; and Pessanha's friend, Alberto Osório de Castro, whose contribution consisted of four sonnets. Montalvor contributed an essay on decadence in literature, Pessoa a sequence of fourteen difficult sonnets entitled "Passos da Cruz," and the poet and philosopher Raul Leal (1886-1964) a tale called "A Aventura dum Sátiro ou a Morte de Adônis," an allegory with homosexual implications about the passing of the gods from one civilization to another.

The only twentieth-century poet in the Portuguese language whose reputation has worldwide proportions, Fernando Pessoa, spent his youth in

South Africa, knew English literature and wrote poetry in English. He began his literary career in Lisbon as a poet of the movement of literary nationalism called *saudosismo,* but he was soon attracted by symbolism. In 1914 he published in *Renascença,* an ephemeral review associated with the movement, two poems under the general title "Impressões do Crepúsculo," which were quite different in manner. One was "O Sino da Minha Aldeia" [My Village Church Bell], a beautiful expression of *saudosismo,* and the other was "Pauis" [Marshes], which was symbolist in its vagueness and its suggestiveness and almost phenomenological in its treatment of the marsh and its atmosphere. This gave rise to a short-lived symbolist movement called *paulismo* of which Sá-Carneiro became an enthusiastic adherent for a brief period. About the same time, Pessoa wrote his prose drama *O Marinheiro* [The Seaman] which pays homage to Maeterlinck and which is the exemplification of another literary theory, *amplição*—apparently, if we judge by the definition, an aspect of symbolism: it is an art that "procura tornar o seu objeto superior a si-próprio, busca nele uma qualquer espécie de além ele"[6] [tries to transform its object into something superior to itself and searches in it for what is beyond itself]. Then, no longer content with symbolism, he experimented with and developed other theories which form the basic elements of Portuguese *modernismo.* Unlike Verlaine he was an intellectual poet who would never have considered that a writer should be dominated by his subconscious instead of his conscious mind—here he recalls Valéry—although he was interested in occult practices, studied Rosicrucianism, and corresponded with and translated a poem by Aleister Crowley, a British astrologer and magician. Instead there is something quite *conceptista* about his doctrine, embodied in many of his best-known poems, that the writer and therefore human beings feign an existence, feelings, a whole inner life, that they finally come to accept as their own. Yet certain elements of symbolism continue to be present during his artistic development, especially its pessimism and the predominantly musical imagery. Pessoa was well known by other Portuguese poets of his time, but he published only one book, *Mensagem* [Message] (1934), before his death. Thereafter his fame grew with successive posthumous editions of his uncollected prose and verse, and his influence is still the paramount one in Portuguese poetry.

Mário de Sá-Carneiro died by suicide at the age of twenty-six, and he was a productive poet only during his last three years. He was closely attached to Pessoa, and it is possible that his poetic development, had he lived, might have paralleled that of his friend. But even during this short space of time he did produce a fairly large body of work, including a play, a novel, two collections of short stories or novellas, as well as the fairly large quantity of verse on which his reputation rests; and he collaborated with a friend on the translation of a play by François de Curel, *Les Fossiles.* His collected poems, *Indícios de Ouro* [Traces of Gold], came out posthumously in 1937. Sá-Carneiro's first volume of poetry, *Dispersão* (1914), is symbolist in essence, but it shows the influence of the manner of *modernismo.* In the later poems he begins to deviate significantly from symbolism, especially in his use of the metaphor less as a symbol than as a device for expressing his emotion directly. An unattractive, puffy young man, supported for a while in Paris by an allowance that was abruptly cut off, he was painfully aware of his limitations, especially in his sexual life. In fact, his one permanent liaison seems to have been with a prostitute who, his writings indicate, showed him little or no affection. His poetry shows his loneliness, his narcissism, and his pessimism; technically it is characterized by musicality, pervasive synesthesia, imagery that is rich in color and marked by the extravagant use of the word *gold* and its synonyms and derivatives. The "Epigrafe" of *Indícios de Ouro* is representative of his symbolism and his identity crisis:

> A sala do castelo é deserta e espelhada.
> Tenho médo de Mim. Quem sou? De onde cheguei?
> Aqui, tudo já foi . . . Em sombra estilizada,
> A côr morreu—e até o ar é uma ruína . . .
> Vem de Outro tempo a luz que me ilumina—
> Um som opaco me dilui em Rei . . .
>
> [The castle's hall is deserted and lined with mirrors.
> I fear Myself. Who am I? Whence do I come?
> Here, all is over. . . . The color has died
> In stylized shade—the very air is a ruin—
> The light that shines for me comes from Another time. . . .
> An opaque sound dilutes me into a King. . . .]

In this period from 1890 to 1920 approximately, symbolism had been flourishing in Brazil, where some of the Portuguese were known. Guerra Junqueiro's *Os Simples,* with its four or five symbolist poems, was read by the poets of the 1890's; and the fame of Eugénio de Castro, which was so considerable in Europe, had of course reached the other side of the Atlantic. Pessanha, however, could not have been known at all, for he had published very little before the collection in *Centauro* in 1916. Pessoa and Sá-Carneiro must have been known to a selected few because of *Orpheu,* which was edited in its first number by Ronald de Carvalho and by Montalvor, who was well known in Brazil. *Centauro* should have reached Rio, but it seems to have created no stir there. Though it is not possible that Cruz e Sousa (1861-1898), the greatest Brazilian symbolist, had ever heard of Pessanha, Cruz e Sousa's name may have reached Pessanha's eyes, for his fame passed beyond national boundaries a few years after his death. Rubén Darío saw the *Últimos Sonetos* when they appeared in Paris in 1905, and when in the following year he visited Rio de Janeiro he became acquainted with more of João Cruz e Sousa's work. From that time a certain amount of influence of the Brazilian is seen in Darío's work, and Darío translated one of his poems. Other Spanish-speaking writers who learned about Cruz e Sousa and admired him were Juan Más y Pí, a Spaniard who spent some time in the south of Brazil and who brought him to the attention of Leopoldo Lugones; Ricardo Jaimes Freyre, who lectured about him in Buenos Aires; and the Peruvian diplomat, Ventura García Calderón, who visited Brazil more than once and considered Cruz e Sousa the equal of Baudelaire.[7] He was better known in Portugal, since his lyrics were often reprinted there in magazines and an article about him by Oliveira Gomes had appeared as early as 1898 in *A Arte.* Moreover, Gustavo Santiago's three articles published in *Cidade do Rio* in 1899 must have reached Portugal, where Santiago had lived and where he had strong literary connections. Cruz e Sousa's most famous prose poem "Emparedado" [Walled In] from *Evocações* (1898) is even worked in a curious way into the plot of a strange decadent novel *Nova Safo* [A New Sappho] (1912) by the Visconde de Vila Moura (1877-1935), in which the Lesbian heroine enlarges "Emparedado" into a poem that she calls "Emparedada." She says that the "Black Poet" had been the victim of color prejudice and had used his suffering as the material of his prose poem. In the same way she had composed her "Emparedada," her masterpiece, to bare the intimate sorrows that had been caused by "os preconceitos de toda a ordem que lhe entravavam a ação" (pp. 10-11) [the prejudices of all kinds that had thwarted and hindered her].

The anguish of Cruz e Sousa was not due to the kind of psychological pressures afflicting Pessanha, the illegitimate child of a long-suffering mother, or Pessoa and Sá-Carneiro, each of whom in early childhood had lost a parent and seen the arrival of a usurping step-parent. His were the problems of a superior, cultured black artist living in a society dominated by European theories of white superiority. The fact that so large a number of the leaders of this society were mulattos was explained by what could now be called genetic transmission. The white was naturally superior, the black naturally inferior, and the mulatto who was superior owed his good fortune to the white part of his ancestry. Cruz e Sousa had no such good fortune, for he was the black son of parents who had been slaves. As a child he was reared by a white family that cherished and encouraged his intelligence and talent, but in his early adolescence these foster parents died and he was forced to face the almost completely white society of Santa Catarina with little protection. He endured snubs, was often insulted, and because he never had the kind of government sinecure that was frequently given to Brazilian writers, he was always in financial straits. He developed a complex of inferiority that left its mark on the poems in prose and verse which recount his dreams and visions of unrealized desires for white women; these women may be symbolized by an aloof Virgin above the altar of a church who looks down on an unworthy, adoring monster. There is more realism in his writing about his desire for black women, for it was a desire that was capable of realization, and indeed his beautiful wife Gavita was black. Yet, though there is a strong representation of his sexual drive and the black woman's physical beauty, the affective bond is colored by the problem of race and his pity for one who is condemned to sadness because of it. It is a love for a beautiful woman with a gentle spirit, and it is also a love of pity for one who bears within her the sadness of a condemned race.[8]

It was Cruz e Sousa's two books, *Missal* and *Broquéis* [Shields], both published in 1893, that formally brought symbolism into public view. A former Parnassian who had written anti-slavery articles and verse, he was writing poems in a new manner. This was part of his problem: his symbolism was so abstract and free that it appeared unintelligible to a public nurtured on the simplicity of the romantics and the clarity of the Parnassians. Few readers, few critics, grasped what he was trying to do, although the most influencial critic of the time, Sílvio Romero, was apparently moved and almost hypnotized by the poems he read. He says: "Em frases indeterminadas, aparentemente desalinhadas, sabe, por não sabemos que interessante e curiosa magia, atirar o pensamento do leitor nos longes indefinidos, sugestionando-lhe a imaginativa"[9] [In vague, apparently disorganized phrases, by some unknown, interesting and curious magic, he is able to draw the reader's thoughts to indefinite distances and hypnotize the imagination]. Probably the effect was similar to that produced upon the art public of the 1920's when di Chirico's and Dali's paintings of vast surrealistic spaces were first exhibited. Other writers derived this hypnotic effect of his poetry from the rhythms of his African heritage or the monotonous beat of African tam-tams. Some thought his repetitions and alliterations were due to linguistic features of African languages that his ancestors may have spoken. All this is far-fetched, for he had not heard those languages or the tam-tams in Santa Catarina. In his alliterations and repetitions, in his stress upon sound and rhythm, he was merely applying the symbolist theory of the importance of music in verse. Yet, though it is true that his poetry is more auditive than visual, he was conscious of the value of visual images. Like Baudelaire and his French followers he used much color in his work. At first he worked to produce the effect of white, perhaps under the influence of the impressionist painters, perhaps due to his unconscious desire to be white. He was little interested in Mallarmé's blue. Then, as his later work became increasingly morbid, black assumed a growing importance, and it became the dominant and symbolic color in "Emparedado." His use of color and repetition is in evidence in his poem "Braços" [Arms] from *Broquéis*:

> Braços nervosos, brancas opulências,
> brumais brancuras, fúlgidas brancuras,
> alvuras castas, virginais alvuras,
> latescências das raras latescências.

> [Nervous arms, white opulences,
> misty whitenesses, shining whitenesses,
> chaste purities, virginal purities,
> lactescences of rare latescences.]

Overwhelmed by his feeling of social rejection and his personal problems, he grew more narcissistic during the five years between *Broquéis* and *Missal* (1893) and his death. In "Emparedado," which is dedicated to Night, the blackness of the world is the symbol of the prison that walls him in; he is the victim of a cosmic despair, within dreams of a black race and an Africa of which he knew nothing at all, an Africa that was a phantasmagoria of maddening sun, barbarous forests and empty deserts. It expresses the loneliness of one who has achieved complete awareness of the fact that he is neither a white Brazilian nor a black African. As anguished as ever Rimbaud can have been, Cruz e Sousa writes in "Emparedado":

> Mas, que importa tudo isso?! ¿Qual é a côr da minha forma, do meu sentir?
> Qual é a côr da tempestade de dilacerações que me abala? Qual a dos meus
> sonhos e gritos? Qual a dos meus desejos e febre?

> [What can it all mean? What is the color of my shape and my feeling? What is
> the color of the lacerating tempest that shakes me? What is the color of my
> dreams and shrieks, of my desires and fever?]

Still, in his own anguish he could pity other outcasts. He says in his "Crianças Negras" [Black Children] that he must write

> das crianças que vêm da negra noite,
> dum leite de venenos e de treva,

dentre os dantescos círculos do açoite.
filhas malditas da desgraça de Eva.
[of the children who come from black night,
nourished on the milk of poison and darkness,
from within the Dantean circles of the whip,
doomed offspring of the curse of Eve.]

When Cruz e Sousa died of tuberculosis in 1898, he left behind many friends and disciples. Four who had been close to him were Nestor Vítor (1868-1932), a poet and a critic and his literary executor; Alphonsus de Guimaraens (1870-1921), the second great figure in the constellation of Brazilian symbolism; Emiliano Perneta (1866-1921) who had been his colleague on the *Folha Popular;* and B. Lopes (1859-1916) who had also been a colleague on the *Folha.* Mário Pederneiras (1868-1915) had been a colleague on *Novidades.* Two others who came too late to know him were Eduardo Guimaraens (1892-1928) and Augusto dos Anjos (1884-1914). The symbolist poets were natives of all the different regions of Brazil, from the southernmost state of Rio Grande do Sul, the birthplace of Eduardo Guimaraens, to the northeastern state of Paraíba, the home of Augusto dos Anjos. Their work was published in magazines of the capital like Mário Pederneiras's *Fon Fon,* founded in 1907, and in provincial reviews like *O Cenáculo,* which ran from 1895-1897 in Curitiba, capital of Perneta's Paraná. In all, according to Andrade Muricy, twenty-nine symbolist journals existed at different times in different parts of the country.

The second great poet of the symbolist movement was Alphonsus de Guimaraens, a member of a literary family well known in the province (later state) of Minas Gerais. An enthusiast of Cruz e Sousa, he led a very different life and wrote very different poetry from that of the black poet. Cruz e Sousa raged in narcissistic despair against himself and a society that scorned him, and against a destiny that had raised him up only to cast him down. Though poor, Guimaraens was of a respected and prominent family. He was well educated and for most of his life was a judge in a beautiful, historic but forgotten town of Minas Gerais, where he barely managed to keep himself and his enormous family above the poverty line. His work is neither rebellious nor despairing, but it is tinged with symbolist melancholy. His chief affinity with Cruz e Sousa was his obsession with white as a color. Like many other symbolists he was a Catholic, and a more consistent one than Verlaine. He was a medievalist, too, and ecclesiastical themes and medieval religious language are constants in his poems, the first three volumes of which are entitled *Kiriale* (1891-1895), *Dona Mística* (1892-1894), and *Setenário da Dores de Nossa Senhora* [The Seven-Day Feast of the Sorrows of Our Lady] (1896-1898). This devotion to religious subjects is expressed in appropriate imagery and a vocabulary charged with archaisms. The French poet whom he most admired was Verlaine, whom he translated; like Verlaine he was a musical writer, and he was the most popular of the symbolists.

Cruz e Sousa worked on the *Folha Popular* with B. Lopes, a picturesque mulatto from the state of Rio de Janeiro who had already made a name for himself, and a considerable one at that, as a Parnassian. But even before Cruz e Sousa had become a symbolist, Lopes had written some verse which, to quote Wilson Martins, "havia lançado os primeiros pseudopodos do que seria entre nós o Simbolismo"[10] [had put out the first pseudopods of what would come to be our Symbolism]. With Cruz, Emiliano Perneta and Oscar Rosas (1862-1925), a friend of the black poet's from Santa Catarina, he formed the first group of symbolists, and he published two symbolist volumes, *Brasões* [Escutcheons] (1895), whose title recalls *Broquéis,* and *Val de Lírios* [Valley of Lilies] (1900). Emiliano Perneta, a finer poet, lived only two years in Rio, and then returned to his native Paraná, where he was the leading writer in a small state, and the subject of much tribute, which was well deserved. He was a poet who developed from a Guerra Junqueiro phase of social criticism, through symbolism, to classicism. In his early decadent period he was attracted by Satanism and Don Juanism. He wrote sensual poetry and found subject matter and manner in the Song of Solomon and the life of Solomon in the Book of Kings (I), which inspired him to write his fine "Versículos de Sulamita," from *Illusão* (1911). He was long a disciple of Mallarmé, and in one of his best sonnets, "De um Fauno," he restates the familiar Mallarmé theme. He was not one of those poets who deepen our perception with transcendental symbols. His symbols serve rather to strengthen and to beautify a statement of what we already perceive. Consider for example the last lines of "Sol" from *Illusão,* in which the effect of the sun on all nature is described as it is represented in a drop of water:

> . . . aquela gota d'água
> Que depois de fulgir, assim como uma estrela,
> Derrete-se na luz, funde-se dentro dela!
>
> [. . . that drop of water,
> which ceasing to gleam, melts like a star
> into the light and becomes one with it.]

Mário Pederneiras, who had received his early journalistic training with Cruz e Sousa on *Novidades,* later became the editor of one of the principal organs of the movement, *Fon Fon.* Pederneiras was a poet of genuine feeling, whose early work with its alliteration, neologisms, strange word combinations and unusual plurals and obsessive repetitions seems to be lifted straight out of *Missal.* The following are two lines from "Natal d'Alva" in *Agonia* (1900):

> Horas primeiras, morbidas, brumáceas,
> Fôfas, do fôfo flácido d'arminhos . . .
>
> [Hours early, morbid, misty,
> Fluffed with the flaccid fluff of ermines . . .]

As he grew older he worked in the direction of simplicity and metrical freedom and his admirable "free verse" about his native city of Rio de Janeiro recalls the nostalgic, musical tone of much of Verlaine. He gives the atmosphere of old Rio in "Trecho Final" [Last Phase] from *Outono* (1921):

> Meia-tinta de côr dos ocasos do Outono,
> Sonho que uma ilusão sobre a vida nos tece,
> E perfume sutil de uma fôlha de trevo,
> São, decerto, a feição deste livro que escrevo
> Neste ambiente de silêncio e sono,
> Nesta indolência de quem convalesce.
>
> [A half tone from Autumn sunsets,
> A dream woven for us by life's illusion.
> The subtle perfume of a leaf of clover,

> Are the true quality of this book I write,
> In this atmosphere of silence and sleep,
> In this convalescent indolence.]

Another very fine symbolist is Eduardo Guimaraens (1892-1928), who spent his life in Rio Grande do Sul. In spite of his distance from Rio and the even greater distance from Portugal, he was well enough known to be invited at the age of twenty-three to contribute to *Orpheu,* and a series of his poems which he also published in his *Divina Quimera* (1916) appeared in the second number of the great *modernista* magazine, the number edited by Pessoa and Sá-Carneiro. A man of great culture, Eduardo Guimaraens was well acquainted with other literatures, an admirer of D'Annunzio, Jammes and Poe, and the translator of Tagore, Baudelaire, Verlaine, Heine and Dante.

Although this brief review of Brazilian symbolists must of necessity be incomplete, one poet who cannot be forgotten is Augusto dos Anjos, perhaps the most widely read of all the group. His one volume *Eu* [I] (1912) has been a constant best-seller and had its thirty-first printing in 1971. The popularity is hard to understand, not because he was not a good poet—for he was a very good one—but because his work seems both anti-poetic and difficult in subject matter and style. The content must be repulsive in a great many cases to a fastidious person; and even a glance at the titles of some poems will give the idea that dos Anjos should be incomprehensible to the average reader. Consider for example such titles as "O Deus-Verme" [The God Worm], "O Meu Nirvana" [My Nirvana], "O Poeta do Hediondo" [The Poet of What Is Repugnant], "O Lupanar" [The Brothel] and "A um Carneiro Morto" [To a Dead Ram]. He was a chronic sufferer from a lung disease, and the illness, coupled with his poverty, which increased as his family increased, produced in him a nihilistic view of the world that resulted in an overwhelming despair. He appears different in vocabulary and style from the other symbolists, for his images and language are drawn from science and the philosophy of Haeckel. The final effect is not, however, that of a series of lessons in science put into verse, but rather of a mystical philosophy expressed in a language which was daring and surprising and with which he must have become acquainted during his long illness. One sonnet, which is both repulsive and scientific, "Agregado infeliz de sangue e cal" [Wretched mixture of blood and lime], is dedicated to his first child who was "born dead without having reached seven months of age." Its sextet follows:

> Porção de minha plásmica substáncia,
> Em que lugar irás passar a infáncia,
> Tràgicamente anónimo, a feder?!
>
> Ah! Possas tu dormir feto esquecido,
> Panteìsticamente dissolvido
> Na *noumenalidade* do NÃO SER.

> [Portion of my plasmic substance,
> In what place will you pass your infancy,
> Tragically anonymous and stinking?
>
> Ah, forgotten fetus, may you be able to sleep,
> Pantheistically dissolved
> In the *noumenality* of NON-BEING.]

Both Portugal and Brazil produced a considerable amount of symbolist drama and prose narrative. There was no Maeterlinck or D'Annunzio, nor even a Huysmans or a Fournier, and symbolist poetry was far superior to the drama and the fiction. But the same may be said about other literatures, too, for symbolism was basically the movement of poetry and more especially of lyric poetry. In Portugal there was one writer of prose who because of his originality, his vision and his powerful imagination deserves to be well known in other lands. As a youth Raul Brandão (1867-1930) became a symbolist and was a member of the group of *nefelibatas* of the city of Oporto which published a little book in 1893 of the same name. In his first novel *História de um Palhaço* [The Story of a Clown] (1896), he expresses the theme that life is a tragic farce in which people have lost faith in everything and live in a perpetual dream or nightmare. His greater novels, such as *Os Pobres* (1906) and *A Farsa* (1903) are fiction that is also prose poetry. Impressionistic, chiaroscuro representations of human tragedy, and especially the tragedy of poverty, they are organized in brief scenes and portraits, flashes and vignettes, in which theatres, churches, dark streets and ugly, contorted faces unite to form a single, vast symbol of human life. Brandão had learned from Dostoievski; and, though his work is not on the vast scale of Dostoievski's, he was always a great and an impressive writer.

There are other symbolist fictionists who merit mention. One is Mário de Sá-Carneiro, who has already been spoken of as a poet. His fiction—the collections of short stories in *Princípio* (1912) and *Céu em Fogo* [Sky on Fire] (1915) and the novel, *A Confissão de Lúcio* (1914) — is decadent and preoccupied with disturbed and ambiguous personalities, sadism, and male and female homosexuality, represented by Portuguese and other expatriates living in Paris or visiting in their own land. Another decadent writer of fiction was the aristocratic, anti-democratic Visconde de .Vila-Moura, the author of *Nova Safo,* the Lesbian novel that has been discussed above. António Patrício, who has been discussed as a symbolist poet, was also the author of short fiction and drama some of which is disturbingly beautiful. In *Serão Inquieto* [Restless Evening] (1910) the hero of one particularly interesting story "O Homem das Fontes" [The Man of the Fountains] is obsessed with the idea, that could only have occurred to a symbolist, of building a palace of water and setting it to music. This theme of the fusion of music with another art has reference to the symbolists' favorite composer, Wagner, and in an intercalation the narrator comments that the dream was a chimera, doomed to failure, as Wagner had failed to fuse the arts in his music dramas.

António Patrício's dramas may still be read with interest, and one, *O Fim* (1909), was revived recently because of its pertinence to a continuing problem of Portuguese politics. It is the allegory of a country condemned to death by its rulers' intransigent opposition to change and the self-destructiveness of the people. D. João da Câmara (1852-1907) was also a historical dramatist, but one of his contemporary symbolist dramas grasps the imagination. It is *O Pântano* [The Marsh] (1894). In it the world is symbolized by the *pântano,* and its fetid exhalations are the forces against which human beings struggle in vain. Pessoa's prose drama, *O Marinheiro* [The Seaman] (1913), with its dense atmosphere, its mysterious occupants of a medieval castle and its single setting of a room enshrining a maiden in a coffin, coupled with its motionless, static quality, shows the influence of Maeterlinck. *Belkiss* (1894) by Eugénio de Castro is an opulent, highly

decorated drama about the unrequited passion of the heroine for King
Solomon. It is better written than Wilde's *Salomé*, but it lacks the dramatic
shock of that play.

In Brazil there is no figure in the drama or fiction of symbolism who can
be compared with the great poets of the movement. Lima Barreto's beautiful
*Vida e Morte de M. J. Gonzaga de Sá* (1919) uses symbolism to produce
artistic effects but is in truth a novel of direct statement about Brazilian
problems in the period of the author's life, 1881-1922. Graça Aranha, who
was one of the outstanding literary figures on the Brazilian scene during his
whole career, wrote a play, *Malasarte* (1911), in Portugese and French, the
leading character of which is intended to represent or symbolize the country.
Malasarte is a kind of Peer Gynt, Til Eulenspiegel or Pedro Urdemales, who
comes out of Brazilian and Peninsular folklore, and the play centers upon a
contemporary problem. But the intention is better than the achievement.
Aranha was also the author of one of the most famous novels of the century,
*Canaã* [Canaan] (1902), which is frequently classified as symbolist. It has
elements of symbolism as it has elements that are pure naturalism, but the
symbols are traditional literary ones and do not set forth or probe into the
depths of human psychology as the important symbols of symbolism do. The
great interest of the novel is in its place in the literature of ideas, in its
discussion of Brazil's racial composition and of its national future, and in the
position of the immigrant in contrast with the white, upper-class Brazilian
and the mulatto who represents a very large sector of the population.

It is quite comprehensible that Henrique Coelho Neto (1864-1934), a
writer of fiction, drama and criticism, who was at times a realist, romantic,
regionalist and naturalist, should have incorporated many techniques and
themes of symbolism into his work. His first book, *Rapsódias* (1891), a
collection of prose tales and poems, is indeed symbolist and is filled "de neve,
princesas, magos, florestas, e deuses, escritas num estilo deliberadamente
poético" [with snow, princesses, magicians, forests, gods and goddesses and is
written in a deliberately poetic style], says Wilson Martins.[11] There is
considerable symbolism in his other fiction, but even *Rei Negro* (1914) is no
more a work of symbolist fiction than *Canaã*. Coelho Neto was as prolific a
writer as Camilo Castelo Branco, Galdós or Balzac, and his work was uneven,
but at his best he is a writer of power. How interesting is the symbol in the
novella, "Bom Jesus da Mata" [Christ of the Woods] from *Treva* [Darkness
of Night] (1906): a sculptor dying of tuberculosis in the backlands of Brazil
creates a statue from a strangely shaped log that is accepted as miraculous by
the people and that he himself comes to worship in a moment of mass
hysteria during a pilgrimage (*romaria*). Finally, perhaps the most interesting
symbolist novel of all, because it seems the most modern, is *No Hospício* [In
the Insane Asylum] (1905) by Rocha Pombo (1857-1933), a poet and the
author of a monumental history of Brazil. It is about a youth who has lost his
reason after being imprisoned in a mental hospital through the machinations
of a powerful man whose daughter he had dared to love. The asylum is the
symbol of an insane world that drives its inhabitants to madness.

The world was different after the First World War. There had been great
economic and political changes and new developments in psychology which
had affected the arts. The cultural unity of Portugal and Brazil, which had

not been destroyed when Brazil became independent, was severed. Symbolism and its narcissism were thrust into the background by *modernismo* which, though it was not the same in the two countries, led to artistic advances in both and produced an enduring effect in both. Yet, symbolism did not disappear completely; it lives on in Portuguese neo-realism and surrealism and in Brazil in the novels of Jorge Amado, the theater of Jorge Andrade and Ariano Suassuna, and the poetry of Jorge de Lima, Murilo Mendes and Cecília Meireles.

*Queens College, CUNY*

## NOTES

[1] Tristão de Alencar Araripe Júnior, *Literatura Brasileira: Movimento de 1893* (Rio de Janeiro: Empresa Democrática Editora, 1896), pp. 69-70.

[2] *Brotéria,* 90, No. 3 (1970), 305-19.

[3] Eugénio de Castro, *Obras Poéticas* (Lisbon: Parceria A.M. Pereira Ltda., 1971), V, 17.

[4] "Camilo Pessanha e António Patrício," in *Estrada Larga* (Oporto: O Comércio do Porto, n.d.), pp. 136-39.

[5] João Gaspar Simões, *Perspectiva Histórica da Poesia Portuguesa: Século XX* (Lisbon: Brasília Editora, 1976), p. 57.

[6] Quoted by Teresa Lopes, "Pessoa, Sá-Carneiro," *Colóquio,* December 1971, p. 19.

[7] Andrade Muricy, *Panorama do Movimento Simbolista Brasileiro* (Rio de Janeiro: Instituto Nacional do Livro, 1952), I, 67-71.

[8] See Raymond Sayers, "The Black Poet in Brazil: The Case of Cruz e Sousa," *Luso-Brazilian Review,* 15, Supplementary Issue (1978), 96.

[9] *Histórica da Literatura Brasileira,* 3rd ed. (Rio de Janeiro: José Olímpio, 1943), V, 308.

[10] *História da Inteligência Brasileira* (São Paulo: Cultrix, 1978), IV, 109.

[11] Ibid., IV, 374.

Charcoal drawing by Julio Ruelas. Reproduced from *Revista Moderna,* 2, No. 2 (1899), 64.

# Symbolism in Spanish American Literary Periodicals, 1896-1910

## Catherine Vera

The literary journals examined in this study represent major geographic focal points in the development of *modernismo,* and in the growth of understanding of symbolism in Spanish America: Argentina (*El Mercurio de América, La Biblioteca*); Peru (*Prisma*); Venezuela (*El Cojo Ilustrado*); and Mexico (*El Mundo Ilustrado*).[1] The year 1896 is important for the study of symbolism in Spanish American literature, for it marks the publication by Rubén Darío of two works, *Prosas profanas* and *Los raros,* reflecting Darío's awareness of, and appreciation for, Parnassian and symbolist writers.

*El Mercurio de América* (1898-1900) kept its readers aware of new trends in European and American literature by means of a continuing section on letters in America, Italy, France, Brazil, and Spain. *La Biblioteca* (1896-1898) features many articles by its editor, Paul Groussac, which focus on the role of art in America and the nature of the American—specifically, Argentinian—reading public. The Mexican publication *El Mundo Ilustrado* (founded as *El Mundo* in 1894) spans the entire period studied in this paper and offers original works by Spanish American and foreign writers as well as critical essays by such important men of letters as Rubén Darío, Luis G. Urbina, and Dr. M. Flores. *El Cojo Ilustrado* (1892-1915) of Venezuela and *Prisma* (1905-1907) of Peru reflect attitudes of writers in these countries towards vanguardist tendencies at home and abroad. The fragmentation that one would expect in a study of literary reviews located geographically so distant from each other is not a predominant factor in the critical articles appearing during the years covered by this paper. Leading Spanish American writers and critics were well aware of publications by their colleagues in other countries, and the leading literary journals regularly published works by writers from beyond their national borders.[2] The critical writings about *modernismo* and its relations to symbolism and other movements in these major journals, if considered collectively, offer an encompassing view of Spanish American *modernismo* during the maturity of the movement's trajectory.

The problem of defining the literary and social aspects of Spanish American *modernismo* continued to be a preoccupation of critics[3] even until the beginning of World War I. Enrique Gómez Carrillo, in 1907, conducted a poll in his Parisian publication, *El Nuevo Mercurio,*[4] in an attempt to find a definition of the amorphous literary movement. The Guatemalan asked Spanish American writers associated with *modernismo* "1. ¿Cree usted que existe una nueva escuela literaria o una nueva tendencia intelectual y artística? 2. ¿Qué idea tiene usted de lo que se llama modernismo? 3. ¿Cuáles son entre los modernistas los que usted prefiere? 4. En una palabra: ¿Qué piensa usted de la literatura joven; de la orientación nueva del gusto y del porvenir inmediato de nuestras letras?"[5] [1. Do you believe that a new literary school, or that a new intellectual and artistic tendency exists? 2. What do you believe *modernismo* to be? 3. Which *modernista* writers do you prefer? 4. Briefly, what is your opinion about this young literature with such a new appeal; and what do you believe to be the future of our literature?].

Clemente Palma, in *Prisma,* responded to this questionnaire by saying that "el modernismo está pues caracterizado hoy por una completa indeterminación, por una falta de orientación precisa"[6] [*modernismo* is characterized today by a complete lack of direction, and by a lack of precise orientation]. Amado Nervo in *La Aurora* (Mexico), in answer to the same question, laments the vagueness attached to the "tan socorrida palabreja"[7] [often sought-after word (*modernismo*)], even though he fears that the confusion he perceives is due to his own lack of historical perspective.[8] Current criticism, however, confirms both Nervo's and Palma's perceptions of the confusing complexity of Spanish American *modernismo,* by noting an absence of stability and ideological definition inherent within the large diversity of artistic criteria espoused by those Spanish American writers associated with this complex and broadly interpreted literary phenomenon, *modernismo.*[9]

"*Nommer* un objet, c'est supprimer les trois quarts de la jouissance du poème qui est faite du bonheur de deviner peu à peu; le *suggérer,* violà le rêve" [To *name* an object, is to take from it three-fourths of the enjoyment of the poem, which consists of the satisfaction of guessing what it is little by little; to *suggest* it (the object), that is the ideal], affirms Stéphane Mallarmé.[10] The esthetic views and poetic achievements of Mallarmé are notably present in the reviews under consideration. Darío's necrological article on Mallarmé in *El Mercurio de América* (October 1898) demonstrates a perspicacious insight into his poetry and a thorough knowledge of its themes, theory, and content. He states his reluctance to assess the merits of this great and controversial contemporary poet, a judgment which, in his opinion, should be postponed as "trabajo por hacerse dentro de cincuenta años"[11] [a task to be undertaken fifty years in the future]. In 1897, Enrique Gómez Carrillo had commented in *El Cojo Ilustrado* on the "arte misterioso y sugestivo" [mysterious and suggestive art] of Mallarmé.[12] Mallarmé is also the subject of an article in the same publication, in 1909, which praises the French poet's ability to suggest with sounds "fenómenos espirituales"[13] [spiritual phenomena].

The suggestive use of words and sounds by Spanish American writers is noted by several critics. "Castalia Bárbara," by the Bolivian Ricardo Jaimes Freyre, contains, according to an article in *El Mercurio de América,* "la sugestión de las ideas y sensaciones"[14] [the suggestion of ideas and sensations]. In dealing with the same work, Eugenio Díaz Romero calls Jaimes Freyre "el poeta de la *nuance* y del sueño"[15] [the poet of *nuance* and of dreams]. Again in *El Mercurio de América,* vagueness is praised: the author and critic, José María Vargas Vila, praises the imagery of César Zumeta, in which waves "se esfuman y se pierden, en una bruma dorada . . . donde duermen, ya para siempre, los amores idos"[16] [become foam and are lost in a golden haze . . . where lost loves sleep forever].

Although vagueness was generally accepted as a basic aspect of poetry during the *modernista* years, as the new century advanced, this lack of precision was challenged. Clemente Palma in 1906 in *Prisma* ridicules this dreamlike quality by asking for precise details: did the poet receive his inspiration from the Muse by "lámpara eléctrica, candil o velón de cera?"[17] [electric light, lantern, or wax candle?] Also with irony, contemporary vagueness is attacked by Dr. M. Flores in *El Mundo Ilustrado* in 1910, as he exemplifies contemporary verse by the following "poem":

¡Ah!

. . . . . . . . . .

. . . . . . . . . .

. . . . . . . . . .

. . . . . . . . . .

. . . . . . . . . .

¡Oh!

Flores indicates that in the empty space between the " ¡Ah! " and the " ¡Oh! " where, "al parecer no se dice nada, nuestra imaginación lo suple todo. El poeta, nos decimos, ha querido pintar la vida humana"[18] [apparently the poet says nothing, our own imagination supplies everything. The poet here, we tell ourselves, wants to explain the meaning of human existence].

Poe Carden, in his article, "Parnassianism, Symbolism, and Decadentism in Spanish American Modernism," points to the American understanding of these concepts as vague and overlapping, but also as having "worship of beauty" as a common element.[19] The frequent appearance of poetry by José María de Heredia and Théophile Gautier, both in translation into Spanish and in the original French, in important literary journals, would seem to indicate a general acceptance of the concept of "Art for Art's sake." A sampling of critical commentary about Parnassian work, however, indicates an ambivalence of opinion as to the mission of a work of art. The Colombian writer, José María Vargas Vila, in *El Mercurio de América,* in 1900, praises the work of the Venezuelan, César Zumeta, in terms consistent with the Parnassian approach: that Zumeta and others "tienen su dios: el Arte. Tienen su culto: la Belleza"[20] [have their god: Art, and their cult: Beauty]. On the occasion of the death of José María de Heredia, Clemente Palma, in *Prisma,* praises the French poet's perfection of form and his ability to create eternal beauty.[21] However, the setting apart of Art as being its own justification receives criticism from José María Vargas Vila in the article cited above; for, although he praises the work of Zumeta, he also indicates that "para mí el Arte es un medio, no un fin; un útil, no un culto"[22] [for me, Art is a means, not an end; a useful tool, not a cult]. Víctor Pérez Petit, in *El Mercurio de América,* in 1898, finds a "Cameo" of Gautier to be "esfumado en claridades lechosas, mortecinas, súbitamente cadavéricas" [colored in a deathly milk-like paleness, shocking like a cadaver] and totally lacking in a most important element in a work of art: expression of human emotions, which Pérez Petit finds in abundance in the work of Gabriele D'Annunzio.[23]

The confusion existing in France concerning the definition of criteria for literary schools had a counterpart in the literary circles of Spanish America, especially with the use of the terms Parnassianism, symbolism, decadentism, and *modernismo*. In 1896 Enrique Gómez Carrillo, in *El Cojo Ilustrado,* equates Parnassianism with romanticism.[24] As late as 1907, Amado Nervo, in *La Aurora,* equates *modernismo* with decadentism.[25] In 1897 and in 1904, symbolism was pronounced dead.[26] There was, however, an increasing awakening in America to "los nervios modernos" [modern feelings] causing "imperiosa necesidad de expresión"[27] [an overpowering need to be expressed]. Clemente Palma prudently writes in *Prisma* that "la vaguedad de significación del término con relación al espíritu del movimiento no significa que ésta no exista"[28] [the vagueness of the meaning of *modernismo* with relation to the content of the new movement does not preclude the existence of the movement].

Paul Verlaine, in his "Art poétique," begins by exhorting: "De la musique avant toute chose"[29] [Music above all else]. Musicality in verse, that reached a pinnacle in Spanish American poetry with works such as "Marcha triunfal" by Rubén Darío, and "Nocturno" and "Día de difuntos" by José Asunción Silva, received little favorable comment by critics in the reviews studied. Pérez Petit in *El Mercurio de América,* in 1898, acclaims the ability of poetry by D'Annunzio to calm his spirit "con inusitadas melodías"[30] [with unusual melodies]. José Ojeda in the same journal indicates that a poet is a person "que proclama la primacia del ritmo sobre el número"[31] [who proclaims the predominance of rhythm over syllable counting]. Eugenio Díaz Romero echoes the attitude of Ojeda in 1899 in reference to "Castalia Bárbara."[32]

Musicality of verse, however, had its critics in Spanish America from the early years of *modernismo* until well into the twentieth century. As early as 1896, in *El Cojo Ilustrado,* Enrique Gómez Carrillo indicates his belief that poetry which emphasizes the musical quality of words alone can become nonsense, as he exclaims " ¡Dios mío! ... debe de hacer dudar en América y en España del gusto de Francia y de la sinceridad de mis poetas jóvenes! "[33] [My God! ... this (nonsense) ought to make people in America and Spain doubt the sense of propriety in France and the sincerity of my young poets!] Paul Groussac, in *La Biblioteca,* believes that if music is the basis for poetry, then modern man should go directly to music to calm his spirit, thus making written poetry obsolete.[34] F. Navarro y Ledesma in "Poetas americanos: Rubén Darío y su escuela" is disturbed by syntactical errors committed by new poets for the sake of sound.[35] Clemente Palma, in 1905, when writing of "El triunfo del mármol" of Elías David Curiel, in *Prisma,* deplores this poet's "faltas de sentido"[36] [lack of reasoning]. This same critic, in 1906, laments that the suggestive qualities of the sounds of words have become more important to poets than clarity of intellectual expression. He writes that "da pena ver cuantas ideas que podían haber sido bellamente explotadas han sido malogradas por las intonserías modernistas y los snobismos cursis del poeta-pedagogo"[37] [it is a shame that so many ideas which could have been beautifully expressed, have not reached their potential because of snobbish *modernista* disharmonious expression]. Later, in 1910, Dr. M. Flores, in *El Mundo Ilustrado,* quotes a nonsensical nursery rhyme and then, ironically, explains that "lo que interesa, para gozar del arte moderno, y gozar intensamente, es prescindir de lo que dice . . . (aun si) esto no dice nada"[38] [in order to enjoy modern art with great intensity, one must pay no attention to what it says . . . even though it may say nothing].

A discussion of music in verse leads directly to a discussion of the technique of synaesthesia. The major theorists and practitioners of this technique in poetry (Théophile Gautier, with his equation of verse with sculpture; Charles Baudelaire, who in "Correspondances," equates fragrance with the sense of touch of a child's skin; Arthur Rimbaud who equates color with sound in "Voyelles") were well known in Spanish America and influenced many major works, such as "De blanco" by Manuel Gutiérrez Nájera. Critics publishing in the periodicals researched for this study were keenly aware of synaesthesia: F. Navarro y Ledesma, in *El Mundo* (1897), sees in the work of Francisco A. de Icaza "un *fondo* plástico de tan rico valor"[39] [a subject of rich plastic value]. Pérez Petit takes cognizance of synaesthesia in his description of "Poema Paradisiaco" of D'Annunzio, as he exclaims " ¡Oh, los dulces versos de claror de ópalo, los hermosos versos blancos como un girón de rayo lunar, los melancólicos versos llenos de inenarrables nostalgias, de soñolientas y errabundas rapsodias! ¡Cuán dulces y acariciadores!   ¡Cuán fugitivos y tenues, y apesadumbrados! "[40] [Oh, sweet verses with a pale opalescence, beautiful verses which are white like a moonbeam, melancholy verses full of inexpressible nostalgia, sleepy and errant rhapsodies! How sweet, and how carressing! How fast in flight and tenuous and mournful!]. Vargas Vila compares poetry to painting.[41] A staunch critic of synaesthesia, however, is to be found in the Mexican, Dr. M. Flores, who, in his article "La Babel del Arte," sees in the mingling of art forms and sensations a lack of communication which he compares to the Biblical Tower of Babel.[42]

The term "decadent" was often used by Spanish American critics in a pejorative sense, relating to non-traditional life-styles of writers in *le Quartier Latin* with a Satanic influence on literature which was contaminating Spanish American letters and destroying public morality. The Cuban, Nicolás Heredia, sees decadentism as "a school without ideals and therefore characteristic of worn-out souls and a society in the dotage." He continues by describing European culture as "dulled by satiety," and therefore not relevant to his contemporary Cuba.[43] Clemente Palma, however, in a series of articles about decadentism in *Prisma* (1905-1907), speaks of decadent dissipation as the ruination of many good writers, links decadentism in literature with a high suicide rate, and concludes by characterizing decadentism as a childhood disease suffered by most young writers.[44] Dr. M. Flores in *El Mundo Ilustrado,* in 1904, explains literary decadence as a result of the "mal del siglo," or "spleen" and affirms that "del spleen al suicidio no hay más que un paso"[45] [from "spleen" to suicide there is but one step]. Dr. Flores is also concerned about a lack of morality present in the creative artist. He concludes that this nucleus of negative traits defining the artist "inevitablemente se refleja en el arte y se manifiesta en las anomalías de los sentimientos y de la razón"[46] [inevitably is reflected in his art and in other abnormalities in his sentiments and reasoning]. The Colombian poet, José Asunción Silva, in a very personal confession relating to his life-style—his feeling of "hastío" [boredom] which even drug-induced experiences fail to alleviate, and his lack of mental clarity due to drug abuse—expresses the hope that death will soon overtake him and "curarme del horrible, del tenebroso mal de vivir"[47] [cure me of the horrible, shadowy evil of living].

The *modernista* writer's search for novel experiences led him not only to "les Paradis Artificiels" [Artificial Paradises] of opium and hashish, as described by Charles Baudelaire,[48] but also to faraway lands with new, fresh, undiscovered ways of life and forms of artistic expression. Experiencing the Far East, either through travel or by means of the imagination, became associated with *modernismo*. The Orient of Pierre Loti, the Goncourts, Gauguin, Gómez Carrillo, and others became a theme in Spanish American *modernismo,* attracting such important writers as the Cuban, Julián del Casal, and the Mexican, José Juan Tablada. Enrique Gómez Carrillo has a series of articles appearing in *Prisma* during the years 1905-1907 about Japan, Korea, and China. *El Mundo Ilustrado* published numerous articles about life and customs in the Orient.

The Spanish American *modernista* in his search for novel effects, shares with writers of the symbolist and decadent mood an exquisitely refined verbal expression, combined with exotic and unfamiliar words. The well-known poem by Rubén Darío, "Sonatina," presents an excellent example of words rarely used poetically, such as "crisálida"[49] [chrysalis]. The use of unusual vocabulary made clarity of expression difficult and prompted declarations like "Tuércele el cuello al cisne de engañoso plumaje" [Wring the neck of the swan with its deceptive plumage] by Enrique González Martínez, and "La virtud está en ser tranquilo y fuerte; con el fuego interior todo se abraza" [Virtue is to be found in being calm and strong; it is with inner strength that all is encompassed] by Rubén Darío.[50] Both Clemente Palma in *Prisma* (during 1905 and 1906) and Dr. M. Flores in *El Mundo Ilustrado* (in 1910) ridicule the extravagant freedom in word usage and the creation of neologisms by *modernistas.* Other critics lament the large number of incompetent writers of this extravagant poetry, who, by sterile imitations of poetic images ("el cisne" [the swan], for example), caused an explosion of mediocre poetry. Most critics, whether they approved of the use of unusual vocabulary or not, agreed that the opaque verbosity of poetasters substantially reduced the number of readers of good poetry.[51]

The problem of the degree of sophistication among members of the American reading public is a most interesting question posed to turn-of-the-century Spanish American poets. There was little doubt that *modernista* poetry could be appreciated only by a minority. Víctor Pérez Petit in *El Mercurio de América* speaks of the reading public as "los escogidos"[52] [the chosen ones]. Vargas Vila describes the Spanish American reading public as "sin la cultura, sin la iniciación" [without the culture, without the initiation] needed to understand *modernista* literature.[53] In that same essay Vargas Vila exclaims: " ¡Escribir de Arte en América, y para América! ¡Sublime abnegación! ¡Noble empeño de almas soñadoras! "[54] [Writing about Art in America and for America! A complete impossibility! A noble task for dreamers!]

The question of sources of inspiration for *modernista* poets was also an issue of concern for the critics in Spanish America; they often displayed resentment of the high esteem many *modernista* writers had for France and for French literary leadership because of the fine Parnassian and symbolist poets. In *Mallarmé entre nosotros* Alfonso Reyes describes the accuracy with which Darío had been able to assimilate the style of Mallarmé and comments that "Darío, que era tan niño, se deja llevar por el deseo de imitar la lengua de Mallarmé"[55] [Darío, who was such a child, let himself get carried away by a desire to imitate Mallarmé's language]. There was concern in Spanish America for America to "create" a literature, rather than "copy" foreign modes of expression as a child might do.

At the turn of the century, there were many Spanish American writers who believed that artistic creation could occur in America without the dominance of French literature. Many critics voiced disapproval of France as being the main source of artistic inspiration in Spanish America. Leopoldo Lugones in *El Mercurio de América* indicates that Americans are tired of "confitería parisiense" [Parisian foolishness] and that in America "tenemos sed de vida intensa, de viento agreste; el campo virgen nos llama, pese al sobredorado de nuestras molduras europeas"[56] [we are thirsty for intense life, for country wind; the virgin countryside calls us, in spite of the glittering of our European models]. Luis Berisso, also in *El Mercurio de América,* admits that "indudablemente, el arte nuestro, comparado con el europeo, no existe casi; anda en pañales todavía" [without a doubt, our art, compared with European art, hardly exists; it is still in diapers] ; yet he believes that this young American art should be nurtured.[57] F. Navarro y Ledesma in *El Cojo Ilustrado* equates political independence from Europe with a need for "autonomía poética"[58] [poetic autonomy], a sentiment shared by Manuel Ugarte, who, in *La Aurora,* writes that American art "será libre, sano, audaz y joven como la tierra en que ve la luz"[59] [will be free, healthy, bold, and young, like the land that gives it life].

Manuel Ugarte continues in his article, "Las nuevas tendencias literarias," to discuss American art. He expresses the belief that "la belleza no puede ser una cosa transplantada y exótica, sino un brote nacional y espontáneo, una raíz hecha flor"[60] [beauty cannot be something transplanted and exotic, but a national and spontaneous shoot, a root that becomes a flower]. Bartolomé Mitre sees the presence of the rudimentary elements necessary for the formation of American art.[61] Clemente Palma blames the American reliance upon European inspiration on both American insecurity in relation to Europe and on the relative lack of difficulty in copying rather than in creating.[62] American art, claims Manuel Ugarte in *La Aurora,* should be solid and clear because the people of Spanish America are, in his view, "más bastos, más duros, más sólidos y más sanos" [more rough, hard, solid, and healthy] than the people of Europe, and therefore need a form of artistic expression "en consonancia con nuestras naturalezas silvestremente rústicas, donde tejen todavía su nido los deberes, las bondades y los entusiasmos de la primera edad" [in tune with our rustic nature, in which work, goodness, and the enthusiasm of an early age are still making their nest].[63] The growth of Spanish American literature, reason Ugarte, Mitre, and Palma, will be handicapped both in content and in form by superficial and artificial attitudes and an abundance of imitation.

Due to the eclectic nature of Spanish American *modernismo,* our study of the role of symbolism within that literary movement has necessarily dealt also with Parnassian principles and the Spanish American understanding of the decadent mood in literature. In this study of important literary journals published between 1896 and 1910, it is evident that literary critics applied disparate and often conflicting aesthetic criteria when evaluating a work of art.

Until the turn of the century, the qualities of vagueness, suggestiveness, and musicality of verse associated with symbolism were generally accepted as techniques which were not detrimental to the writing of good poetry. With the passing of time, however, these techniques were challenged. Both Clemente Palma and Dr. M. Flores felt that poetry should appeal to reason rather than to emotions and, therefore, advocated clarity in the presentation of the intellectual content of a poem. Other critics, such as Paul Groussac and F. Navarro y Ledesma feared detrimental attitudes which could affect the Spanish language if poets continued to challenge traditional syntax at their convenience and to create neologisms with frequency. As the century advances, the trend among literary critics in the journals studied is to exact greater adherence to traditional syntax and greater emphasis on content over form. While this critical attitude grows, however, vanguardist tendencies leading in some cases to a complete predominance of the suggestive values of sound and rhythm also continue to thrive, reaching culmination in works by writers such as Nicolás Guillén and Vincent Huidobro.

The search for the exotic by use of the Orient as a literary theme is not criticized in the reviews under consideration in this study. The search for the exotic by use of a contrived vocabulary of unusual words of obscure meaning, especially in the later years, is a subject of concern for the literary critics who published in the reviews studied here. An important expression of the desire to avoid the exotic and the frivolous is to be found in the sonnet "Tuércele el cuello al cisne," published in 1911 by the Mexican, Enrique González Martínez. It is in this sonnet that he proposes the wise owl, not the beautiful swan, as a new and important poetic symbol.

It seems proper to conclude, then, that the enormous impact of French letters upon Spanish America during the years 1896-1910 has had at least two important and lasting effects in the development of Spanish American literature. France provided America with new ideas and excellent works of art to serve as literary models. Spanish American writers both adopted and modified literary currents from France; and a rich, creative literature, *modernismo,* evolved. Nevertheless, this same presence of French letters made many Spanish Americans acutely aware of a relative lack of literature inspired by American motifs. This awareness, inspired in part by a comparison of American and European artistic expression, led critics and writers to search for artistic expression having roots deep in Spanish American reality.

*William Jewell College*

# NOTES

[1] Other literary reviews cited in this study include: *La Aurora* (Mexico: 1906-1909); and *Artes y Letras* (Mexico: 1904-1914).

[2] For example, the Mexican publication, *El Mundo Ilustrado,* during the years 1900-1905, published works by authors from Argentina, Bolivia, Colombia, Costa Rica, Cuba, Chile, Ecuador, El Salvador, Guatemala, Honduras, Mexico, Nicaragua, Panama, Peru, The Dominican Republic, Uruguay, and Venezuela. European countries represented include Spain, Germany, Belgium, Denmark, France, Italy, Poland, Portugal, Russia, and Sweden. The importance of French literature to this review is great. *El Mundo Ilustrado,* between 1900 and 1905, published 170 works by 65 different French authors.

[3] Recent studies, such as "Reflexiones en torno a la definición del Modernismo" by Ivan A. Schulman in *Cuadernos Americanos,* 147 (1966), 211-40, and "¿Es posible definir el Modernismo?" by Raúl Silva Castro in *Cuadernos Americanos,* 141 (1965), 172-79, reflect a continuing quest for precision in defining the term *modernismo.*

[4] The short-lived Parisian literary review, *El Nuevo Mercurio,* directed by Enrique Gómez Carrillo, consists of twelve issues printed in 1907. For more information about this review, see Schulman, pp. 216-18.

[5] This questionnaire was reprinted in *La Aurora,* 1 (15 Sept. 1907), 4.

[6] Clemente Palma, "Notas de Artes y Letras," *Prisma,* 3 (16 Apr. 1907), 9.

[7] Amado Nervo, "El modernismo," *La Aurora,* 1 (15 Sept. 1907), 4.

[8] Ibid. Nervo indicates that at least 20 years will be necessary for a critic to look back on *modernismo* with understanding.

[9] Yerko Moretic, "Acerca de las raíces ideológicas del modernismo hispanoamericano," in *El modernismo,* ed. Lily Litvak (Madrid: Taurus, 1975), pp. 53-54.

[10] Albert Schinz, *Nineteenth Century French Readings,* II. *Realism 1850-1885; Symbolism 1885-1900* (New York: Holt, 1939), p. 730.

[11] Rubén Darío, "Stéphane Mallarmé" in *Obras completas,* Vol. IV, *Cuentos y novelas* (Madrid: Afrodisio Aguado, 1955), p. 913. Alfonso Reyes devotes a note to the article of Darío in *Mallarmé entre nosotros* (Mexico City: Ediciones Tezontle, 1955), pp. 23-30. Reyes notes Darío's special use of language and his impressive knowledge of Mallarmé's works. Reyes reproduces several paragraphs of Darío's article.

[12] Enrique Gómez Carrillo, "La vida parisiense: la poesía contemporánea, 1884-1897," *El Cojo Ilustrado,* 6 (1 July 1897), 250. Gómez Carrillo also speaks in this same article of the work of Mallarmé as "gota de sol en diamante negro" [a drop of sunshine on a black diamond].

[13] Lucien Muhfeld (translated into Spanish by José Austria), "Mallarmé," *El Cojo Ilustrado,* 43 (15 Nov. 1909), 608. The author states that "los sonidos hieren, halagan, etcétera, nuestros sentidos y luego *sugieren* los fenómenos espirituales" [the sounds wound, flatter, etc., our senses and then *suggest* spiritual phenomena].

[14] José Ojeda, "Ensayo de crítica: 'Castalia Bárbara,' por Ricardo Jaimes Freyre," *El Mercurio de América,* 2 (Nov.-Dec. 1899), 198.

[15] Eugenio Díaz Romero, "Castalia Bárbara," *El Mercurio de América,* 2 (Sept.-Oct. 1899), 127.

[16] José María Vargas Vila, "Prefacio," *El Mercurio de América,* 3 (July-Aug. 1900), 68.

[17] Clemente Palma, "Notas de Artes y Letras," *Prisma,* 2 (16 Apr. 1906), 29.

[18] Dr. M. Flores, "El decadentismo explicado," *El Mundo Ilustrado,* 2 (15 May 1910), n. pag.

[19] Poe Carden, "Parnassianism, Symbolism, and Decadentism in Spanish American Modernism," *Hispania,* 43 (1960), 549.

[20] Vargas Vila, "Prefacio" (see above, n. 16), p. 70.

[21] Palma, "Notas de Artes y Letras," *Prisma,* 1 (16 Oct. 1905), 24.

[22] Vargas Vila, "Prefacio," p. 70.

23 Víctor Pérez Petit, "Los modernistas, II. Gabriel D'Annunzio," *El Mercurio de América*, 1 (Aug.-Sept. 1898), 104.

24 Gómez Carrillo, "Crónica parisiense," *El Cojo Ilustrado*, 5 (15 Feb. 1896), 178.

25 Nervo, "El modernismo" (see above, n. 7), p. 4.

26 Gómez Carrillo, "La vida parisiense: la poesía contemporánea, 1884-1897" (see above, n. 12), p. 518. Here Gómez Carrillo states that "el simbolismo acaba de ser enterrado" [symbolism has just been buried]. Later, Fernando Araujo in "Recuerdos del simbolismo," *El Cojo Ilustrado*, 13 (15 Feb. 1904), 129, states that symbolism "está muerto y enterrado" [is dead and buried].

27 Nervo, "El modernismo," (see above, n. 7), p. 4.

28 Palma, "Notas de Artes y Letras," *Prisma*, 3 (16 Apr. 1907), 9.

29 Arthur Canfield and Warner Patterson, *French Poems* (New York: Holt, Rinehart and Winston, 1960), p. 407.

30 Pérez Petit, "Los modernistas, I. Gabriel D'Annunzio," *El Mercurio de América*, 1 (20 July 1898), 17.

31 Ojeda, "Ensayo de crítica" (see above, n. 14), p. 204.

32 Díaz Romero, "Castalia Bárbara" (see above, n. 15), p. 129.

33 Gómez Carrillo, "Crónica parisiense," (see above, n. 24), p. 178.

34 Paul Groussac, "La Biblioteca de Buenos Aires," *La Biblioteca*, 1, No. 1 (1896), 182.

35 F. Navarro y Ledesma, "Poetas americanos: Rubén Darío y su escuela," *El Cojo Ilustrado*, 7 (15 June 1898), 439.

36 Palma, "Notas de Artes y Letras," *Prisma*, 1 (1 Nov. 1905), 21.

37 Palma, "Notas de Artes y Letras," *Prisma*, 2 (16 Apr. 1906), 29.

38 Flores, "El decadentismo explicado" (see above, n. 18), n. pag.

39 Navarro y Ledesma, "Poetas americanos: Francisco A. de Icaza," *El Mundo*, 2 (4 July 1897), 12.

40 Pérez Petit, "Los modernistas, II. Gabriel D'Annunzio" (see above, n. 23), p. 101.

41 Vargas Vila, "Prefacio," pp. 68-69.

42 Flores, "La Babel del Arte," *El Mundo Ilustrado*, 7 (8 December 1901), n. pag.

43 Quoted by Poe Carden in "Parnassianism, Symbolism, and Decadentism in Spanish American Modernism" (see above, n. 19), p. 547. Originally published in *Puntos de Vista* (Havana, 1892), pp. 172-73.

44 Palma, "Notas de Artes y Letras," *Prisma*, 1 (1 Nov. 1905), 21; "Decadencia y Apogeo," *Prisma*, 2 (15 Aug. 1906); "Notas de Artes y Letras," *Prisma*, 3 (16 Feb. 1907), 20.

45 Flores, "El spleen," *El Mundo Ilustrado*, 9 (3 July 1904), n. pag.

46 Flores, "El decadentismo explicado" (see above, n. 18), n. pag. Other articles by Dr. M. Flores concerning the relationship of art to public morality include: "La influencia moralizadora del Arte," *El Mundo Ilustrado*, 9 (16 Feb. 1902), n. pag.; "El Arte y la Moral," *El Mundo Ilustrado*, 8 (15 Sept. 1901), n. pag.

47 José Asunción Silva, "De sobre mesa (fragmento)," *El Cojo Ilustrado*, 7 (1 Sept. 1898), 626.

48 Charles Baudelaire, "Les paradis artificiels," in *Oeuvres complètes* (Paris: Seuil, 1968), pp. 566-616.

49 Rubén Darío, "Sonatina," in *Obras completas*, V (Madrid: Afodisio Aguado, 1953), 774-75.

50 Enrique González Martínez, "Tuércele el cuello al cisne," in Eugenio Florit and José Olivio Jiménez, *La poesía hispanoamericana desde el modernismo* (New York: Appleton, 1968), p. 145; Rubén Darío, "Yo soy aquel que ayer no más decía," in *Obras completas*, V, 861-65.

[51] Palma, "Notas de Artes y Letras," *Prisma,* 1 (1 Nov. 1905), 21. In this article he uses irony to ridicule the use of such words as "nidos ornitonófonos" [ornithological nests]. Palma also equates *modernista* vocabulary with Esperanto, "Notas de Artes y Letras," *Prisma,* 2 (16 Apr. 1906), 29.

[52] Pérez Petit, "Los modernistas, I. Gabriel D'Annunzio" (see above, n. 30), p. 28.

[53] Vargas Vila, "Prefacio," p. 76.

[54] Ibid., p. 74.

[55] Reyes, *Mallarmé entre nosotros* (see above, n. 11), p. 23.

[56] Leopoldo Lugones, "Del amor, del dolor y del vicio," *El Mercurio de América,* 1 (Aug.-Sept. 1898), 99.

[57] Luis Berisso, "De mi diario," *El Mercurio de América,* 1, No. 1 (Nov. 1898), 266.

[58] Navarro y Ledesma, "Poetas americanos: Rubén Darío y su escuela" (see above, n. 35), p. 438.

[59] Manuel Ugarte, "Las nuevas tendencias literarias," *La Aurora,* 1 (15 Apr. 1909), 3.

[60] Ibid.

[61] Bartolomé Mitre, "Letras americanas," *La Biblioteca,* 2, No. 7 (1897), 69.

[62] Palma, "Notas de Artes y Letras," *Prisma* 1 (1 Nov. 1905), 21.

[63] Ugarte, "Las nuevas tendencias literarias," p. 3.

# EL CULTO DE LOS MUERTOS.

Illustration by Julio Ruelas. Reproduced from *Revista Moderna de México,* 4 (Nov. 1903), 194.

# Julián del Casal and the Cult of Artificiality: Roots and Functions

## Luis Felipe Clay Méndez

> *haz, ¡oh, Dios! , que no vean ya mis ojos*
> *la horrible Realidad que me contrista.*
> —*Julián del Casal*[1]
>
> *[Grant, oh, Lordi, that my eyes no longer see*
> *the horrible Reality that afflicts me.]*

Despite traditional interpretations that persisted in stressing an innate deficiency that determined Julián del Casal's character, a new and more accurate consideration of the social, political, and cultural pressures that weighed upon him is being brought to bear.[2] It is no longer valid, therefore, to simplify his artistic pose under the mistaken assumption that his production was conceived exclusively within, and related only to, an alienated point of view. Partly accountable for this sophism was the fact that it stemmed basically from an analysis of Casal's poetry. The prose, much more copious and revealing, still awaits being properly incorporated into the Cuban artist's overall production. This study will have as its main objective the itemization of the antecedents—literary and environmental—that motivated, shaped, and maintained the cult of artificiality as expressed primarily in Casal's prose.

Julián del Casal approached literature as a way to release both his talents and his anxiety. In doing so, he manifested a tendency to depersonalize himself in order to better achieve cohesion with other writers who advocated similar emotional aberration, disenchanted with the oppressive environment and firmly committed to changing it.[3] After a considerable amount of eclectic reading by Casal, French poetic schools became the most propitious source from which he could draw sound inspiration as well as a mode of expression. Of these the one that provided the best and most accessible means of change and escape was French Symbolism. The powerful capabilities inherent in the cult of artificiality, which was a pervasive element in that movement, became Casal's overriding premise, broken down to its essential components. From the symbolists Casal inherited a priority of purpose that could be synthesized by the dictum that "the first duty in life is to be as artificial as possible."[4] Eagerly adopting this dictum as an intellectual obsession in the manner of Joris-Karl Huysmans, Casal then developed the principles of what Gustavo Duplessis calls "la estética de lo artificial"[5] [the esthetic of the artificial], which guides and limits the scope of his most recurrent themes.


## Withdrawal from Society

One evident cause of Casal's devotion to artificiality was an intense desire to withdraw from the social and political constituents of the world around him, perpetrated by the stagnant form of government that imperial Spain imposed on Cuba, with its archaic regulations and ill-fated goals. The resulting social climate was one of deprivation and overt materialism, which contrasted sharply with the refined and exquisite creed espoused by Casal.[6] Unable, therefore, to negotiate the patulous "abyss" that separated him from his fellow men, Casal opted for total separation by isolating himself in a virtually impenetrable and artificial world of his own. By means of evasion, which resulted from his convictions and not from instinctive impulses, Casal attempted to minimize the impure influences of his milieu while simultaneously devoting his efforts to more dependable reinforcements. In this artificial realm of alienation Casal was able to delve into his own self, a process that Ricardo Gullón calls "confinamiento en el yo"[7] [confinement in the self], which is the center of artistic creation. The writer, as Casal himself points out, "acude a sí mismo, única fuente de consuelo, para adormecer sus penas con la cadencia de las estrofas que arranca de lo más profundo de su corazón"[8] [resorts to himself, the only source of consolation, in order to appease his sorrows with the cadence of the stanzas that he tears out of the depths of his heart].

Solitude provides both shelter and a mood conducive to meditation and illumination. Casal infers this transition when he recalls his farewell to a bookstore owner who had told him the story of a young man who lived much like Casal himself: "sin decir una palabra, estreché su mano, cogí el sombrero y me refugié en mi soledad, donde he pensado mucho y donde pienso todavía en aquel extraño joven que, para conjurar su spleen, ha hecho del sufrimiento una voluptuosidad" (I, 237) [without saying a word, I shook his hand, took my hat and sought refuge in my solitude, where I have thought a lot and where I still think about that strange young man who, in order to exorcise his despondency, has turned suffering into voluptuousness]. The apparent solidarity—suggested by "I shook his hand" and "I still think"—transcends to a level of spiritual perversion with "my solitude" serving as a catalyst. Worthy of mention in this regard is the deliberate use of the possessive adjective ("mi soledad"), normally omitted in Spanish, employed here to underline the personal nature of solitude. But Casal's awareness that others also had an affinity for solitude led to a further awareness that there exists a brotherhood of marginal entities who share a common purpose in suffering and shattered aspirations. Since they are in an alien environment, however, they are unable to sustain their creed and are equally unable to share those alien values. "Whatever the beginning of his solitude," Ralph Harper has written, "an outsider knows he is not like most men; and the knowledge of his difference hurts. The nineteenth and twentieth centuries in art and real life have left a frieze of outsiders of all kinds, ranging from epic and tragic heroes to orphans and refugees. They are all brothers of communion of displacement and loneliness."[9]

As an "outsider," Casal eventually makes solitude an ideal that presupposes "vivir obscurecido, solo, arrinconado e invisible para todos" (III, 85) [living in obscurity, alone, set aside and invisible to everyone]. Nevertheless, there is suffering associated with this flight, stemming from the confrontation—as Rodríguez-Fernández puts it—of the self and the alien world.[10] Casal himself clearly outlines the causal relationship: "aquel hombre ha vivido un día entre sus semejantes y, desencantado de ellos, se ha retirado a la soledad, sin dignarse mostrar su desprecio a los demás" (III, 27) [that man has lived one day among his fellow men and, disenchanted with them, has withdrawn to solitude, without condescending to show his scorn toward others].

Eventually, Casal recognizes that his "lúgubre aislamiento" (p. 46) [gloomy isolation] has become obsessive since, as he admits, "en cualquier lugar he de encontrarme solo" (p. 51) [I will feel alone anywhere]. This is when the anguished writer begins to consider death as the ultimate solitude:

Procuraré irme a vivir en un barrio lejano, cerca del mar, para aguardar allí la muerte, que no tardará muchos años en venir. Mientras llegue, viviré entre libros y cuadros, trabajando todo lo que pueda literariamente, sin pretender alcanzar nada con mis trabajos, como no sea matar el tiempo. (III, 85)

[I will try to go and live in a faraway neighborhood, near the sea, to await death there, which will not take many years to come. While it is arriving, I will live among books and paintings, working literarily as much as I can, without pretending to attain anything with my work other than killing time.]

Casal has tried to arrange his remaining years so that they will be as artificial as possible, surrounding himself with works of art and adopting nihilistic aspirations that will isolate him from the outside world. It is by no means accidental that his final location is distant from everything and near the sea, a powerful symbol of escape and hope frequently utilized by French Symbolists.[11]

The sea provides an extension of self-confinement and a way to alter the physical circumstances by linking them with an artificial environment where the bemused spirit might find solace and inspiration. Again, we must establish a direct relationship between the impoverished state of Casal's homeland and the respite inherent in travel; accordingly, Casal then summoned three components of artificiality and "built for himself a secluded world of oriental art, of sensory perceptions, of imaginary wanderings"[12] that was diametrically opposed to the real world. Casal favors this avenue of escape because he can carefully reconstruct his visions to conform to a particular need at any given moment. His vacillating moods account for paradoxical expectations in the "bello país desconocido" (p. 217) [beautiful unknown country]. In a poem entitled "Nostalgias" (p. 135), Casal lets his mind wander like Rimbaud's "drunken boat"[13] and whimsically changes the make-up of his imaginary landscape: "soplo helado del viento" [frozen breath of the wind], "campos olorosos" [odorous fields], "llanura africana" [African plain], "bambú corpulento" [strong bamboo tree], "flor de loto" [lotus flower]. or "taitiano archipiélago" [Tahitian archipelago]. Behind all the confusion there is a unifying desire to flee, with no specific heading, to "otro cielo, otro monte,/ otra playa, otro horizonte,/ otro mar,/ otros pueblos, otras gentes/ de maneras diferentes/ de pensar" [another sky, another hill,/ another beach, another horizon,/ another sea,/ other towns, other people/ with a different way/ of thinking].

Casal realizes that he cannot make his dreamland too definite, lest it become perilously like a natural place, physically accessible. It is precisely for this reason that, after having dreamed of Paris and made plans to visit it, when he found himself in Europe he categorically refused to fulfill his dream. He explains this incident in terms of not wishing to see his visions turn into a disappointing reality:

> Porque si me fuera, yo estoy seguro que mi ensueño se desvanecería, como el aroma de una flor cogida en la mano, hasta quedar despojado de todos sus encantos; mientras que viéndolo de lejos, yo creo todavía que hay algo en el mundo, que endulce el mal de la vida, algo que constituye mi última ilusión. (I, 229)
>
> [Because if I left, I am sure that my reverie would vanish, like the aroma of a flower taken in the hand, until becoming stripped of all its charms; while seeing it from afar, I still believe that there is something in the world that may sweeten life's evil, something that constitutes my last illusion.]

This vital stance is representative of Julián del Casal's devotion to artificiality and his preference of illusion over a reality that could prove to be disappointing and even more deceiving than make-believe. Since distance was necessary to the development of his vision, Casal always maintained as an ultimate goal the enticingly exotic land where "todo es bello, rico y tranquilo, donde la fantasía ha construido y decorado una China occidental, donde la vida es dulce de respirar, donde la dicha está casada con el silencio. Allá es preciso que vayamos a vivir, allá es preciso que vayamos a morir" (II, 151) [everything is beautiful, rich, and tranquil, where fantasy has constructed and decorated an occidental China, where life is sweet to breathe, where happiness is married to silence. There we must go to live, there we must go to die].

### Against Natural Law

Similar to the way that social, economic, and political conventions promote self-confinement and an obsessive desire for exotic climes, the physical environment—both primary nature and the man-made metropolis—triggers in devoted advocates of artificiality an immediate and uncompromising tendency to rejection. Despite the intrinsic antithesis of the two alternatives, the artist is unable to cope with either one since, in a materialistic environment, he is denied an atmosphere in which he can survive esthetically. Nature represents a competitive creative force that overwhelms the artist with its inflexible manner, justifying the symbolists' aversion to natural law, which Paul Verlaine (to cite but one example of many that are available) delineates in his poem "L'Angoisse" ["Anguish"]: "Nature, rien de toi ne m'émeut, ni les champs/ Nourriciers, ni l'écho vermeil des pastorales/ Siciliennes, ni les pompes aurorales,/ Ni la solennité dolente des couchants" ["Nature, nothing in you moves me, not the fruitful/ Fields, not the roseate echo of the pastorales/ Of Sicily, not the grandeur of the dawns,/ Not the solemn ruefulness of sunsets"].[14] The negative aspect of these lines complements the attitude shared by other nineteenth-century writers, who viewed nature as an entity that had little to offer the tired senses: its omniscient powers are wasted and reduced to a cyclical pattern of monotony.

This finitude renders nature inferior to the boundless powers of artifice, which is capable of ridding objects of "sus defectos naturales" (II, 81) [their natural defects]. Artists envision the day when the triumph will be absolute, when synesthetic combinations will be achieved that are not possible in the realm of natural law: "Si las piedras preciosas tuvieran aromas, como los tendrán algún día, porque el Arte se encargará de curarlas de esa imperfección natural." (III, 46) [If only precious stones had aromas, as they will have some day, because Art will be responsible for curing them of that natural imperfection]. Casal looks forward to this day and also to a certain country that will attest to this victory: "Es un país singular, superior a los otros, como el Arte lo es a la Naturaleza, donde ésta está reforzada por el ensueño, donde está corregida, embellecida, refundida" (II, 152) [It is a singular country, superior to others, as Art is superior to Nature, where the latter is reshaped by reverie, where it is corrected, beautiful, recast].

Further evidence of nature's shortcomings is the corruptibility of its accomplishments. Charles Baudelaire, an ardent exponent of the enmity between artist and nature, often captures it through images of putrefaction in his poetry, as in "une Charogne" ["A Carcass"]: "Le soleil rayonnait sur cette pourriture,/ Comme afin de la cuire à point,/ Et de rendre au centuple à la grande Nature/ Tout ce qu'ensemble elle avait joint" ["The sun shone hotly on all this rotteness/ As if it were in some sense boiling,/ As when Nature in her absolute nothingness/ Cares nothing for her creature's spoiling"].[15] The poem epitomizes nature's impassiveness and obvious lack of interest in man's debased and putrid existence. Emulating this champion of the perverse and macabre, Casal also takes morbid pleasure in describing the putrefying process within himself:

> De me cráneo, que un globo formaba
> erizado de rojos cabellos,
> descendían al rostro deforme,
> saboreando el licor purulento,
> largas sierpes de piel solferina
> que llegaban al borde del pecho,
> donde un cuervo de pico acerado
> implacable roíame el sexo. (p. 150)[16]
>
> [From my skull, shaped like a globe
> bristling with red hairs,
> descended, to the deformed face,
> savoring the purulent liquor,
> long serpents of purplish skin
> that arrived at the edge of my chest,
> where a raven with a steel beak
> implacably gnawed at my sex.]

Since nature has been exposed both for its imperfections and for its perishability, in Casal's view, mankind no longer "acude a refugiarse en los brazos de la naturaleza, porque sabe que no tiene alma" (I, 168) [seeks refuge in the arms of nature, knowing that it has no soul]. Hence, it follows, if one reasons as Baudelaire did, that, since nature is heartless, "everything natural in man is bad and whatever is good is artificial and acquired—from virtue to face-paint."[17] Nature is therefore diametrically opposed to the essential components of the artist's ethical and esthetic make-up. Casal expressed this through an antipathy even for those artists—such as gifted singers—who had God-given talents and did not have to endure the agony of concentration, study, and hard work before succeeding, as writers did: "Yo los odio, como odio todo aquello en que predomina la obra de la naturaleza y en que apenas se reconocen las huellas del estudio, de la paciencia y de la propia personalidad" (III, 57) [I hate them, as I hate everything in which the work of nature predominates and in which traces of study, patience, and even the personality itself are barely recognized].

Casal himself was living proof of nature's inadequacy since he was sporadically plagued by the ominous signs that foreshadow an early death and that forced him to withdraw to more healthful places. His infirmity, consequently, can be taken to account for the value inversion that chooses instead of "el olor de un bosque de caoba,/ el ambiente enfermizo de una alcoba" (p. 190) [the odor of a mahogany forest,/ the sickly atmosphere of a bedroom]. These preventive measures suggest the special care required by a delicate being because of "la pobreza de su organismo, que lo obligaría a vivir, como una planta de invernadero, tras las vidrieras de la casa paterna, buscando la sombra y huyendo de la luz de sol" (I, 230) [the weakness of his organism, that would force him to live, like a nursery plant, behind the windows of his paternal home, seeking the shade and fleeing from the sunlight]. Sunlight, being a product of nature, is destructive and threatens to "exterminate" the "freshness" of any feeble vegetable (p. 62). The ability to survive in the shade heralds another type of triumph—however perverted—over the devastating effects of nature.

Casal's embittered resentment of natural law appears at a very early stage of his thematic development, when the poet chastises nature for instilling a sense of boredom:

> ¡Qué insípidos tus dones conocidos!
> ¡Cómo al verte el hastío me consume!
> Muere al fin, creadora ya agotada,
> o brinda algo de nuevo a los sentidos . . .
> ¡Ya un color, ya un sonido, ya un perfume! (p. 119)

> [How insipid are your known talents!
> How tedium consumes me when I see you!
> Die once and for all, creator already spent,
> or offer something new to the senses . . .
> Either a color, or a sound, or a perfume!]

It is precisely the inalterable quality of the Cuban landscape that prevents Casal from finding any redeeming value in it, as we can see in a letter written shortly after his return from a convalescing excursion to the country, where he felt "el hastío más insoportable a la vista de un cielo siempre azul, encima de un campo siempre verde. La unión eterna de estos dos colores produce la impresión más antiestética que se puede sentir" (I, 241) [the most unbearable tedium at the sight of an ever-blue sky above an ever-green field. The union of these two colors produces the most antiesthetic impression that one can feel]. Incapable of tolerating the unchanging exhuberance of his countryside, Casal professes "el impuro amor de las ciudades" (p. 190) [the impure love of the cities], where there exists a pervasive artificiality more attuned to his aberrant psyche. Nevertheless, subjected as he was to sporadic changes of mood brought about by a sudden aggravation of his pathological symptoms, Casal also admits that he is unable to maintain emotional stability in a synthetic world of human beings whom he finds terribly irritating: "creo que mi neurosis, o como se llame mi enfermedad, depende en gran parte de vivir en la ciudad, es decir, rodeado de paredes altas, de calles adoquinadas, oyendo incesantemente estrépito de coches, ómnibus y carretones" (III, 85) [I believe that my neurosis, or whatever my illness might be called, stems in part from living in the city, that is to say, surrounded by high walls, cobblestone streets, incessantly hearing the deafening noise of coaches, omnibuses, and carts]. His alienated spirit and refined tastes clashed in the city with the daily reminders of another type of existence that was extremely active, mechanized, and chaotic. Moreover, urban life can ultimately lead to a rhythm that denotes the same despised invariability as that encountered in the countryside.[18] As George Ridge has pointed out, the decadent hero "detests the great city, his megalopolis, which holds him captive through the fatal appeal of its artificiality."[19] On the one hand, the city contains every conceivable perversion and symbolizes man's victory over nature; on the other hand, its environment is comprised of multitudes that augment "la sensación más triste que se puede experimentar: la del aislamiento entre la multitud" (II, 99) [the saddest sensation that can be experienced: that of isolation within a crowd].

Since the urban setting is incapable of fulfilling his insatiable appetite for artificiality, Casal must create a synthetic reality within the immediate reality. For this purpose he resorts to various ploys, from dressing like a monk and living an ascetic existence to surrounding himself with oriental objects that created an ambiance of exotic preciousness. He clung to this world by refusing to recognize the signs that threatened to dissolve his illusive reality: "Los globos de luz eléctrica, colgados entre las columnas rojas, eran lo único que desvanecía a ratos mi ilusión. Pero yo procuraba no mirarlos jamás" (III, 57) [The electric light bulbs, hung among the red columns, were the only things that at times made my illusion vanish. But I tried not ever to look at them]. This state of mind, however, was not tenable for long. Consequently, realizing the precarious and ephemeral function of this kind of self-deceit, Casal also tried to produce artificiality through the use of drugs, a means of escape utilized by Baudelaire in his journeys to "the real land of Cockaigne."[20]

Casal's relationship to drugs was more esthetic than practical and his hallucinatory experiences were normally related to literary trances or the commitment to modify reality: "Durante la lectura, mi pensamiento se sumerge, desde la primera página, en una especie de letargo cataléptico, del que no quisiera nunca salir. Cada párrafo me produce el efecto de una bocanada de éter" (I, 207-08) [while reading, my thoughts are submerged, from the first page, in a kind of cataleptic lethargy which I would never want to leave. Each paragraph produces in me the effect of a whiff of ether]. Literature, like ether, becomes a cathartic agent and has an effect similar to the one outlined in "La canción de la morfina" [The Song of Morphine], in which the drug is animated for the purpose of enticing the reader with its powers:

> Amantes de la quimera,
> yo calmaré vuestro mal:
> soy la dicha artificial,
> que es la dicha verdadera. (p. 69)
>
> [Lovers of the chimera,
> I will calm your sickness:
> I am artificial happiness,
> which is true happiness.]

This assertion of a perverted truth by the morphine is one of the chief justifications for using hallucinatory agents. Through drugs the artist is able to confuse the delicate balance that separates reality from artificiality. Furthermore, while he is under the influence of drugs, he can expand the sensorial boundaries that stimulate creation by unleashing the limitless dimensions of synesthesia:

> doy al cuerpo sensaciones;
> presto al espíritu alas.
>
> Percibe el cuerpo dormido
> por mi mágico sopor,
> sonidos en el color,
> colores en el sonido. (p. 70)
>
> [to the body I give sensations;
> to the spirit I lend wings.
>
> The body that lies asleep
> under my magic stupor
> perceives sounds in color
> and colors in a sound.]

Precisely because of this esthetic inducement, Casal, like many other artists of his time, fell prey to the drug habit. As Guerard has stated: "few believers in Art for Art's sake are free from the *À Rebours* taint, the willful quest of the abnormal."[21] All symbolist-decadent perversion had its roots either in the rejection of the prevailing circumstances or in some sort of sordid experimentation purported to broaden the scope of artistic creativity. The latter, in the case of Casal, will compensate for the cultural myopia of colonial Cuba.

### The Power of Art

Although Julián del Casal remains somewhat aloof and confessional in his poetry, his prose provides his readers with an objective and accurate account of the cultural stagnation of his time, which should be considered among his most recurrent and significant themes. The overall picture is one of deprivation, beginning with "la indiferencia glacial, la falta de estímulo y la poca estimación que acompañan a los que viven aquí dedicados a los trabajos intelectuales" (II, 28) [the glacial indifference, the lack of stimulation, and the little esteem that accompany those who live here dedicated to intellectual work]. These factors, among innumerable others are responsible for Casal's defeatist question: "¿Puedo aspirar a algo, en nuestro medio social, que esté en consonancia con mi carácter, con mi educación o con mis aspiraciones?"

(I, 228) [Can I aspire to anything, in our social medium, that is in consonance with my character, my education, or my aspirations?]

In such a demoralizing milieu the artist may succumb, for his "inteligencia se atrofia, y su carácter se agria, cayendo en la más negra misantropía" (II, 71) [his intelligence is atrophied, and his character becomes bitter, falling into the blackest kind of misanthropy]. Only artists who can pursue and maintain a commitment to esthetic ideals may overcome the cultural circumstances, and Enrique José Varona is—like Casal himself—one of them:

> un gran escritor en un medio propicio para realizar toda clase de empresas, menos para las intelectuales, lo cual demuestra que poseía una vocación más sólida que ningún otro escritor cubano y que es un hombre que ama verdaderamente su Ideal, amor que no se ha visto justipreciado por su pueblo, porque no teniendo éste más que el de la vida material, difícil le sería comprender que un individuo pueda perseguir otro más noble, más elevado, más inmaterial. (I, 251-52)
>
> [a great writer in an environment conducive to the accomplishment of all kinds of plans, except intellectual ones, which shows that he possessed a more solid vocation than any other Cuban writer and that he is a man who truly loves his Ideal, a love that his people have not appreciated because they, having love only for a material life, could hardly understand how an individual could pursue a nobler one, more elevated, less materialistic.]

Casal establishes an antithesis between literary dedication and the prevailing values, underscoring the merit of artists who survive under such adverse conditions. This contraposition becomes a prevalent stylistic element in Casal's production, employed whenever the young writer addressed an intrinsic duality: "Su pensamiento anhelaba ascender en pos de las águilas hacia el sol y tuvo que marchar tras los reptiles hacia el lodazal" (I, 262) [His thoughts longed to ascend after the eagles toward the sun and had to march behind the reptiles toward the swamp].

Devotion to art establishes the polar, elevated world seen above, where the follower of this cult can develop it, nourishing what Guerard calls "a perversity inherent in the artistic temperament, a shrinking from the bustle of the market place, a nostalgia for the solitude of the Ivory Tower, a timidity which half-reveals the haunting secret of self-diffidence."[22] In this stance there is a resulting "estado de alta espiritualidad"[23] [state of high spirituality] derived from the willful acceptance of "la penitencia purificante de la vida" (I, 37) [the purifying penitence of life] that either protects the artist from denigrating stains or cleanses him afterward. The esthete may then consider himself a martyr who "ha sacrificado su existencia en aras de su ideal" (III, 62) [has sacrificed his existence on the altar of his ideal].

In addition to affording a mystical purification of life, the devotion to art can indeed supply protection to "el confiado caminante que pasa por el sendero de la vida, aspirando el olor de las flores abiertas y bebiendo la lumbre de los astros" (III, 35) [the confident traveler who goes along the path of life, inhaling the aroma of open flowers and drinking the brightness of the stars]. Anyone who identifies with refined and dignifying things is worthy of "la mirada consoladora de las estrellas" (I, 213) [the consoling glance of the stars] since artistic devotion is a powerful ally, providing "el talismán que conjura al maleficio, el ácido que aniquila al microbio, la fuerza que arranca la pistola al suicida, la moneda de oro en el fango del arroyo, la tea fulgurante que deshace el pavor de las tinieblas" (I, 258) [the talisman that conjures the spell, the acid that annihilates the microbe, the force that tears the pistol away from the would-be suicide, the gold coin in the mud of the stream, the bright torch that dispels the fear of the darkness]. The deliverance is immediate:

> Cuando tu cuerpo, acribillado de heridas, caiga sangrando sobre las piedras del camino; cuando tus labios, cerrados para siempre, exhalen el último suspiro; ceñiré a tu frente el lauro de los inmortales y te abriré las puertas de mi templo. ¿Quieres seguirme? Piensa en que me aborrecen las muchedumbres, porque soy *El Arte*. (II, 83)
>
> [When your body, riddled with wounds, falls bleeding on the rocks of the road; when your lips, closed forever, exhale the last sigh; I will place on your forehead the wreath of the immortals and open for you the doors of my temple. Do you want to follow me? Remember that the multitudes abhor me, because I am *Art*.]

The symbolism here is overwhelming; the dual options represent the multiple vicissitudes of life ("wounds," "rocks," "the sigh," and "the multitudes"), counterpoised by the withdrawal that is inherent in artificiality, the "temple."

Casal readily accepts this invitation, hoping that artistic devotion will succor him and alleviate his suffering:

> Para olvidar entonces las tristezas
> que, como nubes de voraces pájaros
> al fruto de oro entre las verdes ramas,
> dejan mi corazón despedazado,
> refúgiome del Arte en los misterios. (p. 16)
>
> [To forget then the sadnesses
> that, like clouds of voracious birds
> on the golden fruit among the green branches,
> leave my heart in pieces,
> I take refuge in the mysteries of Art.]

This confidence in art has an immediate advantage: the conscientious esthete can eventually disregard the "voracious birds" that threaten him with the new realization that "el verdadero artista no se debe ocupar del prestigio que le concede el público, sino perfeccionarse en su arte y nada más" (III, 85) [the true artist should not concern himself with the prestige that the public bestows on him, but with the perfection of his art and nothing else]. Such a striving for perfection is the basis of what Auerbach has called in the French Symbolists "the Idolatry of art."[24] Casal's self-imposed and rigid standards were extremely difficult to attain; and, unwilling to acquiesce to prevailing norms, he was rarely satisfied with his own work. What Casal wrote about José Arburu could have been said of Casal himself: "nunca quedaba satisfecho con sus obras, porque había colocado muy alto su ideal" (I, 282) [he was never satisfied with his works because he had set his ideal very high]. Casal's epitaph attests to his overriding and primary esthetic drive: "Amó solamente la Belleza/ Que ahora encuentre la Verdad su alma" (p. 55) [He loved only Beauty/ Let his soul now find Truth].

In his never-ending quest for an innovative expression and for intellectual and sensory stimulation, Julián del Casal promoted an extension of literature.

Through a diffusion of techniques he attempted to establish a continuity between the written word and the plastic arts. His collection "Mi museo ideal" [My Ideal Museum] consists of ten sonnets that correspond to an equal number of paintings by the French symbolist artist Gustave Moreau. Each of the poems is a verbal painting that approximates the chromatic richness of a particular canvas while simultaneously probing its meaning; the poems reveal the palette of a painter who has a keen sense of color, an artist who feels through his senses.[25]

The apprenticeship of Julián del Casal was a long, steady, and conscientious one, beginning with the appreciation and emulation of compatible approaches by other artists, like Joris-Karl Huysmans who, according to Casal, "traspasa las fronteras literarias, refundiendo los procedimientos más refinados de las otras artes, especialmente los de la orfebrería, el mosaico y la pintura" (I, 177) [goes beyond literary boundaries, recasting the most refined procedures of other arts, especially those related to gold or silver work, mosaic, and painting]. It is quite fitting that Casal used the French writer to illustrate the extensive scope of literature. Huysmans created a character—Des Esseintes—with whom the bemused Casal might be identified, a refined spirit who also had "unrealizable ideals and was beginning to outline his experiments in colour."[26] Undoubtedly, Casal himself began to manipulate color when he first lamented "que nuestra pluma no tenga, en estos momentos, la fineza de un pincel" (II, 25) [that our pen does not have, in these moments, the fineness of an artist's brush]. Eventually he developed this technique, and his profound admiration for plastic expression provided the incentive: "Habiendo sentido siempre un gran amor por la pintura, yo había tratado de hacer, en aquella composición, dos cuadros poéticos, uno en el estilo de Perugino y otro en el estilo de Rembrandt" (I, 267) [Having always felt a great love for painting, I tried to make, in that composition, two poetic paintings, one in the style of Perugino and another in the style of Rembrandt].

Bearing in mind that the underlying intention is to form an artificial realm as discordant with the environment as possible, it should come as no surprise that Casal avails himself of the illusive capabilities of the plastic arts. Once he has achieved his purpose, the painter can reap its benefits:

> la hora de arrinconar la tela esbozada, pasar la espátula sobre la paleta y aprisionar el color en sus frascos, dejando que su espíritu, como halcón desencantado, se aleje de la tierra y se remonte a los espacios azules de la fantasía, donde las quimeras, como mariposas de oro en torno de una estrella, revolotean sin cesar. (I, 265)

> [the time for laying aside the sketched canvas, for passing the knife over the palette and closing the colors in their tubes, allowing his spirit, like a disenchanted falcon, to withdraw from the earth and to flee to the blue spaces of fantasy, where chimeras, like golden butterflies around a star, flutter incessantly.]

By means of a powerful symbol of elevation and freedom, the writer has achieved the levitation of a deserving spirit to an artificial and ethereal region of recognition and dreams. Supplementary images—"blues," "butterflies," and "a star"— enhance the dignifying nature of this realm. Since both literary and plastic arts espouse no other objective than "el de satisfacer una necesidad espiritual" (II, 177) [the satisfaction of a spiritual necessity], they can share the attainment of this level of fulfillment and reward, where "el Arte se conserve, en las más puras cimas" (I, 177) [Art may be kept on the purest summits].

Access to this artificial world in which dreams, aspirations, hopes and recompense amalgamate harmoniously, was possible only for superior beings whose entire lives were an exemplary devotion to estheticism of one sort or another, and who possessed a spirit that was "impaciente por abrir las alas" (III, 64) [impatient to spread its wings]. In Casal's view, Rafael Díaz Albertini and Gaspar Villate were such spirits: "Albertini transportaba las llamas desconocidas, en las notas de oro de su violín, al paraíso azul del Ideal y Villate, por medio de sus creaciones, iba ascendiendo a la Cumbre Sagrada, donde la Gloria aguarda a sus elegidos" (III, 60) [Albertini transported the unknown flames, in the golden notes of his violin, to the blue paradise of the Ideal; and Villate, by means of his creations, was climbing to the Holy Summit, where Glory awaits the chosen ones]. Again we must notice the ascending motion imparted by the use of appropriate images. Casal himself fervently strove to reach this world of artificiality and consequent spirituality. As a poet, he was cognizant of the potential innate in his literary production:

> Aves mis versos son, que se detienen
> en las páginas blancas de tu libro,
> pidiéndote, con voz arrulladora,
> que les dejes hacer en tu alma un nido. (p. 212)

> [My verses are birds that stop
> on the white pages of your book,
> asking you, in a lulling voice,
> to let them build a nest in your soul.]

Unfortunately, a prolonged stay in this artificial region is untenable. Despite the unquestionable protection it offered to the aberrant spirit, there is always the inexorable return to the real world, expressed by Casal in terms of a descending motion:

> Así mi ensueño, pájaro canoro
> de níveas plumas y rosado pico,
> al querer en el mundo hallar cabida,
>
> encontró de lo real los muros de oro
> y deshecho, cual frágil abanico,
> cayó entre el fango inmundo de la vida. (p. 143)

> [Thus my reverie, a song bird
> of snowy feathers and rosy beak,
> wanting to find a place in this world,
>
> found the golden walls of reality
> and, in pieces, like a fragile fan,
> fell into the filthy mud of life.]

Casal's artificial creation crumbles due to the constant pressures of his materialistic milieu; and, however hard he tries to sustain his visions, he is constantly haunted by overwhelming signs that herald his fall. Literature, art, dreams, and any other means of artificiality are supportive only to a certain degree, inasmuch as "Al salir del magnífico establecimiento, mi espíritu se sintió dolorosamente impresionado por el espectáculo de las calles. Me parecía haber descendido desde la altura de un antiguo palacio italiano, poblado de maravillas artísticas, hasta el fondo de inmundos subterráneos, interminables y angostos, llenos de quejas, gritos y blasfemias" (II, 77) [Upon leaving the magnificent establishment, my spirit felt itself painfully impressed by the spectacle of the streets. It seemed as if I had descended from the heights of an ancient Italian palace, filled with artistic marvels, to the depths of filthy tunnels, endless and narrow, filled with grumblings, screams, and blasphemies]. This is a Dantesque descent to the infernal atmosphere of the surroundings that, through brutal contrast, clarifies the need for these evocations.

Even though Julián del Casal was unable to find constant security in artificiality, he was able to sustain it long enough to provide himself with respite from a reality that he strongly abhored. To these moments of solitude and tranquility we owe a unique and personal blending of literary and esthetic influences and the expression of an anxiety that was genuine. Casal's message will have enduring relevance as long as there are beings who cannot cope with their immediate circumstances and who seek ways to evade them.

*Illinois State University*

## NOTES

[1] "Tras una enfermedad," in *Poesías* (Havana: Consejo Nacional de Cultura, 1963), p. 123. Throughout this paper references to the poetry of Julián del Casal—page numbers only, given parenthetically in the text—will be to this edition. The translations are mine.

[2] For an example of the traditional interpretation consult Rufino Blanco Fombona, *El modernismo y los poetas modernistas* (Madrid: Mundo Latino, 1929), p. 29. The new interpretation was spearheaded by Ivan A. Schulman in *Génesis del modernismo* (Mexico City: El Colegio de México, 1968), pp. 16-17.

[3] Juan J. Geada y Fernández says in "Introducción a la Selección de Poesías de Julián del Casal," *Colección Libros Cubanos*, 23 (1931), xxxviii: "Por el gran número de autores que leía, podemos llegar a la conculsión de que fue tal la influencia por ellos ejercida, que la personalidad real de Casal fue sustituyéndose por una personalidad puramente artística. Desde entonces no se ajustaba a la realidad del vivir de los demás. Vivía en su propio ambiente, hijo de sus lecturas en amoroso consorcio con la fantasía" [Because of the great number of authors that he read, we can reach the conclusion that their influence was such that the real personality of Casal was replaced by a purely artistic personality. From then on he could not adjust to the reality of other people's lives. He lived in his own environment, offspring of his readings in amorous consortium with fantasy].

[4] Roland N. Stromberg, *Realism, Naturalism, and Symbolism: Modes of Thought and Expression in Europe, 1848-1914* (New York: Harper, 1968), p. 238.

[5] Gustavo Duplessis, "Julián del Casal," *Revista Bimestre Cubana*, No 3 (1945), p. 268.

[6] Schulman states that Casal lived "en medio de fuerzas contradictorias, polares, condenado a comparar con dolor el profundo e intransitable abismo entre sus gustos refinados y exquisitos y los valores materialistas y positivistas que lo circundaban" (p. 17) [in the midst of contradictory, polar forces, condemned to compare with sorrow the deep and unbreachable abyss between his refined and exquisite tastes and the materialistic and positivistic values that surrounded him].

[7] Ricardo Gullón, *Direcciones del modernismo* (Madrid: Gredos, 1963), p. 96.

[8] Julián del Casal, *Prosas,* 3 vols. (Havana: Consejo Nacional de Cultura, 1963-1964), I, 168. Henceforth, all prose quotations will be indicated in the text by volume number and page number. The translations are mine.

[9] Ralph Harper, *The Seventh Solitude: Metaphysical Homelessness in Kirkegaard,Dostoevsky and Nietzsche* (Baltimore: Johns Hopkins Press, 1965), p. 5.

[10] Mario Rodríguez-Fernández, *El modernismo en Chile y en Hispanoamérica* (Santiago de Chile: Editorial Universitaria, 1967), p. 47.

[11] See, e.g., Stéphane Mallarmé, "Sea Breeze," in *An Anthology of French Poetry from Nerval to Valéry in English Translation with French Originals*, ed. Angel Flores (New York: Doubleday, 1958), p. 147 (cited hereafter as Flores), and Arthur Rimbaud, "Delirium (II)," in *Baudelaire, Rimbaud, Verlaine: Selected Verse and Prose Poems*, ed. Joseph M. Bernstein (New York: Citadel, 1947), p. 186 (cited hereafter as Bernstein).

[12] John E. Englekirk, Irving A. Leonard, John T. Reid, and John A. Crow, *An Anthology of Spanish American Literature*, 2nd ed. (New York: Appleton, 1968), II, 394.

[13] See Flores, p. 109.

[14] Flores, pp. 85 and 338.

[15] Bernstein, p. 30.

[16] Casal's "Horridum Somnium" bears a remarkable resemblance to Baudelaire's "Un Voyage à Cythère" ["A Voyage to Cythera"]: "Les yeux étaient deux trous, et du ventre effondré/ Les intestins pesants lui coulaient sur les cuisses,/ Et ses bourreaux, gorgés de hideuses délices,/ L'avaient à coups de bec absolument châtré" ["The eyes were holes, and from the ruined gut/ Across the thighs the heavy bowels poured out,/ And crammed with hideous pleasures, peck by peck,/ His butchers had quite stripped him of his sex"] (Flores, pp. 43 and 314).

[17] A. E. Carter, "The Cult of Artificiality," *University of Toronto Quarterly*, 25 (1956), 455.

[18] "Todas las noches, en La Habana, son iguales. Siempre vemos el mismo cielo, tachonado de los mismos astros; aspiramos el mismo ambiente impregnado de los mismos olores; recorremos las mismas calles, alumbradas por los mismos mecheros de gas; penetramos en los mismos cafés, invadidos por las mismas gentes. . . . Vivimos condenados a girar perpetuamente, en el mismo círculo, sin poder escaparnos de él. Así la vida nos parece abominable, y brota incesantemente de nuestros labios impíos la súplica diabólica de Baudelaire:
*O Satan! aie pitié de ma longue misère*" (II, 27).

[All the nights in Havana are alike. We always see the same sky, spattered with the same stars; we breathe in the same atmosphere, impregnated by the same smells; we walk the same streets, illuminated by the same gas lights; we enter the same cafés, invaded by the same people. . . . We live to girate perpetually, in the same circle, without being able to escape from it. Thus, life appears abominable to us, and from our impious lips incessantly comes Baudelaire's diabolical supplication:
*Oh, Satan, have pity on my long misery!*]

[19] George Ross Ridge, *The Hero in French Decadent Literature* (Athens: Univ. of Georgia Press, 1961), p. viii.

[20] Bernstein, p. 120.

[21] Albert L. Guerard. *Art for Art's Sake* (New York: Schocken, 1936), p. 292.

[22] Ibid., p. 337.

[23] Rafael Ferreres, *Los límites del modernismo* (Madrid: Editorial Torres, 1964), p. 68.

[24] Erich Auerbach, "The Aesthetic Dignity of the *Fleurs du mal*," in *Baudelaire: A Collection of Critical Essays*, ed. Henri Peyre (Englewood Cliffs, N.J.: Prentice-Hall, 1962), p. 168.

[25] Cf. Duplessis (see n. 4, above), p. 255.

[26] Joris-Karl Huysmans, *Against Nature*, trans. Robert Baldick (Suffolk: The Chaucer Press, 1976), p. 211.

# *Modernista* Pythagorean Literature: The Symbolist Inspiration

## Theodore W. Jensen

Literary Pythagoreanism, whose importance in the English-speaking world has been underlined in brilliant studies by Hollander and Heninger,[1] has only recently begun to receive deserved attention as a most important phenomenon of Spanish American *modernismo.*[2] Much remains to be clarified, especially concerning the peculiar nature of *modernista* Pythagoreanism and its sources and influences. This study will focus attention on the relationship between *modernista* Pythagoreanism and French symbolism.

It appears that, like *modernismo,* symbolism is an elusive term, giving rise to numerous polemics and disagreements. Yet most scholars probably would agree that the idea of "correspondences" is an important characteristic. This writer proposes that these correspondences are the source of all symbolist manifestations. By "correspondences" in the symbolist sense, we are referring to the poetic gift of externalizing the internal ineffable by a "magical" manipulation of Word, accomplished by the poet-seer's mystic perception of cosmic correspondences (called by Baudelaire the Universal Analogy).

Most writers point to Swedenborg's "doctrine of correspondences," used by him to interpret his dreams, as the symbolists' source. Yet this doctrine is traceable to Plotinus and the Neoplatonists.[3] And in truth, the originator of the doctrine of correspondences in Western thought was Pythagoras. He taught that the universe was composed of contesting opposite forces, embraced and unified by a divine cosmic harmony. Called "Kosmos" by Pythagoras, the first to use that term,[4] this harmonious universe was determined by him to be peopled by beings who are themselves each a "kosmos" in miniature, "organisms which reproduce the structural principles of the macrocosm."[5] From this idea of interactions between micro and macrocosm stems the theory of correspondences, which became the basis for most theories of the occult, and eventually for both the occult and poetic-oriented symbolist correspondences. Let us recall the first two stanzas of Baudelaire's sonnet "Correspondances," often cited as a type of symbolist manifesto:

> La Nature est un temple où de vivants piliers
> Laissent parfois sortir de confuses paroles;
> L'homme y passe à travers des forêts de symboles
> Qui l'observent avec des regards familiers.

Comme de longs échos que de loin se confondent
Dans une ténébreuse et profonde unité,
Vaste comme la nuit et comme la clarté,
Les parfums, les couleurs et les sons se répondent.

[Nature is a temple where living pillars
Let sometimes emerge confused words;
Man crosses it through forests of symbols
Which watch him with intimate eyes.

Like those deep echoes that meet from afar
In a dark and profound harmony,
As vast as night and clarity,
So perfumes, colours, tones answer each other.]6

*The Golden Verses of Pythagoras* (circa 388 B.C.) by the Pythagorean
Lysis, reprinted and interpreted by Antoine Fabre d'Olivet as *Les vers dorés de
Pythagore expliqués* (1813), state that Pythagoras discovered his philosophy
while gazing at the heavens one night, near a temple:

> The base columns, architrave and triangular pediment suddenly represented, in
> his eyes, the triple nature of man and the universe, of the microcosm and the
> macrocosm crowned by the divine unity, itself a trinity. The Kosmos,
> controlled and penetrated by God, formed "the sacred Quaternion, the source
> of Nature, whose cause is eternal."7

Could Baudelaire have been thinking of the *Golden Verses* when he wrote
"Correspondances?" It cannot be proved. But there is ample reason to
expect that he and later symbolists were quite familiar with the figure of
Pythagoras.

A perusal of book jacket advertisements of the era reveals that there were
a multitude of writings extant concerning Pythagoras. What is more, Helena
Blavatsky's *Isis Unveiled* was unveiled in 1875, and that widely read and
highly influential tome is replete with Pythagorean doctrine.8 The French
spiritualist leader, Edouard Schuré, published another vital Pythagorean
source in 1889, *Les Grands Initiés*. Even before these works appeared, great
French authors were manifesting interest in the "first philosopher." The
occult aspect of Victor Hugo's Hellenism was represented by the figure and
ideas of Pythagoras.9 Gérard de Nerval—described as a Pythagorean-inspired
symbolist by Arthur Symons10—revealed his familiarity with the *Golden
Verses* in his well-known sonnet "Vers Dorés," wherein he quotes a statement
attributed to Pythagoras, "Tout est sensible" [All things live]. Louis Ménard,
a Parnassian precursor whom Arturo Marasso terms "the father of
Symbolism,"11 wrote poems like "Le Rishi," "L'Athlète," and "Panthéon,"
which refer to metempsychosis, Pythagorean harmony, and the music of the
spheres.12 Ménard was an advocate of Pythagorean metempsychosis, and his
metaphysics were drawn to a great degree from Pythagorean sources.13 And,
returning finally to Baudelaire, he gives forth a rather "decadent" image of
the harmony of the spheres in "Une Charogne" and touches on
metemphychosis in "La vie antérieure";14 and *Les Fleurs du Mal* has been
associated, at least in part, with Pythagorean number symbolism.15

Having established at least some historicity and credence for Baudelaire's
perhaps having a Pythagorean model in mind when he composed
"Correspondances," let us examine this most interesting—and most
Pythagorean—concept as it relates to the symbolists.

John Senior, in effect, suggests that the entire basis of symbolist literature is occult.[16] I believe that this view is correct because the theory of correspondences—implying that actions in the microcosm may influence the macrocosm, and vice versa—is occult, be it manifested as Pythagorean metaphysics, voodoo, or symbolist verbal illumination. Pythagoras as the first philosopher, the Haitian witch doctor, and the symbolist *voyant* all have that in common. In symbolist literature, there were three major applications of the theory of correspondences which most attracted the Spanish American *modernistas:* verbal mystification-illumination; poetic musicalization; and a flirtation with the occult.

The symbolist *voyant* and the *vate modernista* pursued a technique of verbal mystification-illumination. By their use of symbol in the manipulation of word, they strived to convey to the reader a glimpse of their cosmic vision/poetic vision which otherwise might never be experienced. While Anna Balakian[17] may today make distinctions between the romantic concept of correspondences and a less-mystical symbolist variety; between the differing styles of Baudelaire, Verlaine and Rimbaud; and between allegory and symbolism; *modernista* writers seem not to have done so. Influenced by Symons, and later by Remy de Gourmont,[18] they perceived a mystical core in symbolist correspondences. The Mexican poet and critic Octavio Paz presents this description of *modernista* poetry: "El universo es un sistema de correspondencias ... En toda la poesía modernista resuena un eco de los 'Vers dorés'"[19] [Its universe is a system of correspondences.... In all *modernista* poetry resounds an echo from the "Vers dorés"]. Then, in his first narrative reference to Pythagorean doctrine, the Nicaraguan leader of the *modernista* movement—Rubén Darío—shows definitively the *modernista* linkage of correspondences and Pythagoras:

> Los astros del cielo están en relación con nuestros destinos. Nuestras almas están influidas por la música pitagórica: hay en nuestro ser una parte que nos viene de la altura luminosa. Pues bien, así como los celestes astros están en continuo movimiento—y si lo suspendiesen cesaría el orden en la máquina del universo—, nuestra naturaleza nos impulsa también a no permanecer fijos en un solo punto.... Necesario nos es la traslación.[20]
> [The stars in the heavens are related to our destinies. Our souls are influenced by Pythagorean music: There is in our being a part that comes to us from the luminous heights. Well then, just as the celestial stars are in continual movement—and if they were to stop it, order in the machine of the universe would cease—our nature impels us also not to remain fixed in one place. Movement is necessary for us.]

Even when the *modernistas* used the synesthesia lauded in Baudelaire's "Correspondances," the sensory juxtapositions could be viewed as an inevitable part of perceiving the unity of all in the divine Monad. The Argentine *modernista,* Leopoldo Lugones, offers a superb example of this Pythagorean basis for the use of synesthesia in his short story "La metamúsica" (1898) [Metamusic], wherein a musician-inventor creates a device which translates music into colors and then reproduces geometrically the structure of the cosmos. Says the musician:

> El universo es música.... Pitágoras tenía razón, y desde Timeo hasta Kepler, todos los pensadores han presentido esta armonía. Eratóstenes llegó a determinar la escala celeste, los tonos y semitonos entre astro y astro. ¡Yo

creo tener algo mejor; pues habiendo dado con las notas fundamentales de la música de las esferas, reproduzco en colores geométricamente combinados, el esquema del Cosmos![21]

[The universe is music. Pythagoras was right, and from Timaeus to Kepler, all thinkers have had a presentiment of this harmony. Eratosthenes managed to determine the celestial scale, the tones and semi-tones between one star and another. I believe I have something better since, having run into the fundamental notes of the music of the spheres, I reproduce, in geometrically combined colors, the scheme of the Cosmos!]

It is difficult in this context not to think of the decadent writer Huysmans in *À Rebours* where des Esseintes, by the use of his *orgue à bouche* tries to transform musical sounds into tastes. A further link to Pythagoras is forged when the musician, during a demonstration of his machine, declares: "Lo que estás escuchando es una armonía en la cual entran las notas específicas de cada planeta del sistema" (p. 90) [What you are listening to is a harmony in which enter the specific notes of each planet of the system].

The use of metaphor keys or symbols appealed also to the romantic sensibilities of the *modernista* poets. Only the "initiate" might perceive the deeper meanings of some hermetic verse. This more mundane use of symbol often can still create a real communication between poet and reader that transcends the everyday potential of the written word. An example of this is when both Rubén Darío and his close friend the Mexican *modernista* Amado Nervo used the neologism "pitagorizar" ["pythagorize"] in their poetry. Nervo uses it in "El agua multiforme" from *La hermana agua* (1901) [Sister Water]:

> Hoy soy torrente inquieto y ayer fui agua tranquila;
> hoy soy, en vaso esférico, redonda; ayer apenas,
> me mostraba cilíndrica en las ánforas plenas,
> y así pitagorizo mi ser, hora tras hora:
> hielo, corriente, niebla, vapor. . . .[22]

[Today I am an anxious torrent and yesterday I was calm water; Today I am, in a spherical glass, round; yesterday I showed myself cylindrical in full urns, and so I pythagorize my being, hour after hour: ice, running water, mist, vapor. . . .]

It is unveiled the same year by Darío in his poem "Ama tu ritmo" (1901) [Love Your Rhythm], which Marasso called a "Pythagorean initiation":[23]

> Ama tu ritmo, y ritma tus acciones
> bajo su ley, así como tus versos;
> eres un universo de universos
> y tu alma una fuente de canciones.
>
> La celeste unidad que presupones
> hará brotar en ti mundos diversos,
> y al resonar tus números dispersos
> pitagoriza en tus constelaciones.
>
> Escucha la retórica divina
> del pájaro del aire y la nocturna
> irradiación geométrica adivina;
>
> mata la indiferencia taciturna
> y engarza perla y perla cristalina
> en donde la verdad vuelca su urna.[24]

[Love your rhythm, and rhythm your actions under its law, as well as your verses; you are a universe of universes and your soul a fount of songs. The celestial unity you presuppose will cause to sprout in you diverse worlds, and upon echoing your dispersed numbers, pythagorize in your constellations. Listen to the divine rhetoric of the airborne bird and divine the nocturnal geometric emanation; kill taciturn indifference and link pearl after crystaline pearl where truth tips her urn.]

*Pitagorizar* in both cases is meaningless to the non-initiate. Yet is suggests not only the idea of metempsychosis in Nervo's usage, but the associated ideas of harmony, rhythm and movement towards perfection, towards eventual incorporation in the divine Monad, from the most concrete and earthbound form (ice) to the least earthbound form which ascends (vapor). The same idea of movement towards perfection is inherent in Darío's usage also: poetic and metaphysical perfection. This type of lesser correspondence, that between metaphor and secret meaning, was characteristic of Pythagoras and Pythagoreans; and symbolist technique lent itself to that purpose also, although the association by *modernistas* with Pythagoras probably came via Nerval and Helena Petrovna Blavatsky.[25]

Nerval wrote "Tout est sensible" [All things live]; Victor Hugo wrote "Vents, ondes, flammes;/ Arbres, roseaux, tout vit. Tout est plein d'âmes"[26] [Winds, waves, flames, trees, reeds, all live. All is full of souls]. And Darío wrote:

> cada hoja de cada árbol canta un propio cantar
> y hay un alma en cada una de las gotas del mar;
> el vate, el sacerdote, suele oir el acento
> desconocido....[27]

[Each leaf of each tree sings its own song, and there is a soul in each one of the drops in the sea; the seer, the priest, is accustomed to hearing the unknown accent....]

There is no reason to question the seriousness of these poetic statements. As Senior points out, "when Gérard de Nerval [quoting Pythagoras] ... says that everything is alive, he means it, literally."[28] If that is the poet's belief, then words become more active partners of the poet, rather than tools. Besides being perhaps an anticipation of surrealism, this idea is not even so foreign to certain modern French structuralists (Lacan, Benveniste) in their theories about the relationship of language and subjectivity; and Boon has written a book on Lévi-Strauss in the literary atmosphere of symbolism.[29] In spite of recent proclamations to the contrary, the metaphysical cannot be separated from symbolist correspondences nor from *modernista* correspondences. That metaphysical base is Pythagorean; and the *modernistas* perceived it as such. Lugones, in his openly Pythagorean collection *Las fuerzas extrañas* (1906) [Strange Forces], even tries to provide scientific support for the Pythagorean idea that all things live, which he uses to present an explanation for occult forces:

> La sensibilidad es la radioactividad de la materia ... toda materia posee sensibilidad.... La vida de los cristales ha demostrado ya hasta la evidencia que la sensibilidad no es una propiedad exclusiva de la materia llamada orgánica.... El pensamiento es una forma de la energía.... Cada pensamiento es una individualidad.... Si el pensamiento es la energía primordial, todas las fuerzas (energía manifestada) son pensamiento, es decir, seres inteligentes.[30]

[Sensibility is radioactivity of matter ... all matter has sensibility.... The life of crystals has even demonstrated already the evidence that sensibility is not an exclusive property of organic matter. . . . Thought is a form of energy. . . . Each thought is an individual. . . . If thought is primordial energy, all forces (manifested energy) are thought, that is to say, intelligent beings.]

Paul Verlaine in "Art Poétique" (1874) [Poetic Art] unveiled a new musical preoccupation of the symbolists with his poetic statement "De la musique avant toute chose" [Music before everything]. Music-like verse could evoke correspondences or sensations just as had the visual symbols of Baudelaire. From that point on the poet would attempt to adopt the properties of music to poetry. In order to musicalize their verse, symbolists—consciously or not—were drawn towards a sympathy with some Pythagorean beliefs. The *modernistas* took to this idea with enthusiasm, but—typically—they again interpreted it as Pythagorean in nature. For example, we have already noted that Schulman has identified Pythagorean music in the poetry of the early *modernista* from Cuba, José Martí. Leopoldo Lugones wrote an essay entitled "La armonía pitagórica" (1936) [Pythagorean Harmony] which makes reference to "la noción musical de la aritmética pitagórica"[31] [the musical notion of Pythagorean arithmetic], discusses the idea of correspondences between number and music (rhythm), and brings to mind his story "La metamúsica," wherein he states that the universe is music. José Vasconcelos also wrote an essay, "Pitágoras (una teoría del ritmo)" (1919)[32] [Pythagoras (A Theory of Rhythm)], in which he stressed the idea of correspondences between number and music, expressed as rhythm. And we have seen already in "Ama tu ritmo" that Darío expressed it poetically. He even viewed Isadora Duncan as one who danced to the rhythm of Pythagorean music.[33] Amado Nervo reveals his Pythagorean musical vision in "Música" (1916) [Music]:

> Sólo las claves, sólo las pautas y las notas,
> revelarán al mundo sus bellezas ignotas.
> Platón oyó a los orbes su concierto ideal,
> y Beethoven, a veces, lo escuchó en el mutismo
> nocturno. Todo es música: los astros, el abismo,
> las almas . . . ¡Y Dios mismo
> es un Dios musical![34]

[Only the keys, the rules, and the notes will reveal to the world their unknown beauties. Plato heard the ideal concert of the spheres, and Beethoven, at times, listened to it in the nocturnal quiet. All is music: stars, abyss, souls. . . . And God himself is a musical God!]

But it was Rubén Darío who perhaps best communicated this correspondence between music and poetry, and its linkage with Pythagoras, in his autobiographical novelistic fragment, *El oro de Mallorca* (1913) [The Gold of Mallorca]:

Pitágoras y Wagner tenían razón. La Música en su inmenso concepto lo abraza todo, lo material y lo espiritual, y por eso los griegos comprendían también en ese vocablo a la excelsa Poesía, a la Creadora. Y que el arte era de trascendencia consoladora y suprema sabía por experiencia propia, pues jamás había recurrido a él sin salir aliviado de su baño de luces y de correspondencias mágicas.[35]

[Pythagoras and Wagner were right. Music in its immense concept embraces everything, material and spiritual, and consequently the Greeks comprehended also in that word Sublime and Creative Poetry. And that art was of a consoling and supreme importance he [Benjamin Itaspés, a musician and Darío's alter

ego] knew through personal experience, since he had never turned to it without
leaving soothed by its bath of lights and magical correspondences.]

Worthy of note is the linking here of Wagner and Pythagoras. Darío viewed
Wagner as the renovator of the Pythagorean idea that music creates a bridge
between man and the cosmos. *Modernistas,* as well as symbolists, admired "le
dieu Richard Wagner"[36] [the god Richard Wagner].

Previously we have touched upon the inherent occult significance of
Pythagorean correspondences. While the figure of Pythagoras seems not to be
a frequent one in symbolist literature, the presence of the father of Western
occultism is undeniable in symbolist esoterica. Indeed, Pythagoras is reputed
to have been the originator of the term "esoteric."[37] Senior, in his study of
symbolists and the occult, portrays Western occultism as being essentially
platonic[38] and describes Eliphas Lévi as "the single greatest occult influence
on Symbolism."[39] A close scrutiny of Lévi's occult symbolism reveals it as
Pythagorean in nature. This is understandable, given Lévi's deep attraction to
Pythagorean doctrines while studying at the theological college of
Saint-Sulpice (which we recall as a major locus in Huysmans' novel *Là-bas*):

> Twice daily each seminarist had to make his "examination of conscience"
> which was based on maxims and precepts contained in the *Golden Verses of
> Pythagoras,* one of those non-Christian works which, like the *Meditations* of
> Marcus Aurelius, had been taken up by Christians for the universal morality
> and wisdom they contained. Whether or not Constant [Lévi] had at that time
> read Fabre d'Olivet's esoteric interpretation of the verses, they certainly must
> have made a deep impression on him.[40]

Lévi's choice of which passage to translate from *The Golden Verses* shows him
being attracted at an early age to the magical facet of Pythagoreanism. That
Pythagoras continued to interest him later is evident in his *Histoire de la
magie* (1860) [*History of Magic*], wherein he devotes a chapter to the
"Mathematical Magic of Pythagoras" and quotes from his early extract from
Saint-Sulpice.[41]

Symbolist writers carried on a flirtation with the occult. That term is
chosen to point out that some, like Mallarmé who wrote an essay on magic
and had occultist friends,[42] seemed not to embrace occultism with the fervor
of others, like Huysmans (who once accused the Marquis Stanislas de Guaita
of murdering the Abbé Boullan by black magic), or the less-known decadent,
"Sar" Joséphin Péladan.[43]

The *modernistas* also were drawn to the occult sciences. As previously
noted, Darío, Nervo and Lugones were theosophists. Darío and Lugones were
also Masons, Lugones even advancing to the 33rd Degree.[44] Darío, at least,
was familiar with Rosicrucian literature.[45] Nervo and Darío read books on
spiritualism and mesmerism, and "sought the company of mediums."[46]
Lugones also attended spiritualist meetings and, along with Darío, apparently
did believe in supernatural forces; he is reputed to have studied the occult
sciences from the time he was an adolescent.[47]

But the *modernistas* were not drawn into the Satanism and black magic
which fascinated some decadents. Their occultism was limited, rather, to a
search for supernatural truths to explain the inexplicable—a cerebral exercise
and a spiritual one. They perused what the black arts had to offer; they were
never ones to overlook any possible source of inspiration. But, unlike

Huysmans, they were repelled by the negativism of black magic. Rather than serving as models for the *modernistas,* the decadent symbolists functioned to point the way towards occultism in general, and thus indirectly towards Pythagorean esoterica.

The Pythagorean nature of much *modernista* occultism is seen in works such as Amado Nervo's well-known occult novel, *El donador de almas* (1899)[48] [The Donor of Souls], or in his story "Diálogos pitagóricos: La próxima encarnación" (1912) [Pythagorean Dialogs: The Next Incarnation], which connects Pythagoreanism with spiritualism and the well-known occult figure Allan Kardec.

Lugones, in "Un fenómeno inexplicable" (1898) [An Inexplicable Phenomenon], narrates a tale of an Englishman whose studies of occult sciences lead him to attempt to separate his astral spirit from his body during a somnambulistic trance. He fails and in the process loses his "unidad de ser" [unity of being], creating a split personality. He nervously confesses that his "other" has ape-like characteristics. When the narrator traces on a wall the outline of the Englishman's shadow, it is disclosed to have the shape of an ape. This reflects a belief Lugones thought originated with Pythagoras—that prior to death a spiritual double may appear. The double assumes a form which best reflects the inner nature of the man in this life, and which may be the form he assumes in the next incarnation.[49]

Pythagoreanism was a part of the episteme of late nineteenth-century and early twentieth-century France. Even though the symbolists rarely used his name, it is highly unlikely that they were unaware of the Pythagorean base of much of their literature. A direct Pythagorean influence is not proved. Yet the symbolist techniques admired and imitated by the *modernistas* were interpreted Pythagorically by them and served as a further inspiration for *modernista* literary Neo-Pythagoreanism.[50]

*Eastern Montana College*

## NOTES

[1] John Hollander, *The Untuning of the Sky: Ideas of Music in English Poetry 1500-1700* (Princeton: Princeton Univ. Press, 1961) and S. K. Heninger, Jr., *Touches of Sweet Harmony: Pythagorean Cosmology and Renaissance Poetics* (San Marino, California: The Huntington Library, 1974).

[2] Brief but important statements may be found in: Enrique Anderson Imbert, *La originalidad de Rubén Darío* (Buenos Aires: Centro Editor de América Latina, 1967); Arturo Marasso, *Rubén Darío y su creación poética* (Buenos Aires: Editorial Kapelusz, 1954); Alan S. Trueblood, "Rubén Darío: The Sea and the Jungle," *Comparative Literature Studies,* 4 (1967), 425-456. Studies more specifically realted to Pythagoreanism and *modernismo* include: Erika Lorenz, *Rubén Darío bajo el divino imperio de la música* (Managua: Academia Nicaragüense de la Lengua, 1960); Raymond Skyrme, *Rubén Darío and the Pythagorean Tradition* (Gainesville: Univ. of Florida Press, 1975); Ricardo Gullón, "Pitagorismo y modernismo," *Estudios críticos sobre el modernismo,* ed. H. Castillo (Madrid: Gredos, 1968), 358-383; Ivan Schulman, "Modernismo, revolución y pitagorismo en Martí," *Casa de las Américas* (July-Aug. 1972), 45-55; Theodore Jensen, "El pitagorismo en *Las fuerzas extrañas* de Lugones," *Fantasía y Realismo Mágico en Iberoamérica,* Memoria del XVI Congreso Internacional de Literatura Iberoamericana (East Lansing: Michigan State Univ., 1975), 299-307, and "Christian-Pythagorean Dualism in Nervo's *El donador de almas,*" *Kentucky Romance Quarterly,* 3, No. 3 (1981), in preparation.

[3] Cyriel O. Sigstedt, *The Swedenborg Epic* (New York: Bookman Associates, 1952), p. 179.

[4] W. K. C. Guthrie, *The Greek Philosophers from Thales to Aristotle* (New York: Harper and Row, 1960), p. 37.

[5] Ibid., p. 38.

[6] *Selected Poems of Charles Baudelaire,* trans. Geoffrey Wagner (New York: Grove Press, 1974), p. 23.

[7] Edouard Schuré, citing Fabre d'Olivet's *The Golden Verses of Pythagoras,* in *The Great Initiates,* trans. Gloria Rasberry (West Nyack, N.Y.: St. George Books, 1961), p. 18.

[8] Theosophists claim that their order was founded in the third century A.D. by the initiator of the Neoplatonist school, Ammonias Saccas, and that the Neo-Pythagoreans Porphry, Plotinus, and Iamblichus were indeed theosophists (H. P. Blavatsky, *The Key to Theosophy* [Pasadena: Theosophical Univ. Press, 1946], p. 3).

[9] Pierre Albouy, *La création mythologique chez Victor Hugo* (Paris: Librairie José Corti, 1963), pp. 79-83.

[10] Arthur Symons, *The Symbolist Movement in Literature* (New York: Dutton and Co., 1958), pp. 17-19. Published in 1889, this book was widely read in Europe and Latin America and, in spite of subsequent criticisms, was undoubtedly quite influential.

[11] Marasso, p. 28.

[12] Louis Ménard, *Rêveries d'un Païen Mystique* (Paris: Georges Crès et Cie., 1911), pp. 144, 145 and 206.

[13] Henri Peyre, *Louis Ménard* (New Haven: Yale Univ. Press, 1932), p. 303 and Chapter VII ("Philosophie mystique").

[14] Charles Baudelaire, *Oeuvres complètes* (Tours: Librairie Gallimard, 1958), pp. 105-07 and p. 93.

[15] John Senior, *The Way Down and Out: The Occult in Symbolist Literature* (New York: Greenwood Press, 1968), p. 93.

[16] "The basic metaphysical assumptions of symbolism are occult. ... The following chapters attempt to demonstrate that the chief Symbolist poets were to some extent occultists, that insofar as their work contains philosophy it is occult philosophy, and, more important, that the purpose of their poetry is in a sense the communication and evocation of occult experience" (Senior, pp. xvi and 46).

[17] *The Symbolist Movement: A Critical Appraisal* (New York: Random House, 1967).

[18] Gourmont called Verlaine and Mallarmé Parnassians and Baudelairians, and wrote: "All the present literature and especially that which is called symbolistic, is Baudelairian, not doubtless by its external technique, but by its internal and spiritual technique, by the sense of mystery, by the anxious care to hear what things say, by the desire to harmonize from soul to soul, with the obscure thought diffused in the night of the world . . ." (*The Book of Masks* trans. Jack Lewis [New York: Books for Libraries Press, 1967], p. 59).

[19] "El caracol y la sirena," *Diez estudios sobre Rubén Darío,* ed. Juan Loveluck (Santiago de Chile: Zig–Zag, 1967), p. 254.

[20] *El hombre de oro* in *Cuentos* (Madrid: Espasa-Calpe, 1965), p. 23. Note that "traslación," besides implying movement though space, also suggests a change of condition and, like the English word *translation,* intimates transmigration of the soul.

[21] Leopoldo Lugones, *Las fuerzas extrañas* (Buenos Aires: Editorial Huemul, 1962), p. 90.

[22] *Obras completas,* ed. Francisco González Guerrero and Alfonso Méndez Plancarte (Madrid: Aguilar, 1951), II, 1359.

[23] Marasso, p. 157.

[24] *Poesías completas,* ed. Alfonso Méndez Plancarte (Madrid: Aguilar, 1967), p. 617.

[25] In *Isis Unveiled* (New York: J. W. Bouton, 1877), I, 212, Helena Petrovna Blavatsky discusses man's relationship with the Universe in terms similar to some used in

"Ama tu ritmo." Besides the astral soul, she disucsses the "divine spirit" which is an "infinitesimal ray," one of "countless radiations proceeding from the Highest Cause." She points out that Plato's works are written enigmatically because they contain hidden Pythagorean secrets, which only initiates might perceive (I, 287); that Neo-Pythagoreans like Plotinus were "clairvoyant-seers" (II, 591); even that Jesus learned to speak in parables and use metaphors from the "Pythagorean Essenes," in sentences which were "purely Pythagorean" (II, 144).

The three great *modernistas,* Darío, Nervo and Lugones, were all theosophists (Anderson Imbert, p. 52; Miguel Lermón, *Contribución a la bibliografía de Leopoldo Lugones* [Buenos Aires: Ediciones Marú, 1969], p. 196; Alicia Barrios de Madriz, *Lecciones y conferencias de Teosofía* [Guatemala City: Imprenta Galindo, 1967], p. 7).

[26] In "Le Satre," according to Marie-Josèphe Faurie, *Le Modernisme Hispano-Americain et ses sourçes françaises* (Paris: Centre de Recherches de l'Institut d'Etudes Hispaniques, 1966), p. 35.

[27] "Coloquio de los centauros" (1896), in *Poesías completas,* p. 643.

[28] Senior, p. 42.

[29] James Boon, *From Symbolism to Structuralism* (New York: Harper and Row, 1972).

[30] *Op. cit.,* pp. 174-82. The explanation in its entirety is quite dense and consequently has been abbreviated considerably here.

[31] *La Nación,* 12 Apr. 1936, sec. 2, pp. 1 and 3.

[32] *Obras completas* (Mexico: Libreros Mexicanos Unidos, 1959), III, 10-86.

[33] Raymond Skyrme discusses the *modernistas'* concept of a musically structured universe, which Darío tried to translate into poetic form, in "The Pythagorean Vision of Rubén Darío in 'La tortuga de oro,'" *Comparative Literature Studies,* 11 (1974), 233-48.

[34] *Obras completas,* II, 1723.

[35] *La Nación,* 7 Dec. 1913. Reprinted by Allen W. Phillips in *"El oro de Mallorca*: Textos desconocidos y breve comentario sobre la novela autobiográfica de Darío," *Revista Iberoamericana,* 33 (1967), 449-492. We'll not dwell further on Darío, since other manifestations of his musical Pythagoreanism are well documented by Skyrme and Lorenz.

[36] "Hommage," in *Stéphane Mallarmé: Poems* (New York: New Directions, 1951), p. 153. See Mario Praz, *The Romantic Agony* (London: Oxford Univ. Press, 1954), p. 387, for a discussion of the symbolists and Wagner.

[37] Schuré, p. 310. Pythagoras' occult manifestations may be studied in C. J. De Vogel, *Pythagoras and Early Pythagoreanism* (Assen, Netherlands: Van Gorcum and Co., 1966); E. R. Dodds, *The Greeks and the Irrational* (Berkeley: Univ. of California Press, 1959); Theodor Gomperz, *Greek Thinkers* (London: John Murray, 1964); Vincent F. Hopper, *Medieval Number Symbolism* (New York: Cooper Square, 1969); Alister Cameron, *The Pythagorean Background of the Theory of Recollection* (Menasha, Wisconsin: George Banta, 1938); D. P. Walker, *Spiritual and Demonic Magic from Ficino to Campanella* (London: Warburg Institute, Univ. of London, 1958).

[38] Senior, p. 21.

[39] Ibid., p. 36.

[40] Christopher McIntosh, *Eliphas Levi and the French Occult Revival* (London: Rider and Co., 1972), p. 79.

[41] Ibid., p. 80.

[42] Senior, p. 135.

[43] See "The Magical Quest of J. K. Huysmans," and "The Heirs of Eliphas Levi," in McIntosh, pp. 157-194. Balzac, Hugo, Nerval and Rimbaud are also linked with the occult in "Writers and the Occult," pp. 195-205.

[44] Charles D. Watland, *La formación literaria de Rubén Darío* (Managua: Publicaciones del Centenario, 1966), p. 45; Leopoldo Lugones (hijo), *Mi padre* (Buenos Aires: Ediciones Centurión, 1949), p. 124.

[45] Marasso, p. 299.

[46] John E. Englekirk, *Edgar Allan Poe in Hispanic Literature* (New York: Instituto de las Españas, 1934), p. 248; Enrique Anderson Imbert, "Rubén Darío and the Fantastic Element in Literature," in *Rubén Darío Centennial Studies,* ed. González-Gerth and Schade (Austin: Univ. of Texas, 1970), p. 101.

[47] Antonio Pagés Larraya, "Lugones," *Atenea,* 45 (1968), 126; Lugones (hijo), *Mi padre,* p. 267; Lugones (hijo), "Introducción," *Cuentos fatales* (Buenos Aires: Editorial Huemul, 1967), p. 20.

[48] Jensen, "Christian-Pythagorean Dualism in Nervo's *El donador de almas.*"

[49] Schuré, pp. 118-119, attributes this to a teaching of Pythagoras. Blavatsky, *Isis Unveiled,* II, 328, discusses it also. It can at least be traced back to the Neo-Pythagorean Plotinus, in *The Enneads,* trans. Stephan MacKenna (New York: Pantheon Books, 1964), p. 186.

[50] I would like to express my appreciation to my colleague in French, Dr. William Plank, for serving as a sounding board for my ideas concerning French symbolism.

A vignette by Julio Ruelas, dated 1903. Reproduced from *Revista Moderna de México,* 12, No. 1 (Sept. 1907), 54.

# Notes on Contributors

**J. M. Aguirre** is Reader of Spanish at the University of Wales, Cardiff. He is the author of *Calisto y Melibea, amantes cortesanos* (1962), *José de Valdivielso y la poesía religiosa tradicional* (1965), *Antonio Machado, poeta simbolista* (1973), several anthologies of Spanish poetry, and has published many articles in various scholarly journals.

**Luis Felipe Clay Méndez**, Assistant Professor of Spanish at Illinois State University, has a book on Casal in press and articles published or forthcoming in *Cuadernos Americanos, Cuadernos Hispanoamericanos, Anales de Literatura Hispanoamericana, Revista de Estudios Hispánicos,* and *Latin American Research Review.* He has lectured on symbolism and *modernismo* at various American universities and abroad.

**Ricardo Gullón**, Professor of Romance Languages and Literatures at the University of Chicago, has written on both art and literature. His many books include *Autobiografías de Unamuno* (Madrid: Gredos, 1964); *El último Juan Ramón Jiménez* (Madrid: Alfaguara, 1968); *Direcciones del modernismo* (Madrid: Gredos, 1969); *Una poética para Antonio Machado* (Madrid: Gredos, 1970); *Técnicas de Galdós* (Madrid: Taurus, 1970); *Psicologías del autor y lógicas del personaje* (Madrid: Taurus, 1979).

**Theodore W. Jensen**, Assistant Professor of Spanish at Eastern Montana College, has published "El pitagorismo en *Las fuerzas extrañas* de Lugones," in *Otros mundos, otros fuegos: Fantasía y realismo mágico en Iberoamérica* (East Lansing: Michigan State Univ., Latin American Studies Center, 1975). He has articles forthcoming in the *Kentucky Romance Quarterly* and *Forum for Modern Language Studies* (St. Andrews, Scotland).

**John W. Kronik**, Professor of Romance Studies at Cornell University, has written on a wide range of topics concerning Spanish and Spanish American literature in such journals as *Hispanic Review, PMLA, MLN, Symposium, Anales Galdosianos.* His "Rubén Darío y la entrada del simbolismo en España" appeared in *Poemas y ensayos para un homenaje* (Madrid: Tecnos, 1976). His *"La Farsa" (1927-1936) y el teatro español de preguerra* was published in Madrid by Estudios de Hispanófila in 1971.

**Lily Litvak**, Associate Professor of Spanish and Portuguese at the University of Texas at Austin, has written many articles and is the author of *A Dream of Arcadia: Anti-Industrialism in Spanish Literature, 1895-1905* (Austin: Univ. of Texas Press, 1975) and *Erotismo fin de siglo* (Barcelona: Dos Culturas, 1979). She is the editor of *El modernismo* (Madrid: Taurus, 1975).

**Carol Maier,** Assistant Professor of Spanish at Bradley University, has written in *The American Hispanist* about Valle-Inclán's *Luces de Bohemia* as seen in prints by contemporary Spanish artist José Conde Corbal. She has more work in progress about Valle-Inclán and is translating texts of the Cuban poet, Octavio Armand.

**Allen W. Phillips,** Professor of Spanish at the University of California, Santa Barbara, is a prolific writer on Spanish and Spanish American literature. He has published books in Mexico on López Verlarde (1962) and Francisco González León (1964), among others. His recent books include *Cinco estudios sobre literatura mexicana moderna* (Mexico City, 1974), *Temas del modernismo hispánico y otros estudios* (Madrid, 1974) and *Alejandro Sawa, mito y realidad* (Madrid, 1977). He is a Corresponding Member of the Academia Mexicana and has recently been decorated by the Spanish government (Orden de Alfonso el Sabio).

**Geoffrey Ribbans,** Kenan Professor of Hispanic Studies at Brown University, was formerly Editor of the *Bulletin of Hispanic Studies* at the University of Liverpool, England. His books include *Niebla y soledad: Aspectos de Unamuno y Machado* (Madrid: Gredos, 1971) and a critical edition of Machado's *Soledades. Galerías. Otros poemas* (Barcelona: Labor, 1975).

**Raymond S. Sayers,** Professor Emeritus of Romance Languages at Queens College, CUNY, has published widely in the area of Luso-Brazilian literature. His book, *The Negro in Brazilian Literature* (New York, 1956) was published in Portuguese translation in Rio in 1958. He is the editor of *Portugal and Brazil in Transition* (Minneapolis: Univ. of Minnesota Press, 1968), and the co-translator and editor of *Cecília Meireles: Poems in Translation* (Washington, D.C.: Brazilian-American Cultural Institute, 1977).

**Catherine Vera,** Chairman of the Department of Modern Languages at William Jewell College, has published articles in *The American Hispanist* (on Darío and Gutiérrez Nájera), *Explicación de Textos Literarios* (on Gutiérrez Nájera), *Revista de la Comunidad Latinoamericana de Escritores* (on Efrén Rebolledo), *Abside* (on Urbina), as well as studies on Chocano, Quevedo, and Ernesto Sábato.

# THE EDITORS

**Roland Grass,** Professor of Foreign Languages and Literatures at Western Illinois University, holds A.B. and A.M. degrees from Washington University in St. Louis and the Ph.D. from Columbia University in New York. He has published on Spanish and Spanish American authors in *Cuadernos Americanos, The American Hispanist, Hispania,* the *Diorama de la Cultura* section of *Excélsior,* among other journals, and in *Pikarische Welt* (Darmstadt, 1969) and *Homenaje a Sherman H. Eoff* (Madrid, 1970). His monograph *José López-Portillo y Rojas* appeared in 1970. He was co-editor of *Homenaje a Andrés Iduarte* (Clear Creek, IN: The American Hispanist, Inc., 1976). He contributed "The Symbolist Mode in the Spanish American *Modernista* Novel, 1885-1924" to a volume on symbolism edited by Anna Balakian for the International Comparative Literature Association, in press.

**William R. Risley**, Associate Professor of Foreign Languages and Literatures at Western Illinois University, received his A.B. from Hamilton College in New York State, A.M. from Middlebury College in Vermont, and Ph.D. from the University of Wisconsin-Madison. He has articles on Galdós published or forthcoming in *Hispanic Review* and the *Revista de Estudios Hispánicos* and on symbolist narrative in *Anales de la Narrativa Española Contemporánea*. In the field of contemporary Peninsular fiction he serves on the editorial advisory council of *Anales de la Narrativa Española Contemporánea* and the editorial board of *A Semi-Annual Bibliography of Post-Civil War Spanish Fiction* and is an active reviewer for *World Literature Today*.